CONTENTS

ABOUT THE AUTHORS

Andrew Lockwood is Senior Lecturer in Hotel Management in the Department of Management Studies at the University of Surrey. Following management positions in the hotel and catering industry, he has taught in both further and higher education on courses ranging from craft level to masters degrees. His longstanding research interest is in the management of quality in hospitality operations. He is the author and co-author of numerous books and articles in the field of hospitality management and is co-editor of *Progress in Tourism and Hospitality Research.*

Michael Baker has worked as a manager and a consultant in the public sector and in industry. From January 1990 to the end of 1992 he was Head of the Consumer Industries Section at the National Economic Development Office (NEDO), where he was responsible for NEDO's initiatives in the tourism and leisure sector. One of his responsibilities was the management of activities of the Working Party in Competitiveness in Tourism and Leisure, whose recommendations inspired this research. When NEDO closed at the end of 1992, Michael joined the Department of Management Studies at University of Surrey, where he lectures in Information Technology Management.

Andrew Ghillyer is a PhD candidate in the Department of Management Studies, University of Surrey. He has a first degree in Hotel and Restaurant Administration, a master's in International Hotel Management and ten years of management experience within the hospitality and tourism industries. His current research is focused on organizational perceptions of the concept of empowerment.

Peter Cave is Course Leader for the BA (Hons) International Tourism degree and Senior Lecturer in Tourism Management at the Lancashire Business School, University of Central Lancashire. His research interests include the delivery of service quality in tourism businesses and the role of the public sector in tourism. Prior to joining the university he was Industrial Advisor at the National Economic Development Office for the tourism and leisure industries and was involved in a number of projects, including the market for inbound package holidays and an international comparison of management education and training for tourism. He also participated in the Working Party in Competitiveness in Tourism and Leisure.

FOREWORD

Between 1990 and 1992 I chaired the National Economic Development Council's (NEDC) Working Party in Competitiveness in Tourism and Leisure. This group, made up of practical and experienced people with extensive knowledge of the industry, and with the help of the National Economic Development Office (NEDO) secretariat, worked with enthusiasm and dedication to produce the report, *UK Tourism: Competing for Growth*.

It was always intended that the committee should write the report and leave others to undertake any follow-up tasks it identified. The decision of the Government in June 1992 to dispense with the NEDC and its industry committees, and close NEDO, put finding ways of continuing the work into close focus. The good news is that, despite this, the three most important recommendations were implemented.

The industry recognized that it had been unsuccessful in persuading Government that tourism was important and should be taken into account when policies were formulated. This was in large part due to the fragmented nature of the industry and there being no one body that had credibility as the industry's spokesperson. Following our report, and with the particular support of its then Director General, Howard Davies, the CBI set up the Tourism Action Group under the chairmanship of Sir John Egan. It is rapidly gaining recognition as the industry's key lobbying point with Government.

Second, there was consensus that manpower productivity, particularly in hotels, was uncompetitive. As a result a major productivity research project was funded by the Department of Employment and carried out under the direction of the Hotel and Catering Training Company's research team. More recently CBI has carried out a benchmarking exercise on productivity in three- and four-star hotels, whilst the Department of National Heritage has done similar work on the one- and two-star sector.

Third, the report pointed out that the industry must achieve world class standards in quality and concentrate on its management. We were able to launch a rather more modest research programme to support this. In one of its last acts, NEDO provided matching funds to those provided by four industrial companies and one trade union to search out and publish case studies of good practice in quality management in hospitality.

The contribution Government might play in the area of competition in the tourism industry was a strong theme of our NEDO report. The Department of National Heritage acknowledges this and, led by the present Secretary of State, Virginia Bottomley, is focusing on quality in tourism. Quality in service industries like tourism and hospitality can be thought of as having two components: the state of the physical environment in which the product is delivered, and the way the customer is treated. Government can affect industry's refurbishment and investment activities by its fiscal policy, of course; but it can also influence the way staff behave to customers. The introduction of BS 5750. to the service industries, the Training and Enterprise Councils (TECs), and, through the TECs, the championing of Investors in People (IIP), have helped focus the work of managers, and encouraged the training which is the major component of the programme to raise quality standards. Many of the case studies reflect the influence of BS 5750 (now called ISO 9000) and IIP.

I would like to express my thanks to the sponsors of the research programme, and I commend this book to managers and students alike.

Angus Crichton-Miller

ACKNOWLEDGEMENTS

We would like to thank the sponsors of this research project – without their help and support the project would not have been completed. The sponsors are: British Airways, International Vintners and Distillers Ltd, National Economic Development Office, The GMB, The Rank Organisation, Whitbread and Co. plc.

We would also like to thank all the people who participated in the data collection and who contributed to and commented on our case studies. In particular we would like to thank: Gerry Sweeney of Alpha Flight Services, John Murphy of Haven Leisure, Peter Webber of My Kinda Town, Clive Stephens, Ralph Armond and Carla Prior of The Tussaud's Group, Mike Bachelor of Sutcliffe Catering, Peter Lederer of the Gleneagles Hotel, Ean Scott and Jon Bennett of English Lakes Hotels, Tim Savage of Scott's Hotels, Angie Risley of Whitbread's plc, Simon Read and Laurence Watson of Copthorne Hotels, Ian and Jill Guthrie of Rombalds Hotel, and all the other people who talked to us on our visits around the country. Thank you. And, as always, thank you to our wives and children for their continual love and support.

ONE

Hospitality and quality: an introduction

Andrew Lockwood

COMING CLEAN ABOUT QUALITY

There is a story about a London hotel and a guest's struggle with soap. A guest requested the maid not to leave hotel soap in his bathroom as he had brought his own preferred bath-size brand. He also asked that the maid remove the soap that was in his room, i.e. six unopened bars under the medicine cabinet and three from the shower soap dish. A temporary maid took the soap from the shower dish and moved the unopened soap 'out of the way' to the top of the Kleenex dispenser. However, she left three new bars as this was the standing instruction from management. The following day the guest again asked for all the soap to be removed. The regular maid took the six soaps from the Kleenex dispenser and put them in the soap dish and put the guest's own bath soap in the medicine cabinet. In addition she left three small bars in the medicine cabinet as these were required for all new check-ins. The guest contacted the assistant manager who passed on a complaint to the housekeeper who assigned a different maid to the guest's room. The new maid left another three bars of hotel soap in the medicine cabinet plus three new bars on the bathroom shelf. The guest contacted the housekeeper about the soap and the housekeeper instructed the new maid to stop delivering soap and remove all the extra soaps. Unfortunately, at the same time she removed the guest's own bath soap. The guest now having no soap at all called the concierge who found a completely different brand of soap. The guest again contacted the assistant manager about the problem. The assistant manager's response was that he couldn't understand why there was no soap because the maids were instructed to leave three small bars every day and that he would take immediate action. On the guest's return the following evening there were fifty-four bars of soap waiting in the room. The guest contacted the housekeeper to find out what was going on. The housekeeper had returned the twenty-four bars of soap that had been removed plus the three for that day. At the same time the maid had done the same thing, so accounting for the fifty-four bars.

If this is a true story then it highlights a number of key issues about providing quality in hospitality operations, ranging from problems of communication, through inappropriate instructions, to pure serendipity, but all demonstrating very little regard for the customer's needs. Even if the story is not true, there is evidence that all is not right with the products and services the hospitality industry delivers. For example, as part of the original research undertaken by the NEDC's Working Party on Competitiveness in Tourism and Leisure (NEDC, 1992), a survey was conducted of the types of complaints received by members of the British Inbound Tour Operators' Association (BITOA) about one and two-star hotels. The replies covered over one hundred hotels in Greater London and twenty-three outside. The main areas of concern identified were:

- Cleanliness: none of the respondents felt cleanliness was 'good', the most common reply was 'average', followed by 'poor'. In particular, the items felt to be lacking in cleanliness were bathrooms, bed covers, curtains and carpets.
- Maintenance: a lack of maintenance was seen as leading to either an average or a higher than average level of complaints. In particular, maintenance was seen to be lacking in bathrooms in regard to windows, equipment and locks.
- Bedroom furniture: there was a general feeling that the state of bedroom furniture was poor.
- Overcrowding: there was evidence that overbooking in busy periods leads to over-crowding in hotel rooms
- Security and safety: lack of security was often reported as a cause of complaint by visitors. In particular, lack of security at front desk, easy access to keys, lack of secure locks on bedroom doors, unreliable cleaners and poor supervision, especially at night, were cited.
- Value for money: in general, value for money was a regular source of complaint. In particular, the items giving rise to this perception were comparisons with hotels in the rest of Europe, lack of maintenance and small breakfasts.
- Reception, hospitality and service: the aspects of hospitality and service which were reported as lacking were reception staff whose English was inadequate, shortage of staff, staff rudeness, a lack of training and a low level of hospitality.

The rather sorry picture painted here is of many hotels that pay little attention to the upkeep and cleanliness of their physical facilities, that do not provide their customers with either feelings of safety or value for money, and that do not provide a high level of service or hospitality.

SO WHAT IS HOSPITALITY?

The scale and importance of the hospitality industry is not difficult to see. All anyone has to do is think of the number of times in any week that they need rest or refreshment outside their home. If you add to that days away on business or pleasure and annual vacations, weekend breaks or visits to friends and relatives, then the number of occasions when hospitality services are required grows substantially. However, despite the size of the industry that serves these needs and the growing numbers of courses, books, journals and conferences with hospitality in their title, there is still little agreement about the scope and coverage of the industry as a whole.

At one end of the scale Mullins (1993), in the introduction to his book on hospitality management, recognizes that hospitality is increasingly popular as a generic title for different sectors of the hotel and catering industry but prefers to concentrate 'on the mainstream sector of hotel management'. At the other end of the scale, and from a US perspective, Nykiel (1989) expands the scope to cover all products and services offered to the consumer away from home, including travel, lodging, eating, entertainment, recreation and gaming.

Tracing the development of the concept of hospitality should help to determine where the boundaries of the industry lie. To the ancient Greeks hospitality was tied strongly to religion, and strangers received care and protection during their stay under the eye of Zeus Xenios. Any violation of the duties of hospitality was likely to provoke the wrath of the gods. Greece is still very proud of its history and the provision of hospitality is deeply rooted in their national culture as visitors to modern Greece will testify. This early view of hospitality is reflected in the definition offered by the *Oxford English Dictionary*, 'the act or practice of being hospitable; the reception and entertainment of guests, visitors or strangers with liberality or goodwill'. Recent editions of the *OED* recognize the occurrence of commercial hospitality in a 'room, suite of rooms, etc., in a hotel, TV studio, etc., set aside for the entertainment of guests with drinks'.

These two elements of hospitable interaction and the physical environment, within which this takes place, are developed into a package by Burgess (1982: 50).

> The outer primary interacting element is that of the social relationship fostered by the warm, friendly, welcoming, courteous, open, generous behaviour of the host creating the hospitable social environment. This promotes the positive feeling of security and comfort created by the physical structure, design, décor and location of the facility. Finally the provision of accommodation facilities to sleep, relax and wash, together with the supply of food, beverage, service and entertainment.

This model of a social interaction built around the core of hospitality services – accommodation, food, beverage, service and entertainment – provided within the physical environment of the facility is primarily provider based. The importance of the need for hospitality to satisfy not just the physical needs of the guests, but also their more intangible needs, is highlighted by Nailon (1982: 141). 'Hospitality (is) ... concerned with the provision of physiological and psychological comfort and security within defined levels of service'.

Moving the focus from the provider to the receiver of the hospitality, Reuland and Cassee (1983) suggest that: 'hospitality is a harmonious mixture of food, beverage and/or shelter, a physical environment and the behaviour and attitude of people. This produces a feeling of being at home, an "at-ease" feeling in people who do not belong to the group of people who produce hospitality, but stay under their roof'. It is the feelings generated in the guests receiving the service that assumes the important role. The emphasis has moved from providing hospitality to receiving it. This emphasis on the customers' perceptions of the service they have received is a key tenet of the quality management approach.

The missing element which links the concept of hospitality to the business of the hospitality industry is financial. In any situation where hospitality is provided outside the purely domestic situation, a cost is incurred which must be paid for either directly or indirectly by the person receiving the hospitality. Therefore the definition proffered by Lockwood and Jones (1984) comes from Jan Berger, the editor of the first issue of *Hospitality*, the magazine for members of the Hotel and Catering International Management Association, 'Hospitality is the people business of providing, security, physical and psychological comfort for reward'. This definition covers not just the commercial or profit sector of the hospitality industry, where payment is made directly by the customer, but also the cost or nonprofit sector, where payment is made indirectly. For example, the payment for catering in hospitals is made through taxation; payment for eating at work may involve some payment or subsidy from the employer that could otherwise have been included in wages. All hospitality businesses, therefore, must be aware of the financial implications of the hospitality services they provide to their guests.

Drawing from the core elements suggested by Litteljohn (1990), the hospitality industry can be seen to consist of all those businesses that give their customers any combination of the three core services of food, drink and accommodation, at an appropriate service level, within a physical and social environment that caters for their physiological, psychological and social needs.

This definition creates a very broad scope for the provision of hospitality. The scope is reflected in the companies appearing in the following chapters. Hotels feature strongly in the case histories because they represent a large part of the hospitality industry, and also because they provide a large variety of hospitality services which are all of the quality expected by the customer. A combination of services is also a feature of holiday parks where entertainment is now a core element of their service provision. Food and beverages are provided not just by commercial restaurants but by contract catering companies in industrial, welfare and commercial premises and by companies specializing in catering for the customer on the move.

Two key elements emerge from this discussion of hospitality.

- For hospitality to be delivered, there must be some interaction between the customer and the service provider, usually, but not exclusively, on the premises of the service provider. This stresses the central role of the customer in hospitality operations – without the customer, hospitality cannot be delivered.
- Hospitality consists of a complex blend of tangible and intangible elements of both products – food, drink, entertainment and accommodation – and the service and atmosphere that surround them. It is not possible, therefore, to classify a hospitality business exclusively as either a service operation or a production operation. Every hospitality business will, to a greater or lesser extent, display the characteristics of and suffer the problems and benefits of both.

SO WHAT IS QUALITY?

There are many definitions of quality, all having their own particular slant. From the business perspective, however, one of the most useful and widely accepted defines quality as 'the totality of features and characteristics of a product or service that bear on its ability to satisfy a stated or implied need' (British Standard 4778, 1987). The stated or implied need is that of the customer – the final arbiter of quality. The hospitality industry deals for the most part with customers' implied needs. The customer is unlikely to state them explicitly – although in the contract catering field some of these needs may be built in to the contract with the client. These needs then become a series of expectations in the customer's mind – expectations about the type of food they would like, how they would like to be greeted, how much they are prepared to pay and so on. If these expectations are met or exceeded then the customer will be satisfied and will have had a

Characteristics of the experience

	TANGIBLE	INTANGIBLE
PRODUCT	The food and beverage product Facilitating goods : china, glass, cutlery Information : menu Processes : e.g. eftpos* terminal	Atmosphere Aesthetics Feelings Comfort
SERVICE	Actions Process Speed Script Corrective action	Warmth Friendliness Care Service

Nature of the contact

* electronic funds transfer at point of service

Figure 1.1 The quality characteristics matrix

'quality' experience. If, however, these unwritten expectations are not met then quality will not have been provided for that customer and their needs will be left unsatisfied. These gaps between customer expectations and service provision have been well explored by Parasuraman, Zeithaml and Berry, (1985).

The full range of features and characteristics that go to make up any hospitality experience is extremely wide and will vary from customer to customer. Making sense of these complex expectations is difficult but the framework provided in Figure 1.1 gives some guidance as to how they can be broken down. The matrix shows that the hospitality product consists of a combination of both tangible and intangible elements, relating to the physical characteristics of the provision (the product) and the interpersonal contact that occurs during the service.

Looking at a restaurant operation, for example, the product tangible elements might consist of the actual food presented to the customer and the facilitating goods used to serve the food on or with. The style and nature of the crockery, cutlery and glassware and also the linen and napkins are part of the quality experience. The menu provides tangible evidence of the meal to come by displaying information about the dishes available in words or pictures. The final part is made up of the machine processes that a customer may come across in the hospitality operation. These could include the effectiveness of the EFTPOS terminal or the way the vending machine dispenses a cup of coffee.

The product intangible quadrant covers the atmosphere of the establishment and the aesthetic appeal of the décor, furniture and fittings. Every hospitality operation has its own feel – some feel immediately warm and friendly while others appear cold or clinical. Finding the right décor to give the right feelings to the customer is important. For example, compare the clean, bright businesslike atmosphere of a fast-food operation like Burger King with the warmer, darker, timeless feel of a Café Rouge. It is the product intangibles that help to provide that feeling of comfort, of being at ease that was identified earlier as an important part of the hospitality concept.

Service is often considered intangible. There are still elements of service that can be tangible. The actions that service staff perform for customers are tangible. So too is the way the service process is organised. Speed of service can be measured and in some circumstances - such as home delivery pizza - can be a key indicator of performance. The words that staff use - their service 'script' - also provide hard evidence. Another example of tangible service is the action taken to put something right after it has gone wrong - the service recovery or corrective action - although it must be better not to let things go wrong in the first place.

The service intangible part is hard to describe but is undeniably important. Indeed, for some customers, it is the single most important characteristic of a quality experience. The warmth and friendliness shown through a genuine smile have almost tangible impact. In some operations customers know implicitly that the staff care about them, while in others, customers know that the staff care about very little. It is this feeling of service that managers must strive to provide.

The relative importance of each part of the matrix is difficult to measure and will change from experience to experience and from customer to customer. However, research suggests that the product tangible component is more significant than the product intangible component. The food on the plate carries more weight than the atmosphere. On the other hand the service intangible component is probably more significant than the service tangible. The feeling of being looked after is more important than the speed of delivery (Parasuraman *et al.*, 1985, Nightingale, 1985).

Quality as described above, as the satisfaction of customer needs and expectations, matches the definition used by Crosby (1984) as one of his quality absolutes, that of 'conformance to requirements'. It is, however, of little use to the customers if they receive exactly what they want on one day but their next visit is a disaster, because a key employee has a bad day. This is obviously important in a hospitality operation where so much of the service depends on the performance of individual employees. Quality must also include a strong element of reliability. Crosby (1984) calls this 'zero defects' and stresses that this is the only acceptable quality standard. Everyone in an organization should be striving to do their job right first time, every time.

There is evidence, however, that some organizations are moving away from the idea of simply satisfying the customer and striving to 'delight' the customer. Delighting the customer means exceeding the customer's expectations but there are dangers in this practice. Tenner and DeToro (1992) suggest that delight arises as a result of the value-added characteristics and features that customers did not expect - arousing their latent expectations. But, once these latent expectations are aroused, they become expected the next time. Over time, those little extras will become the expected norm and new 'delights' must be found.

Delivering quality in hospitality operations involves reliably providing the accommodation, food, service and entertainment within an environment that meets customers' expectations, and at the same time, creating opportunities for adding value that will exceed expectations and result in delight and repeat purchase or recommendation. Deming (1982) suggests that while an unhappy customer will go to someone else, a customer who is only just satisfied may also change because they can't lose a lot and they might gain. He argues that profit comes from repeat customers; customers who boast about the product and service they receive and bring their friends with them next time.

WHY IS QUALITY IMPORTANT?

Lewis (1989) suggests that the pressure on all businesses to pay attention to quality comes from three main sources. First, customers are more demanding of the products and services they buy, and the way those products and services are delivered. Even in the UK, customers are no longer reluctant to complain about bad service. Second, the development of sophisticated technology, both hard and soft, allows managers to provide a wealth of potential additional and convenience services, although personal contact is still seen as highly valued. The technology provides the back-of-house means but 'soft-touch' is still valued in delivery. Third, in an increasingly competitive and international marketplace, quality is seen as providing the edge of competitive advantage.

In the face of these pressures, there can be few managers who still hold to the idea that quality is too expensive or too much trouble to be of any real value. Zeithaml, Parasuraman and Berry (1990) offer three areas of benefit that result from an emphasis on quality.

Quality leads to efficiency

Rather than increasing the costs of an operation, an emphasis on quality and quality improvement results in operational efficiencies that more than recoup the investment. The costs of quality can be divided into two types – the costs of conformance and the costs of nonconformance. The costs of conformance are those involved in assuring that everything comes out right and includes all prevention efforts and training. The costs of nonconformance can be divided into appraisal costs and failure costs. Appraisal costs are the costs of inspection to make sure that mistakes are kept down and to try to ensure that any mistakes made are identified before reaching the customer. Failure costs are the costs of having made mistakes. Internal failure costs are those incurred where mistakes are found before they reach the customer. External failure costs are when mistakes are not found before reaching the customer. They include such things as repair and warranty claims, providing replacement goods or services, but for a hospitality operation it is the loss of future business that is the major cost element here. Crosby (1984) suggests that a service firm can waste as much as 35 per cent of its costs on producing non-quality. He estimates that appraisal and failure costs account for approximately 95 per cent of this total, whereas prevention costs account for the other 5 per cent. Turning this ratio around, giving a much higher emphasis to prevention provides a massive potential for reducing the total cost of any service business.

Quality creates true customers

If the efficiency benefits above are combined with the high perceived value identified earlier then the result will be loyal customers who use the operation consistently over a long period and talk about the experience to their friends. The academic literature on services marketing has recently begun to stress the value of long-term customer relationships (Gummesson, 1995), something managers in the industry may find surprising as good hospitality operations have always recognized the importance of loyal customers.

The payoff of quality

Combining efficiency cost savings and loyal customers must have an impact on the bottom line. The Profit Impact of Market Strategy (PIMS) study (Buzzell and Gale, 1987) has shown that the most important single factor affecting a business unit's performance is the quality of its products and services in comparison to its competitors. Similar results have been found in the hospitality industry (Walker and Salameh, 1990). In the short term, the added value of a 'quality' hospitality operation allows profits to be generated through premium prices but in the long-term, business growth and quality improvement efficiencies will maintain higher profit margins.

THE SPECIAL FEATURES OF HOSPITALITY OPERATIONS

Although the best-known approaches to quality management and their gurus (such as Crosby, Deming, Ishikawa, Juran, Shingo, Taguchi and others (see Flood, 1993)), have grown up in the manufacturing sector, there has been increasing focus on service operations and the particular challenges they face in delivering service quality to the customer (Lewis 1989, Zeithaml *et al.*, 1990, Gummesson 1992). As illustrated by the quality matrix in Figure 1.1, hospitality operations not only face the manufacturing challenge of producing food, drink and accommodation, but also have to cope with being a service operation delivering directly to the customer.

The resulting complexity makes managing quality in hospitality operations difficult but not impossible. Fitzgerald *et al.* (1991) suggest four features that distinguish service operations from their manufacturing counterparts. Reviewing these four characteristics for hospitality operations provides insights into the task facing managers.

Intangibility

Unlike a 'pure' service operation, hospitality services do not consist solely of the service performance and the intangible factors that affect this interaction. A large part of hospitality consists of the very tangible product elements of food, drink and accommodation. On the product side there are the tangible elements of the food or room itself. How hot is the food? What does it look like? What size is the bed? How large is the bath, etc? There are also the intangible elements of the atmosphere created. Does the customer feel comfortable, 'at home', secure? On the service side there are the intangible elements of the friendliness or care offered by the hospitality provider, but at the same time it is possible to identify tangible service elements such as the time taken to deliver the service or the effectiveness of the service performed. Did the waiter spill the soup? How long between the order and delivery of room-service breakfast? There is as yet little conclusive proof about which of these two dimensions has the most impact on customer satisfaction.

Heterogeneity

Service outputs are heterogeneous. The standard of performance may vary, especially where there is a high labour content. It is hard to ensure consistent quality from the same employee from day to day and harder still to get comparability between employees. However, this will crucially affect what the customer receives.

Although a customer may expect to find some variability in the service received, the same cannot be said of the product dimension. A steak au poivre served by one unit of a restaurant chain at one end of the country must be consistent with every other steak au poivre served in every other unit of the same chain. A customer will not tolerate a hotel bedroom that is clean and fresh on one visit, but dirty and smelly on a return visit. The tolerance of error on the product side seems much lower than on the service side.

Simultaneity

In many services, such as a visit to the hairdresser or taking a plane flight, the production and consumption occur at the same time. This means that services cannot be measured or inspected before sale and provision to the customer. In a hospitality operation, not only is the production and consumption of service simultaneous but the production side also operates on a very short cycle of operation. This ranges from simultaneous, where food is cooked and served at the table as in the Benihana chain, to decoupled production such as a cook–freeze system. There are also many other possible systems in between (Huelin and Jones, 1990). The time-scale over which quality management tools and techniques can be applied is therefore very short.

Perishability

Services cannot be stored, so removing the buffer of an inventory that can be used to cope with fluctuations in customer demand. Even a hotel bedroom is a perishable product. Empty rooms cannot be stockpiled for a busy day sometime in the future. Once a room or a restaurant seat has been left empty, the potential revenue from the occupation of that space is lost. From the product perspective, raw ingredients or a complete meal can be stored for a short period, depending on the method of storage. Normally, however, the period will be a matter of days rather than years. On the accommodation side, a hotel room will not deteriorate substantially if left empty for a time. Many UK seaside resort hotels close for the winter and even hotels in central London have been known to close down floors of rooms when business is slack.

It has been established that hospitality operations display many of the characteristics of other service operations but with the added complication of a production element. However, even the production side of hospitality is far from straightforward.

The need to provide the appropriate environment within which hospitality can be delivered means that most hospitality businesses need a substantial investment in premises and plant. The average development cost of a five-star hotel in Europe, for example, is £111,600 per bedroom, excluding land costs (Touche Ross, 1992) but falls to 'only' £26,600 for a two-star property. On the other hand, variable costs are low. The materials cost of servicing a hotel bedroom is under £5 per room (Lockwood and Jones, 1990). This high fixed cost/low variable cost structure creates an unusual cost–profit–volume relationship. Generally the break-even volume for hospitality businesses will be quite high. Exceeding this level will result in high profits, but low volumes will result in substantial losses. The number of hotel operations that fell into the hands of the receiver following the trials of the recession of the early 1990s bears forceful witness to this fact.

This would not in itself be too difficult a problem to deal with if it were possible confidently to predict the levels of demand for the operation. Unfortunately, hospitality services suffer from complex fluctuations in demand. Demand will fluctuate over time – hourly, daily, weekly, monthly, annually and cyclically; by departmental function – reception, housekeeping, bar, restaurant, banqueting, conferences; and by the type of customer – group or individual, business or leisure. The result is a mixture of patterns that makes forecasting and subsequent resource scheduling very difficult indeed.

The length of the hospitality production cycle is short, giving little time for monitoring or for the correction of errors. A restaurant operation may buy in fresh produce in the early morning, which is prepared during the same morning, offered for lunch and consumed by early afternoon. The minimum turn-round time for a hotel bedroom is around half an hour, from the guest checking out to the room being available for resale.

The food production process deals with raw ingredients that have a limited shelf life and which, if contaminated, can result in serious illness and death. Hotels are also potentially dangerous places due to mugging, fire and terrorist attack. The appeal of a white-knuckle ride at a theme park is partly based on appearing to be on the brink of safety. Customers entering a hospitality operation are placing themselves in the care of that host, and the operation must employ all due diligence to ensure their safety. Customers must trust the operation, based on only limited evidence.

The hospitality operation is labour intensive and technological substitution is really only possible in back-of-house operations. For example, developments in catering technology have allowed the decoupling of production and service through the use of cook–chill, cook–freeze or sous vide methods. McDonald's industrialized service delivery system ensures high speed, high volume with high consistency over a limited product range and limited human intervention. Decoupling has also found its way into hotel reservations through the use of information technology. Reservations for Forte Travelodge, for example, are all handled centrally and then sent to the individual units electronically. It is in fact much easier to book a room by telephone from the Little Chef next door than to deal directly with the receptionist in the separate accommodation block.

Throughout the complex operations described above, the hospitality operation is pressurized by the physical presence of the customer, monitoring progress with the expert eye of someone who has eaten many meals before, who has slept in many different beds and paid numerous bills.

KEY CHARACTERISTICS

From the above discussion it is possible to identify four defining characteristics that inform any discussion of hospitality operations.

The central importance of the customer

As mentioned earlier, hospitality cannot be delivered without the presence of the customer, who also provides the source of revenue for the continued financial success of the operation. The customer is directly involved in many aspects of the delivery of the hospitality service. The combination of all customers decides the demand pattern for the operation. One customer forms part of the environment for all other customers. The customer is the final arbiter of satisfaction with both the service and product elements and, therefore, the judge of the quality of hospitality provided. Given these factors, it is perhaps surprising that some hospitality providers still think they know better than the customer.

The criticality of capacity utilization

Achieving a satisfactory balance between demand patterns, resource scheduling and operational capacity is one of the most difficult tasks facing hospitality managers. Managing customer demand to result in the optimum volume at maximum value is extremely complex. If there are too few customers overall, the cost structure of the business ensures financial ruin. If there are too many customers, without the required capacity or resources, the quality of the experience suffers and customers leave dissatisfied. Customer volume can be bought by discounting prices at the expense of value per customer. Not discounting can scare potential customers away to the competition. Yield management is crucial, both for accommodation and for food and beverage operations. Scheduling of resources is also critical. If there are too many staff on duty to cover anticipated demand, productivity and profitability suffer: too few staff on duty and service levels fall along with staff morale. The key here seems effective forecasting and yet little progress has been made in unravelling demand patterns to provide accurate predictions. Many operations still rely on the equivalent of a wet finger.

The complexity of operation

All hospitality operations require management with a combination of manufacturing expertise and service skill in a business that operates around the clock, 365 days a year, and is busiest when most other businesses are not. To consistently deliver an appropriate level of product and service quality to each individual customer requires the efforts of many different teams of staff, who must be coordinated to deliver to standard every time. Catering for the needs of a single customer may be difficult enough, but catering to the needs of many different groups of customers, all with slightly different requirements, multiplies the complexity of the problem many times over. The importance of a coordinated team effort between the different functional groups of employees is self evident. However, the industry maintains organizational structures and occupational boundaries that directly contradict this objective.

The reliance on service contact staff

However well planned and designed the hospitality operation is, however well scheduled the resources, in the final analysis the success of any customer experience will be decided at 'the moment of truth' – the interaction between the customer and the service provider. A highly skilled chef can spend many hours preparing the finest dishes and yet they can be ruined by the lack of care of the waiter. Many millions of pounds can be spent furnishing a hotel bedroom but the pushy porter looking for a tip can tarnish the whole weekend break. The point of contact between the customer and the service provider is also an opportunity for the operation to sell its service and to generate additional revenue. Hotel receptionists can significantly increase the profitability of a hotel by upselling – encouraging customers to trade up to more luxurious and more expensive accommodation – or by simply asking if the guest would like to make a reservation for dinner in the hotel restaurant. Referral of business from one operation in a chain to another can also provide added revenue. It is even more surprising, given the key role that the service provider has in ensuring customer satisfaction and in improving revenue and profit levels, that they remain some of the least well paid and least respected members of staff (Guerrier and Lockwood, 1989).

CONCLUSION

Managing quality in hospitality operations is difficult, complicated by the complex blend of production and service elements that need to be managed over the short cycle of operations. There is an obvious need for a systematic and all-encompassing approach to the problem, yet only a few hospitality operations have risen to the challenge. The organizations described in the following chapters have taken on that challenge and the potential rewards for these organizations that do get it right, first time, every time, are enormous.

REFERENCES

British Standards Institue (1987) *Glossary of Quality Terms (BS 4778)* London: BSI.

Burgess, J. (1982) Perspectives on gift exchange and hospitable behaviour. *International Journal of Hospitality Management*, 1(1), 49–57.

Buzzell, R.D. and Gale, B.T. (1987) *The PIMS Principles: Linking Strategy to Performance* New York: Free Press.

Crosby, P.B. (1984) *Quality Without Tears* New York: McGraw Hill.

Deming, W.E. (1982) *Quality, Productivity and Competitive Position* Cambridge: Massachusetts Institute of Technology, Centre for Advanced Engineering Study.

Fitzgerald, L., Johnston, R., Brignall, S., Silvestro, R., and Voss, C. (1991) *Performance Measurement in Service Businesses* London: Chartered Institute of Management Accountants.

Flood, R.L. (1993) *Beyond TQM* Chichester: Wiley.

Guerrier, Y. and Lockwood, A. (1989) Core and peripheral employees in hotel operations. *Personnel Review*, 18(1), 9–15.

Gummesson, E. (1992) *Quality Management in Service Organisations* New York : SQA.

Gummesson, E. (1995) *Relationsmarknadsföring: Från 4P till 30R* Malmö: Liber-Hermods.

Huelin, A. and Jones, P. (1990) Thinking about catering systems *International Journal of Operations and Production Management*, 10(8), 42–52.

Lewis, B.R. (1989) Quality in the service sector: a review. *International Journal of Bank Marketing*, 7(5), 4–12.

Litteljohn D. (1990) Hospitality research: philosophies and progress, in R. Teare, L. Moutinho and N. Morgan (eds), *Managing and Marketing Services in the 1990s* London: Cassell.

Lockwood A. and Jones P. (1984) *People and the Hotel and Catering Industry* London: Holt, Rinehart and Winston.

Lockwood A. and Jones P. (1990) Applying value engineering to rooms management. *International Journal of Contemporary Hospitality Management*, 2(1). [pages not available]

Mullins L.J. (1993) *Hospitality Management: A Human Resources Approach* London: Pitman.

Nailon P. (1982) Theory in hospitality management. *International Journal of Hospitality Management*, 1(3), 135–43.

NEDC (1992) *Costs and Manpower Productivity in UK Hotels* London: NEDC.

Nightingale, M. (1985) The hospitality industry: defining quality for a quality assurance programme: a study of perceptions. *Service Industries Journal*, 5(1), 9–22.

Nykiel, R.A. (1989) *Marketing in the Hospitality Industry* New York: CBI/Van Nostrand Reinhold.

Parasuraman, A., Zeithaml, V.A. and Berry, L.L. (1985) A conceptual model of service quality and its implications for future research. *Journal of Marketing*, 49 (Fall), 41–50.

Reuland, R.J. and Cassee E.T.H. (1983) *Hospitality in Hospitals*, in E. Cassee and R. Reuland (eds), *The Management of Hospitality* Oxford: Pergamon.

Tenner, A.R. and DeToro, I.J. (1992) *Total Quality Management: Three Steps to Continuous Improvement* Cambridge, MA: Addison-Wesley.

Touche Ross (1992) *European Hotel Construction Costs* London: Deloitte Touche Tohmatsu International.

Walker, J.R. and Salameh T.T. (1990) The QA payoff. *Cornell Hotel and Restaurant Quarterly*, 30(4), 57–59.

Zeithaml, V.A., Parasuraman, A. and Berry, L.L. (1990) *Delivering Service Quality* New York: Free Press.

TWO

A systematic approach to quality

Andrew Lockwood

Given the difficulties identified in the previous chapter and the importance of providing quality for any hospitality operation, the need for a systematic approach to quality management is evident. Quality, and the reliability that needs to go with it, cannot be expected to happen by chance. Providing the framework that will encourage the delivery of consistent quality is the prime responsibility of the management team. Although it will be the operative level staff who will come face to face with the customer, and who will produce the service or product the customer has requested, it is the managers who must ensure that any barriers to quality are removed and that quality and quality improvement are constantly encouraged.

This is not an easy task.

FROM QI TO TQM

The development of approaches to managing quality is shown in Figure 2.1. This diagram shows a movement from early approaches to quality that relied on inspection of the finished product, through quality control and quality assurance to total quality management.

Quality inspection

The earliest, and probably the easiest, approach to looking for quality is the inspection approach. This is a simple approach that relies on identifying defects in a product or service before they reach the customer by introducing an inspection stage, or stages. It is based on having a specification of what the product should be like and checking the product against that standard after it has been produced. This checking would normally be done by staff specifically employed for the purpose. If defects are discovered then that product will be rejected as non-conforming and will be sent back for rework – to put the defects

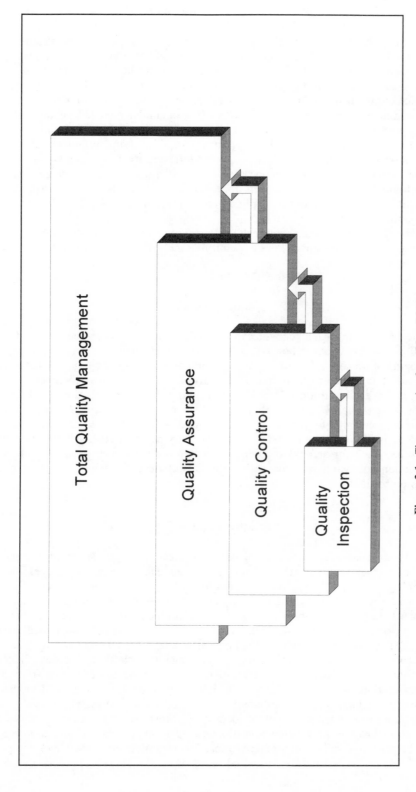

Figure 2.1 The progression from QI to TQM

right – or for scrap. While manufacturing industry has relied on a separate inspection department to carry out this task, this is not a model that has been adopted in hospitality. A simple example of this inspection stage in hospitality is the head chef standing at the hot plate during service and passing dishes across to the restaurant staff only when satisfied with the standard reached. The floor housekeeper checking rooms after servicing by a chambermaid and before release to reception offers a similar model. In neither of these cases, however, could quality inspection be seen as the prime role of their job.

It can be seen that the focus here is firmly on identifying product defects. The emphasis is on the negative elements of quality followed by a rejection of substandard work. The inspector becomes someone the other staff dread and the game becomes one of getting things past the inspector. This approach is also based on product attributes and it is difficult to see how it could be applied in a pure service setting; it really only works for the tangible parts of the operation.

Although this approach will identify the occurrence of non-conformance, the emphasis is on putting things right rather than on identifying the source of the problem and dealing with it at source.

Quality control

The quality control approach recognizes that quality should be designed in to a detailed specification and that quality checks should be made throughout the production process. By developing more sophisticated inspection methods at appropriate points in the production process, this approach will find more errors and will correct them earlier. The emphasis, however, is still on a find and fix mentality. Quality control will not improve product or service quality, it will only highlight when it is not present. A nonconforming product or service must be produced before action will be taken to correct it and this must lead to inefficiency and waste. From the staff perspective, the focus is now on switching the blame for defects to other people or other departments to avoid the 'disciplinary' action against those who make mistakes. Indeed the whole focus of quality control is on mistakes.

Quality assurance

The quality assurance approach recognizes the inherent inefficiency of waiting for mistakes to happen, and makes attempts to design quality in to the process so that things can't go wrong. If they do go wrong, they are identified and corrected as they happen. There is a recognition that lasting and continuous improvement in quality can best be achieved through planning and preventing problems from arising at source. The introduction of quality assurance tools and techniques such as SPC (statistical process control), FMECA (failure mode effect and cause analysis), quality costing, the seven quality tools (histograms, checksheets, pareto analysis, cause and effect diagrams, graphs, control charts, and scatter diagrams), helps to move the emphasis from detection to prevention. At the same time, the approach is likely to include developing a comprehensive quality system, perhaps based on the ISO 9000 series.

Quality assurance is not just about a focus on systems. To be effective, quality assurance must also involve the development of a new operating philosophy and approach that looks to be proactive rather than reactive, that includes motivating and involving people in the process across normal departmental barriers.

Total quality management

The key differences between quality assurance and total quality management are in the focus on the customer and the scale and nature of involvement within and outside the organization. The driving force of any TQM approach is the focus on the satisfaction of customer needs. The whole system of operation should be directed at customer satisfaction and anything that could get in the way of delivering this satisfaction must be removed. This therefore involves the whole organization, including suppliers, in looking for ways of continually improving the products or services delivered. The TQM approach places more emphasis on the people in the organization and their role, through a broadening of their outlook and skills, through encouragement of creativity, through training and empowerment, in measuring their own performance and finding ways to improve it. The emphasis here is on a management-led move towards teamwork and employee participation and motivation which, taking a whole-system perspective, can involve organizations in significant changes in their culture. Whereas it is relatively easily to introduce new systems and procedures, changing the culture is a much more difficult, but essential, task.

The approaches identified above are not mutually exclusive. As the diagram shows, one approach builds towards the next. Just because you have introduced a total quality management approach doesn't mean that you can ignore quality inspection or quality control completely, although there should now be very few defects left to find.

One difficulty facing organizations is knowing where to start their quality initiatives and how to avoid what has become known as 'total quality paralysis'. Many organizations have found that basing their approach around a national or international standard or award provides a framework upon which the organization can build.

THE BS EN ISO 9000 SERIES

In 1979 the British Standards Institute first published their guidelines on quality management systems under the title BS 5750. This standard was based on a series of Ministry of Defence supplier standards, and it is not surprising that it was engineering and manufacturing companies that first took on the standard. This UK standard achieved international success and, with minor amendments, it became the model for the international and European standards published in 1987 as ISO 9000 and EN 29000. When the guidelines were revised in 1994, it was decided to drop the separate BS 5750 title and adopt the international ISO 9000 title instead, as the standards were already identical and to avoid further confusion.

ISO 9000 outlines the key elements required of a quality system and lays down a structured approach on which a system can be based. The guidelines are based on practices that have proved successful in other businesses and they should be applicable irrespective of the size of the company or its industry sector. The standard sets out how to establish, document and maintain an effective quality system that will prove to customers that the company is committed to quality and has the necessary systems and procedures in place to achieve it. It does not, however, specify what the product or service should be like; the requirement for defining customer quality standards is left to the individual organization based on their own customers' needs.

Having followed the guidelines and developed a documented quality system, a company can elect to be assessed by one of several authorized independent bodies – a third-party assessor. The assessor will review the company's documentation and carry out site visits to check that the system is working properly and when satisfied will make the award. Registration lasts for three years but the company is subject to biannual surveillance audits to make sure everything is still going according to plan.

The ISO 9000 series contains a number of different parts that are appropriate for different types of business. ISO 9002 is concerned with 'a quality systems model for quality assurance in production and installation' and is seen as the most appropriate for hospitality operations. The main elements covered by the system include the following.

Management responsibility. No quality system will work properly unless management at all levels are committed to its success. This part of the standard covers the areas of developing a quality policy for the company, providing an organizational structure identifying authority and responsibility for quality, and the procedures for reviewing the overall effectiveness of the quality system.

Quality system. This section asks the company to provide evidence, normally written evidence, of the planning, documentation and implementation of the quality system. This must include a quality manual and written procedures, but only where the skills, training or methods are sufficiently complex to need them.

Contract review. This rather unusual-sounding requirement simply means assessing if the customers' requirements are fully understood and if the operation has the capability to satisfy them. Although originally designed for use with formal written contracts, this also covers any offer for sale to the customer, i.e. any hospitality offer.

Document control. A prime need in a document-based system is to have a system to ensure that all documentation is up to date. The main objective is to make sure that all the personnel who need certain information, data or documents to perform their duties properly are provided with the right information in its most up-to-date form. This may appear an unnecessarily bureaucratic requirement but it is up to the company to decide which documents should be included. Not every document in the company can be said to have a material influence on the quality system and it is only these that should be covered.

Purchasing. The standard covers three aspects of purchasing: the assessment of suppliers and subcontractors, the development of clear purchasing instructions for all goods and services purchased, and the 'verification' of the purchased product, i.e. checking that you got what you ordered, which may involve inspections on your suppliers' premises as well.

Customer supplied product. Although unusual in most hospitality situations, an operation must show as much care about the use of materials provided by the customer as if they were purchasing them themselves. In hotels, for example, this may include wines, flowers, wedding cakes or equipment provided for use during a function. For a contract caterer, this could be the premises provided by the client including the kitchens and equipment.

Product identification and traceability. The purpose of product identification is to keep track of the inputs to a product or service so if there is a problem it can be traced to its source. This is particularly important where food is concerned, and where such a system may provide the basis for demonstrating 'due diligence' in food safety.

Process control. This part of the standard covers making sure that all the activities of the operation are carried out under controlled conditions; that everyone knows what they should be doing and how they should be doing it. This will include the development of detailed work procedures that will ensure the proper planning and co-ordination of work processes.

Inspection and testing. This covers inspection of incoming goods or raw materials, inspection during the production and service process, as well as testing of the finished product. The main objective here is not only to ensure that all specified requirements are being met but also that any nonconforming products are identified and dealt with. Records of all inspection and testing must be kept. These records may include the inspection of bedrooms, details of kitchen hygiene checks and assessment of service staff performance.

Inspection, measuring and test equipment. If testing is going to be accurate, there must be procedures for making sure that the equipment used to do the testing – probably mainly temperature-testing equipment in a catering environment – is regularly checked and calibrated.

Inspection and test status. Those products or services that have been tested must be identified.

Control of nonconforming product. The standard requires that an operation records, identifies and segregates a nonconforming product and that there is an identified procedure for what to do with it then. To give a rather extreme example, if a customer returns a steak for being improperly cooked, there should be a procedure for making sure that the same steak is not sent straight back out to the same customer, or indeed to any customer.

Corrective and preventive action. When the quality system highlights a quality problem, there must be a way of analysing why the problem occurred, then agreement on what action needs to be taken to make sure that it cannot happen again, and a check that these measures have indeed been implemented.

Handling, storage, packaging and delivery. The requirement here is to ensure that the quality of the product is maintained throughout the process. This could include the correct handling of food by staff, the use of appropriate containers and wrappings for food, storage at the correct temperature, and ensuring the speed and temperature of delivery.

Control of quality records. No evidence-based system would be complete without a procedure for the handling of records. These records might include contract review notes, inspection and test reports, materials and test certificates, audit reports, and management review records. The system should identify what records are to be kept, how they are to be filed and referenced and how long they will be retained.

Internal quality audits. The idea of an internal quality audit is very similar to an internal financial audit. The technique is really the same; the operations are examined and assessed against defined criteria, using checklists and samplng procedures, and should result in a report highlighting any errors or deficiencies. The audits should be carried out by personnel independent of those having direct responsibility for the activity being audited.

Training. Training, education and quality awareness are important parts of the standard. The training needs of all personnel should be established and then appropriate training should be provided to meet these needs. In addition the skills and qualifications necessary for a particular job should be decided and steps taken to make sure that job holders have these. Records of all training undertaken must be kept.

Servicing. A new element in the 1994 ISO 9002 standard is that where servicing is a specified requirement then procedures should be established and maintained. The procedures should include performing, reporting and verifying that services meet contract requirements.

Statistical techniques. Another amendment to the standard requires that the operation identifies the need for statistical techniques, and where they are appropriate they should be applied, documented and records maintained. To date, the hospitality industry has not used statistical quality techniques widely but may yet find that control charts and similar techniques could have a beneficial effect.

It can be seen from the description given above that the ISO standard is not prescriptive in telling companies how they should set up their system but simply gives guidance on what elements should be included. The standard does look daunting and the need for documented evidence does seem to add a heavy administrative burden. In fact, however, many companies will have a lot of the documents in place already as part of their normal operation and it is up to the company to decide which additional documents they need and how complicated the paperwork needs to be.

INVESTORS IN PEOPLE (IIP)

IIP is a UK initiative to provide a national standard that can be awarded to companies which can show that their pursuit of excellence and business success has been achieved through the development of their management and staff. The central focus of the standard is not on quality or quality systems. The focus is solely on people and their working performance. However, it is argued that the benefits of pursuing the IIP standard will include adding value to quality programmes by stressing the central importance of people in the delivery of quality. In addition, IIP should help organizations to recognize and meet the needs of individuals, and so promote motivation and morale, releasing their full potential to improve performance. Another benefit is that the standard stresses the importance of all employees recognizing the importance of customers and how they can be satisfied, and encouraging a people-centred approach to customers. Finally, the achievement of the IIP standard should bring the organization public recognition and this will make the company more attractive for customers and for potential high-calibre employees.

The standard provides a framework for assessing the achievements of companies in investing in their people. It does not give a rigid blueprint of how they should go about doing it. Each company, therefore, has the opportunity to develop an approach which suits its own particular needs, circumstances and culture. The standard consists of a series of twenty-four Investors in People Indicators. For each indicator there are guidance notes on what that indicator is intended to cover, and examples of the sort of material that a company will need to include in its portfolio of evidence. Examples of two of these indicators are given in Table 2.1.

Table 2.1 Guidance notes for IIP indicators

Investors in People Indicator	Guidance Notes	What the assessors look for/ask
1.3 There is a written but flexible plan which sets out business goals and targets.	Your longer-term vision is underpinned by clear goals or objectives for the business and a plan for achieving these which includes targets and short-term milestones. The plan is flexible, reviewed and updated as necessary, particularly if there are any major changes affecting the business.	What the assessors may look for: check for evidence that there is a real business plan, not just a budget. Check that it is reviewed at least annually, more often if there have been significant changes. What the assessors may ask: discuss the planning process and business plan with you. Question how you look at the training and development implications of major changes.
3.5 Effective action takes place to achieve the training and development objectives of individuals and the organization.	Check that the training and development identified actually happen, subject to business priorities and budget resources. Look at training and development in the broadest sense, for example coaching, project work, experience in other functions, in addition to formal programmes and courses.	The assessors may follow through the records for a sample of employees, from the identification of need to the training and development action. The assessors may ask a sample of employees what was done about their training and development needs. Did what was planned for them happen? If not, were reasons given to them?

Figure 2.2 identifies the four key stages of commitment, planning, action and evaluation. Once these four stages are in place, the company is assessed by the local Training and Enterprise Council (TEC) either through their own staff or through trained assessors from independent companies. The company must provide the assessors with a portfolio of evidence of practical working documents that they have met the requirements of all twenty-four indicators, but even more weight is placed by the assessors on what they find out through the interviews they carry out with a wide and balanced cross-section of management and staff. In the case of the Moat House Glasgow, 20 per cent of the assessment was based on documentary evidence and 80 per cent on the interviews conducted during the five-day period the assessors spent in the hotel (MacVicar and Brown, 1994).

Commitment

An IIP company makes a public commitment from the top to develop all employees to achieve its business objectives. This will involve a formal letter of intent being sent to the local TEC, but it is also the intention that it should be made public to all stakeholders, including customers and suppliers. The commitment will extend to developing a written, but flexible, business plan, setting goals and targets to be achieved, how all employees will contribute to these, and how to identify and meet their broad development needs. In simple terms, management needs to develop a vision of where the organization is going and communicate this to all employees to show them the role they will play in this future.

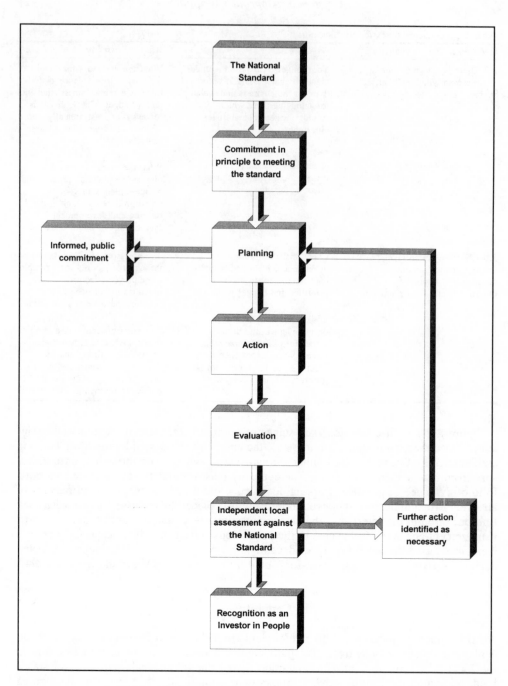

Figure 2.2 Investors in People: the journey

Planning

Within the business plan that is developed, the resources allocated to training and development should be clearly indicated. Management is then responsible for identifying with each individual what their training and development needs are and what will be the best way to meet them to achieve the required standard. This may include the pursuit of qualifications under the appropriate (S)NVQ schemes.

Action

Having developed the plan, the company must be able to prove that it has taken action to train and develop people, starting from their initial needs on recruitment, continually developing and improving their skills, and involving them in that process to contribute to the identification and meeting of their job-related training needs. All training and development activities should be seen to be effective and managers must provide employees with the support they need.

Evaluation

Having undertaken training and development action, the company must continuously assess that the investment they have made is paying off in the competence and commitment of their employees and in the contribution this has made to business performance. This will involve reviewing all training and development activities at the highest levels in the company and, through that, top management commitment and new targets should be communicated to all staff.

Assessments against the standard are made every three years, and a company must be able to show how its achievement of the standard has developed in that time.

In an industry that relies heavily on the performance of its employees to deliver hospitality services to the customers, it is not surprising that, after a slow start, interest in and registrations for the standard are growing very rapidly across all sectors of the industry in both large and small companies. DeVere Hotels was the first national hotel group to win the award, followed by organizations such as Friendly Hotels, Center Parcs and many of the companies that feature in the case studies that follow.

MALCOLM BALDRIDGE NQA

While ISO 9000 and IIP provide a standard against which companies can be assessed to gain external recognition, there are another group of awards conducted, usually on an annual basis, within a competitive framework. Companies submit their applications to enter the competition and following assessment of documentary evidence and site visits the winner in a particular category is announced and applauded. These awards include the UK Quality Award given by the British Quality Foundation, which is closely related to the European Quality Award given by the European Foundation for Quality Management, and the Deming Prize instituted by the Union of Japanese

Scientists and Engineers. However, probably the best-known award internationally is the Malcolm Baldrige National Quality Award (MBNQA).

Only available to companies based in the US, the Malcolm Baldrige National Quality Award is annual award to recognize companies for their business excellence and quality achievement. The award is designed to promote awareness of quality as an increasingly important element in competitiveness, an understanding of the requirements for performance excellence, and the sharing of information on successful performance strategies and the benefits derived from the implementation of these strategies.

The award has three categories: manufacturing companies, service companies, and small businesses. Awards may be given in each category each year. The award examination is based upon a series of performance-excellence criteria developed in partnership with industry. In responding to these criteria, each applicant is expected to provide information and data on the company's improvement processes and results. Information and data submitted must be sufficient to show that the applicant's approaches could be replicated or adapted by other companies. The examination is designed not only to serve as a reliable basis for making awards but also to permit a diagnosis of each applicant's overall management system.

Applications are reviewed and evaluated by the examiners in a four-stage process: Stage 1 – independent review and evaluation by at least five members of the Board; Stage 2 – consensus review and evaluation for applications that score well in Stage 1; Stage 3 – site visits to applicants that score well in Stage 2; Stage 4 – judges' review and recommendations. Each applicant receives a feedback report at the conclusion of the review process, based upon the applicant's responses to the award examination criteria.

The Malcolm Baldridge National Quality Award Criteria are the basis for making the awards and for giving feedback to applicants. The core values and concepts of the award are embodied in seven categories: leadership, information and analysis, strategic planning, human resource development and management, process management, business results, and customer focus and satisfaction. The links between these elements are shown in Figure 2.3.

The framework has four basic elements:

- **Driver.** Senior executive leadership sets directions, creates values, goals, and systems, and guides the pursuit of customer value and company performance improvement.
- **System.** The system comprises the set of well-defined and well-designed processes for meeting the company's customer and performance requirements.
- **Measures of Progress.** Measures of progress provide a results-oriented basis for channelling actions to delivering ever-improving customer value and company performance.
- **Goal.** The basic aims of the system are the delivery of ever-improving value to customers and success in the marketplace.

The distribution of the points score between the various examination categories provides an insight into the relative importance of the various categories in the determination of the award as shown in Table 2.2.

The only hospitality company to date to achieve this prestigious award is The Ritz–Carlton Hotel Company. Now part of the Marriott organization, Ritz–Carlton was an award winner in 1992. The group consists of 25 luxury hotels employing 11,500

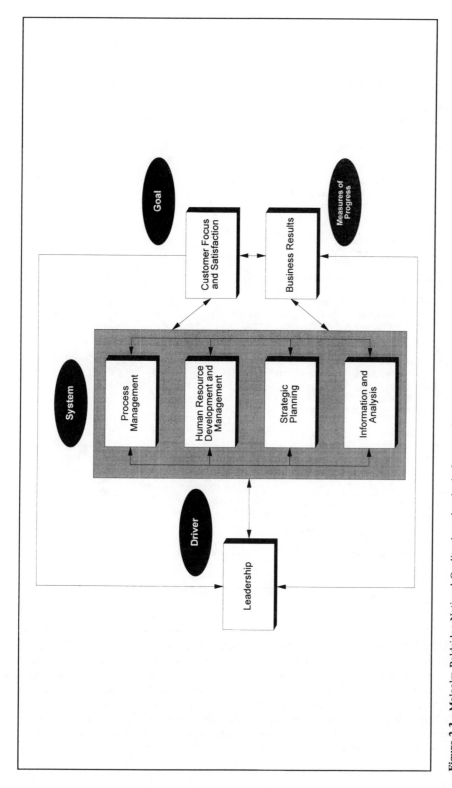

Figure 2.3 Malcolm Baldridge National Quality Award: criteria framework
Source: MBNQA, 1995.

Table 2.2 The allocation of points in examination categories for the Malcolm Baldridge National Quality Award

1995 Examination Categories/Items	Point Values	
1.0 Leadership	90	
1.1 Senior Executive Leadership		45
1.2 Leadership System and Organization		25
1.3 Public Responsibility and Corporate Citizenship		20
2.0 Information and Analysis	75	
2.1 Management of Information and Data		20
2.2 Competitive Comparisons and Benchmarking		15
2.3 Analysis and Use of Company-level Data		40
3.0 Strategic Planning	55	
3.1 Strategy Development		35
3.2 Strategy Deployment		20
4.0 Human Resource Development and Management	140	
4.1 Human Resource Planning and Evaluation		20
4.2 High Performance Work Systems		45
4.3 Employee Education, Training, and Development		50
4.4 Employee Well-being and Satisfaction		25
5.0 Process Management	140	
5.1 Design and Introduction of Products and Services		40
5.2 Process Management: Product and Service Production and Delivery		40
5.3 Process Management: Support Services		30
5.4 Management of Supplier Performance		30
6.0 Business Result	250	
6.1 Product and Service Quality Results		75
6.2 Company Operational and Financial Results		130
6.3 Supplier Performance Results		45
7.0 Customer Focus and Satisfaction	250	
7.1 Customer and Market Knowledge		30
7.2 Customer Relationship Management		30
7.3 Customer Satisfaction Determination		30
7.4 Customer Satisfaction Results		100
7.5 Customer Satisfaction Comparison		60
TOTAL POINTS	**1000**	

people. The key elements of the award-winning entry centred around participatory executive leadership, thorough information gathering, coordinated planning and execution, and a trained workforce empowered to 'move heaven and earth' to satisfy customers. The most important of these elements was identified as having a workforce committed to the Ritz–Carlton Gold Standards, which include a credo, a motto (ladies and gentlemen serving ladies and gentlemen), three steps of service and twenty 'Ritz–Carlton Basics'. The prime aim of all the measures that the company takes is not just to meet guest expectations but to provide them with a 'memorable visit'. According to customer surveys, 92 to 97 per cent of customers leave with that impression.

EFQM

The European Foundation for Quality Management (EFQM) was founded in 1988 by fourteen major European companies, with an objective of increasing awareness of and accelerating the involvement of European companies in TQM to improve Europe's international competitiveness. There are now more than 400 members, ranging from major multinationals and important national companies to research institutes in prominent European universities.

Based on the principle of the Baldridge award, the first European Quality Award (EQA) was presented by His Majesty King Juan Carlos of Spain to Rank Xerox in 1992. Applications for the annual award involve the submission of a company's own self-appraisal information based around the EFQM model as shown in Figure 2.4.

The model shows that customer satisfaction, employee satisfaction and impact on society are achieved through leadership-driving policy and strategy, people management, resources and processes, leading to excellence in business results. Each of these nine elements represents an area to appraise in a company's progress towards quality management. The results aspects are concerned with what the organization has achieved and is achieving, while the enablers aspects are concerned with how these results are being achieved. The percentages for the elements shown on the diagram are the weightings given to the various sections of the model in the determining of final scores by a panel of expert external assessors.

The UK Quality Award was launched in 1994 and is consistent in all respects with the EFQM model. No hospitality organization has yet achieved either the EQA or the UKQA award. However, the British Quality Foundation has established a Tourism and Hospitality Group, and it is to be hoped that, with their encouragement, it will not be long before a hospitality operation wins the award.

HCIMA

In April 1992, the HCIMA hosted a meeting on quality in the hospitality industry at the Institute of Directors in London. It was obvious from this meeting that there was a general agreement that delivering quality was important but that there was still considerable confusion about and antagonism towards quality systems in general and, what was then called BS 5750, in particular. The HCIMA responded by establishing a Quality Assurance Working Group with members from all sectors of the industry and representatives from consultancies and education. The first task that the working group took on was to produce a user-friendly guide to BS 5750, expressing in industry language how the system could be introduced to hospitality operations. *Managing Quality: An Approach for the Hospitality Industry* was published in 1993 and was well received. It has recently been updated to include the 1994 revisions to ISO 9000.

There was, however, recognition that this approach was still relying on the industry's acceptance of ISO 9000, and it was felt that it would be better to develop a quality standard that would include the main elements of ISO 9000 and IIP but would be aimed very specifically at the hospitality industry. The committee have produced such a standard based around the Quality Map shown in Figure 2.5

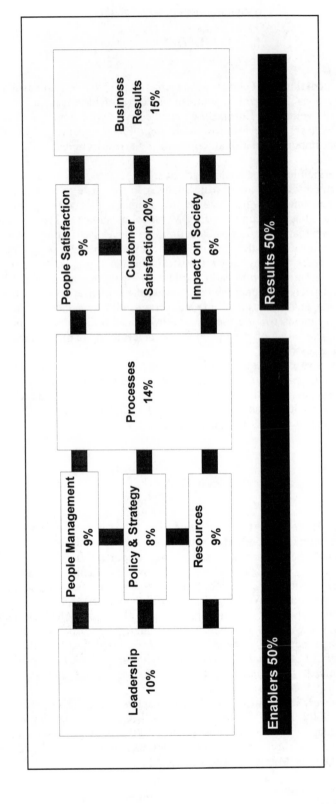

Figure 2.4 The European model for TQM
Source: EFQM, Brussels, 1995.

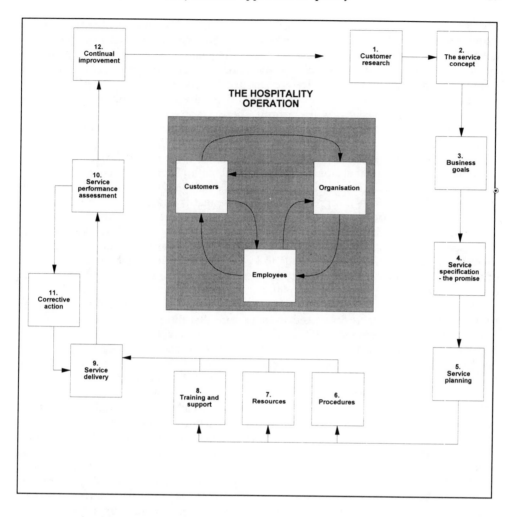

Figure 2.5 The HCIMA quality map
Source: A. Lockwood and HCIMA, 1996

At the centre of the map is the hospitality operation itself. Providing hospitality involves balancing the needs of the three groups which interact to deliver the service. The organization establishes the operation and attracts customers to use its services. These customers come into the operation to be served by the employees of the organization. These employees are rewarded by the organization for their services and, in turn, the customers pay the organization. To be successful everyone must leave the operation happy. The customers must be happy with the service they receive and the amount they pay for it. The employees must be happy that they have been adequately rewarded for their efforts. The organization must be happy that the return it is getting is worth being in business for.

If a company is going to satisfy the needs of its customers, it must obviously first know who the customers are and what sorts of things they like. The company has to carry out customer research. Having gathered information about customer needs, this has to be turned into the mix of products and services that are going to be provided. The plan must include those things that will make this operation different from the competitors. The company needs to develop the service concept that will form the basis of the business.

The company is now in a position to start to think about how to provide this service concept and how the business will perform. There is a need to establish clear business goals. These goals should give a clear picture of where the company wants to be in a certain period of time and how this will translate into achieving financial objectives.

At the moment the service concept is only in outline form and this needs to be made much more explicit so that customers can be told about it. There is a need to put together a service specification. This specification also lets employees know what the business is trying to achieve. In fact, it represents the promise that is being made to all customers.

Now the detailed work can start of turning that promise into a reality for every customer that comes into the operation. This requires some detailed service planning. Time spent on getting the plan right at this stage makes everything that follows much more straightforward. Everybody needs to know what their responsibilities are. All the critical stages in the operation need to be identified and the company needs to be sure that it has the resources to carry the plan out.

Before the operation is ready to open its doors to customers, three further things need to be in place. First, there is a need to make sure that the plans have been converted into a series of procedures and that these have been written down as appropriate. Second, there is a need to make sure that all the resources are available that will be needed to serve the customers. Third, all staff must have received the training and support they will require to do their jobs to the best of their abilities.

Now is the crucial stage that will be the ultimate measure of success. The moment of truth is when the customer comes into the operation and orders a meal or asks for a room. This is the point of service delivery, the point at which the promise to the customer should be fulfilled. It isn't enough to assume that if all is planned properly then it will always work. There has to be some way of checking that everything is going according to plan. There must be some form of service performance assessment. Obviously, if the checking does find that things are not quite as they should be, then things must be put right straight away. It is important to take immediate corrective action and find ways of making sure that the same problem does not come up again.

The operation should now be successful in delivering a range of products and services that customers want in an efficient and effective way. But the story is not quite over. There will always be ways to do things a little bit better and some time and effort should be spent looking for these to make continual improvement. Unfortunately, even with these improvements, customer tastes are constantly changing and an operation must keep up to date with what the competitors are doing. In other words, the cycle needs to start again with customer research.

There is nothing here that is particularly new or particularly complicated. In fact, the benefit of this approach is that most businesses will find that they are doing most of them already. They may be called by slightly different names but the basic ideas will still be there. There is nothing here that will come as a surprise. The ideas presented in the map simply make good business sense. What may be more of a surprise is how far down the road of quality management most businesses have already come.

Besides the simple description of the map, the standard will also include a detailed series of requirements for meeting the standard. The links to ISO 9000 and IIP will also be clearly shown so that an organization can follow the map at three levels: first, as a form of self-assessment to check that they are generally on the right lines, second, as a form of benchmarking to identify best practice and where current operations could be improved and, third, to meet the requirements for external accreditation against either or both ISO 9000 and IIP.

SUMMARY

The systems and award schemes described above offer a number of different models for looking at managing quality within an operation or a company. There are many common elements within these systems:

- the central role of people in the delivery and management of hospitality, as shown in the need for leadership, people satisfaction and training and development;
- the need for documentation that will provide evidence that quality systems are in place and are working, and as a way of providing data for improvement;
- the key requirement to focus on customers at all levels in the operation, and to know what customers want and to find effective ways to meet them;
- the realization that all these efforts are aimed at producing excellent business results.

In the end, however, it does not matter which particular model a company has followed. It is for that company to decide which approach is best suited to the particular needs and culture of each organization and to find a way to implement it effectively. That is the common element that binds the very different organizations described in the following chapters. These companies have found a way forward. They are forging a path through the quality maze that other hospitality operations will need to follow.

REFERENCES

MacVicar, A. and Brown, G. (1994) Investors in People at the Moat House International, Glasgow. *International Journal of Contemporary Hospitality Management*, 6(1/2), 53–60.

Further information on the systems outlined above can be obtained from:

BS EN ISO 9000 Series	BSI Quality Assurance, PO Box 375, Milton Keynes, MK14 6LL. Internet: The International Organization for Standardization: http://www.iso.ch/welcome.html or ISOEasy http://www.exit109.com/ ~ leebee/
Investors in People	Contact your local Training and Enterprise Council via the Yellow Pages
Malcom Baldridge	Internet: NIST Quality Program: http://www.nist.gov/quality_program/

EFQM   European Foundation for Quality Management,
                            Brussels Representative Office,
                            Avenue des Pléiades 19,
                            1200 Brussels, Belgium.
                            Tel: 32 2 775 35 11
BQF   The British Quality Foundation,
                            215 Vauxhall Bridge Road,
                            London SW1V 1EN.
                            Tel: 0171 963 8010
HCIMA   The Hotel and Catering International Management
                            Association,
                            191 Trinity Road, London, SW17 7HN.
                            Tel: 0181 672 4251

THREE

Alpha Flight Services

Andrew Ghillyer

Formerly the airport services division of Forte (UK) plc, Alpha Airports Group was floated as a public company in February 1994, with Forte retaining a 25 per cent stake. The Group consists of two separate divisions: Alpha Retail Trading, which operates a range of duty-free, tax-free and tax-paid retail shops in a total of 26 airport terminals; and Alpha Flight Services, which is responsible for the design, preparation and delivery of airline meals, the logistics and management of airline equipment and the provision of duty-free and sundry stores to over 100 international airlines serving 750 destinations.

Established in 1958 as Forte Airport Services, Alpha Flight Services (Alpha) is now the leading flight caterer in the UK, serving a wide cross-section of airlines, including British Airways, AirUK, Canadian Airlines, Gulf Air, and Britannia Airways, at twenty-six locations in the UK and Channel Islands. The division also has operations in France, The Netherlands, Portugal, the US (Newark and JFK, with two more operations in the planning stage), and joint ventures in Australia and Trinidad.

With a production capacity of over 7500 flights per week, Alpha is responsible for the delivery of approximately 40 million meals per year. Besides the core activity of meal preparation for scheduled and charter airlines, the operations incorporate a complex exercise designed to ensure that food and equipment is ordered, packed, and loaded onto aircraft within precise time frames. Typically, a scheduled Boeing 747 requires more than 40,000 items to be loaded, checked and packed into predetermined stowage on the aircraft. Allowing for choice, dietary and religious requirements, a long-haul flight can be supplied with over thirty different meal types. If, in the words of Rocco Forte, 'a hotel is a disaster waiting to happen', then running a hotel is a kindergarten compared to running a flight kitchen.

Close attention to quality, specification and hygiene control are of paramount importance throughout the process. Detailed planning control is required to ensure product integrity. The prepared meals, with all associated service equipment, beverages, sundry items, newspapers and duty-free stores, are then assembled on a flight-by-flight basis and loaded onto one of a fleet of over 220 purpose-built highlift vehicles for transfer to the aircraft.

RIGHT FOOD, RIGHT PLANE, RIGHT TIME

Close attention to detail in all parts of the operation, including the food production process, precision delivery to aircraft, and final handover to cabin crew, is paramount. 'Getting it right; first time; every time' is an operational credo that is especially pertinent to flight catering, since with a literally captive audience of up to 400 passengers at 9,000 m (30,000 ft), there is no second chance if something goes wrong – if no teapots are loaded, no tea will be served; if insufficient numbers of meals are loaded, some passengers may not get to eat. While a few additional meals are carried in order to provide some element of customer choice, with aircraft weight being the primary determinant in flight distance and number of passengers carried, there is simply no room to carry a large inventory of spares 'just in case', and so for the flight caterer, there is only one chance to get it right. In addition to these complexities of operation, there is also the possibility of passengers (particularly business-class passengers) arriving 20 minutes before a flight without a reservation, for whom a meal must be provided by means of a rapid-response (and, hopefully, still profitable) delivery system.

Under such highly restrictive operational parameters, quality becomes as much an exercise in logistics and statistical process control as it does a grand vision of product excellence and customer service. Everyone remains very conscious of the end-consumer of the product, namely the airline passenger, but the meal specifications set by the client airlines are ultimately sacrosanct, since by the time the meal is placed in front of the passenger by a member of the cabin crew, it is now British Airways' meal or Canadian Airlines' meal, not Alpha's.

QUALITY BUSINESS RELATIONSHIPS

The pursuit of proactive business partnerships with both their client airlines and their own suppliers has been an integral feature of Alpha's commitment to total quality. Their business relationships with their suppliers are conducted, where possible, on the basis of mutual cooperation rather than an adversarial lowest-price approach. Alpha needs the product, the suppliers need the business, and so both parties have a vested interest in making sure the relationship succeeds.

One example of this proactivity has been in the introduction of roteable (i.e. reusable) packaging materials. It is Alpha's policy not to allow cardboard into the manufacturing process, but it was found that bottlenecks were developing in one operation because of the need to remove cardboard inserts and exterior packaging from the delivered supplies. With a product turnaround of 24 hours, there are daily deliveries of supplies and a corresponding daily increase in the mountain of cardboard to be disposed of. Alpha's solution to this problem was to work with their supplier in the development of a roteable packaging system where the product is now delivered in reusable plastic containers. Alpha pays for the containers under the old brewery deposit system, where they receive a credit for each returned container – if they lose them they pay for them. The new system was funded entirely by the supplier, with Alpha agreeing contract terms in return for that financial commitment.

The result has been the removal of 2.5 tons of cardboard from Alpha's production process each week, and the consequent disappearance of a major bottleneck in the production process. By adopting a partnership approach to resolving a problem which, essentially, both parties had, rather than seeking an adversarial 'fix it or else' position, the problem has been solved and the working relationship has been strengthened.

Other examples of award-winning solutions that have been found by working with suppliers rather than against them include:

- New 'aircraft-friendly' highlift trucks were developed in partnership with manufacturers Nordquip Edbro. The new design, which won a 1994 Merit Award from the Inflight Food Service Association (IFSA), incorporates several special features, including ultrasonic sensors and infrared detectors, helping to determine the proximity of the aircraft body and avoiding costly and time-consuming accidents. Another innovative device controls the height of the loading platform once the truck is in position, so that if the aircraft settles during loading, the platform moves with it, preventing damage to the aircraft door sill.
- A new 'CO_2 snowshooting' chilling system was developed in partnership with MG Gas Products in response to increased UK legislation on in-transit refrigeration. The 'AutoSnow Blizzard' supersedes the traditional use of solid CO_2 (dry ice) blocks to maintain low temperatures in airline catering trolleys by directing measured amounts of CO_2 snow into the trolley, thus ensuring even distribution and uniform temperatures throughout. This design was entered into the 1991 Mercury Awards competition for the Inflight Catering Association (IFCA) as 'Project Alaska '91', and was awarded a Gold Medal in the equipment category.

These are advances that have benefited not only Alpha, but also the flight-catering industry in general, as other companies have chosen to adopt the same solutions. The 'snowshooting' system in particular has achieved tremendous success in the UK and most of the airline caterers have now adopted the system.

THE BS 5750 EXPERIMENT

This same proactive approach is also used in all areas of client relations. Alpha's job is to deliver the specification that is agreed with the airline, but typically they have taken the opportunity to go beyond that to strengthen the business relationship. With British Airways, for instance, Alpha has set up a supplier hygiene audit group that visits suppliers regularly to accredit them as fit to supply both Alpha and British Airways. This is not something required in the contract specifications, but it does show the lengths to which Alpha is prepared to go to make sure that every element of the process involved in meeting British Airways' specifications is checked and double-checked.

Another example of this proactive relationship with British Airways is the 'trial' of the BS 5750 quality standard that has taken place in conjunction with (as opposed to 'for') the airline at Alpha's Woolborough Lane unit at Gatwick Airport. As Gerry Sweeney, General Manager for Quality Assurance explains:

> We looked upon BS 5750 as a quality management system which wasn't so far removed from the principles that we had already been applying. We didn't particularly like the idea of going out to another external audit, or the costs which we perceived would be associated with it, but, equally, we felt that we couldn't criticize something

which we knew very little about, having not done it.

We actually found BS 5750 very useful for several reasons. Primarily, it focused the staff and management on very specific control processes, and lead them to document those processes. Unfortunately, there appears to be a lot of overkill in documentation, and, looking back, I believe only 50–60 per cent of that documentation is really required. In practice, we didn't actually change very much – essentially it involved documenting what we already did and, to some extent, changing the documents we had already produced.

There was a large amount of duplication of work, but I think that the bottom line is that BS 5750 is a valid exercise to undertake if you want to focus your management on a quality management system. Some of the key things involved, like 'corrective action', do allow you to document and complete the issue once and for all as opposed to an ongoing situation, and I think we have learnt something out of that process.

This investigation into the potential benefits of BS 5750 was established at Alpha's request, rather than from any external pressure from their client airlines. The perspective taken was simply to find out what was involved, how much it would cost, what the benefits to Alpha would be, and what the added value to the client would be once it was achieved.

The result was that, in retrospect, the costs involved and the high level of duplication of existing documented control processes to meet BS 5750's exacting requirements, did not appear outweighed by any benefits that could be added to their relationship with their clients. A tremendous effort on the part of the staff and management at Woolborough Lane was involved in achieving the quality standard, and a continued effort is required to maintain it, which, in turn, generates tremendous satisfaction for those team members; but from a purely commercial point of view, the effort and expense involved was not matched by any apparent added value for the client.

Having already committed the time and financial resources to the achievement of BS 5750, it will be maintained for the foreseeable future. The perspective that Alpha now takes on the exercise is that it allowed them to assess their own management system and to realize that they were doing quite well in themselves. They are fortunate in that their operating contracts with their client airlines call for many external audits from the airlines themselves, which allow Alpha to remain far more directed towards the exacting nature of their client specifications rather than the generalist approach of the BS 5750 quality standard.

Alpha was the first UK flight caterer, and the third in the world, to achieve BS 5750, but at present, there are no plans to roll it out to the other manufacturing operations. Should a client bring up the idea of accreditation in the future, Alpha is now in a position to discuss both the benefits and costs of achieving the standard, and to help the client airline reach a decision about whether it would bring any added value to their contract.

INVESTING IN PEOPLE

In contrast, the Investors In People (IIP) training programme *has* been rolled out to other operations within the company – three operations in Manchester have been accredited, as has the retail unit at Heathrow, and three other units are currently involved in the process. The commitment to training within the company was such that when Alpha met with the IIP assessors, it was deemed that they were already 'there' to a great extent, and so most of the accreditation process was achieved without involving IIP at the outset. Participation in the programme has been very successful. In particular the impact reviews and the development of team leadership objectives were very closely aligned to the management system which Alpha was already in the process of refining. A further extension of IIP to the other UK units is planned for the future.

PRODUCTION QUALITY

The level of planning control required to handle the logistics involved in delivering over 40,000 items to an aircraft within a precise period, lends itself more to the statistical process control techniques of manufacturing industries than to the more traditional customer service quality techniques of the food service industry. This is demonstrated in the utilization of two manufacturing-based quality control initiatives: 'zero defects' and 'just-in-time' production processes.

Zero defects

In the summer of 1989, an *ad hoc* committee of UK Airline Caterers (Airline Caterers Technical Coordinating Committee – ACTCC) was formed to produce a Code of Good Hygiene Practice for Airline Catering. In 1990, a 'Code of Good Catering Practice' was introduced in which all flight caterers agreed to abide by a standardized system of operation in order to guarantee consistently high performance levels throughout the industry (Table 3.1). Alpha looks upon that Code of Practice as a means of measuring its quality performance, and the elements contained within it have been turned into a detailed unit audit, which forms an integral part of the management appraisal system. With increasingly strict food safety and food hygiene regulations being imposed, the unit audit is Alpha's way of ensuring that their operating procedures and management control systems remain far above the minimum standards required by the legislation.

The units are assessed not on a percentage of attainment, but on a points-based penalty system for specific non-compliance towards the predetermined standards. A maximum score of 5000 points would shut down that operation (which has never happened). In the last audit, their best unit scored only 350 points (most of which related to an already scheduled replacement of equipment), which gives some indication of the serious commitment to the achievement of zero defects that pervades the organization. By awarding penalty points for non-compliance rather than scoring on a percentage grade, it was felt that the units would get the message that there will be no marks given for a good effort. The achievement of the predetermined standard is the level at which their people are expected to operate, and therefore any non-compliance to that standard is then identified as an area for further improvement.

Just-in-time

In view of the tremendous volume of meals being prepared on a daily basis, a flight caterer such as Alpha would be expected to purchase supplies in bulk in order to maximize the revenue savings on margins that are often wafer-thin. As Gerry Sweeney comments:

Table 3.1   List of areas covered in the ACTCC Code of Practice

---

ACTCC Code of Good Catering Practice
Minimum standards and guidelines are specified in the following areas:

1.	Production Processes
2.	Raw Material Supplies
3.	Storage
4.	Pre-processing
5.	Cooking
6.	Rapid Chilling
7.	Chilled Storage
8.	Bakery and Pastry
9.	Meal Assembly
10.	Tray Assembly and Flight Packing
11.	Distribution to Aircraft
12.	Quality Control and Management
13.	Cleaning
14.	Microbiological Guidelines
15.	Personal Hygiene

There are companies in this industry which buy vast volumes of product. They bring it over direct from the manufacturer, store it in huge subcontracted warehouses, employ a security force to look after that subcontracted warehouse, and then employ a delivery fleet to bring that product to their manufacturing base. The unit prices they pay for the product may look cheap, but it's a misperception. Because all of those additional costs are identified in different parts of the business, they never really know how much they end up paying for the product, which means there's no real identification of the true cost – and, lo and behold, they still run out of the product prior to the end of its cycle!

For the last decade, Alpha has been committed to an alternate form of supply that, though not always guaranteeing the lowest unit price, guarantees the freshest quality product at the best possible price, in direct relation to the level of service that their clients want them to provide.

The 'just-in-time' (JIT) process has its origins in manufacturing – in particular in the automobile industry – and is based around the belief that economies generated by volume purchases to achieve low unit costs, are outweighed by the diseconomies of the cost of carrying that inventory before usage. For Alpha, there is an additional diseconomy of loss of product quality in extended storage.

The key principle of JIT is the use of frequent deliveries of small amounts of product as close to an 'as needed' basis as possible, to minimize inventory levels. For Alpha, the commitment to this system over the last decade has led to an operating environment in which their manufacturing plants are built around the production process rather than developing production around the constraints of an existing building structure. In the day-to-day operation of the plant, storage is avoided wherever possible – the raw product is delivered direct to the processing point. Similarly, the cooked products are delivered there direct, as is the salad produce which is delivered up to three times per day.

The commitment to product freshness is obvious, but the gains to be made in terms of reduced inventory levels, reduced stock rotation requirements, and increased product control are also considerable. The Gatwick operation (see Figure 3.1) was the first purpose-built JIT plant in the company, and by introducing this process, inventory levels were reduced from over twenty days to less than five days – a greater than 75 per cent reduction which was directly attributable to the JIT process. When this is multiplied against the stock value for the whole network, substantial savings become possible.

Advocates of the 'just-in-case' inventory method would argue that suppliers charge a premium for such frequent deliveries, but for Alpha the strength of their working relationships with their suppliers (not to mention the considerable volume of product purchases) has allowed them to set up these delivery schedules at minimum cost. In addition, the lost carrying charges more than make up any unit price differential.

Alpha themselves were victims of the 'just-in-case' philosophy for many years. Safety factors were built in to the inventory levels just in case an extra flight came in or there was a problem with the manufacturing process. When they began to examine the frequency of such events – how often they got extra flights, when they got them, how much notice they were given – it was realized that the level of stock far exceeded the worst possible scenario, and so an alternate solution was sought. They have now proved that the old-fashioned (as they would regard them) systems simply do not work. Buying vast quantities to shave pennies off the unit price generates longer-term diseconomies.

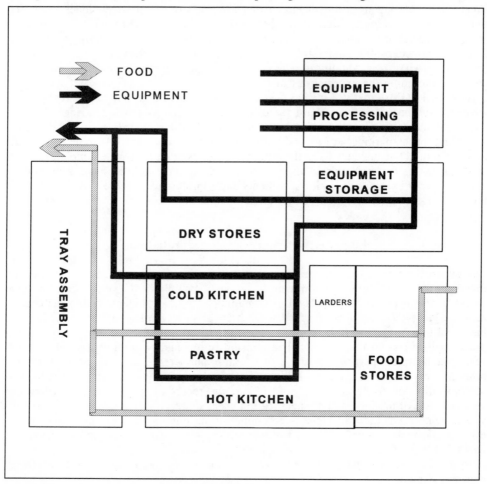

Figure 3.1 Alpha's Gatwick premises: a simplified plan

Such is the company's commitment to this belief, that the unit audit scores down the unit for inventory levels by depth of days.

A QUALITY CULTURE

Despite a 35-year history as a division of Forte, the quality ethic that Alpha puts forward is very much their own. The focus on hotels that predominated the Forte culture allowed the flight services division to operate relatively independently, and the public flotation as the Alpha Airports Group merely underlined that independence. In terms of the specific direction of their quality initiatives, which has always come primarily from their customer base, Alpha looks for strong, successful airlines with precise specifications for the level of service to be provided to their passengers. With a quality culture based so firmly on the exacting requirements of their customers, Alpha's approach to the whole Total Quality Management movement has been to select only those techniques and initiatives that can be closely aligned to their existing operating parameters, rather than seeking to redesign the company to accommodate the latest TQM programme. As such, there are no buzzwords, no motivational hype, and very, very few acronym-based employee programmes. Quality is regarded as the simple matter of meeting and, where possible, exceeding the expectations of the client.

Individual TQM initiatives such as 'zero defects', 'just in time', and statistical process control, have been taken on board to fulfil a specific purpose in managing what is a logistically complex planning control system. Other TQM standards such as 'empowerment' and 'benchmarking' are treated with a little more scepticism. To some degree, the adaptation of JIT techniques from the automobile industry is a strong example of benchmarking, but as for their own industry, Alpha maintains the goal of being a worldwide industry leader by working with their clients and suppliers to develop their own market initiatives rather than seeking to adopt those of their competitors.

Empowerment and team-based initiatives

The apparent absence of any 'grand vision' of quality, as represented by a dramatic inversion of the corporate pyramid or some such metaphorical event, does, to some extent, a disservice to the high level of commitment to quality ideals within the organization. Quality has been approached as a gradual process, and deliberately so. The historical role of Quality Inspector has long since disappeared within the manufacturing process, to be replaced by individual responsibility for quality in all aspects of the business. Similarly, the part-time position of a health and safety manager, with a responsibility for very 'loose' areas of the business has also been removed in favour of individual responsibility for health and safety. In effect, the records kept of time, of people, of temperatures, of product, and of specification checks, are now all performed by the individuals concerned. Indeed, Alpha is committed to an ongoing process by which, wherever practical, the control of every product will be given directly to the individual that handles that product.

At present, Alpha is paying close attention to the use of the team structure. As Gerry Sweeney explains:

The objective of our Team Leader programme is to develop our supervisors and to help them deliver a level of performance which will enable them get the best from their group of people. This has allowed us to 'destructure' our management system to some degree by taking out layers of management, in order to improve our responsiveness to the client.

Such claims of individual responsibility and management 'destructuring' seems to suggest a strong commitment to the concept of empowerment of individual employees, but this is not strictly the case. For Alpha, empowerment answers the question, 'How do we allow our people to operate with the maximum freedom to deliver what is our standard in the best possible way?' That has a very specific meaning in practice.

There are employees who are empowered to act without supervision or the approval of a supervisor or manager. The stores employees responsible for receiving goods, for instance, are empowered to turn away any product that does not meet the specified standard. They undertake an inspection of the product for a predetermined list of criteria, and if any of those criteria are not met, the product is refused, without seeking the approval or authorization of a manager. For most of Alpha's employees, however, the opportunity for such an empowered response is not so readily available. By virtue of the very size and nature of the business, guidance has to come from the centre. Service quality is about the management of a complex process for delivering up to 400 meals and thousands of sundry items to one plane in one go. The opportunity for individual empowerment in that situation is rather limited.

The primary objective in using the team structure is to reinforce the commitment to quality at unit level. By developing the teams to deliver on the exact requirements set out by the corporate management team, Alpha can be sure that the core components of their commitment to their clients are reaching the individual employees rather than being dissipated through a middle-management structure. The unit audits further reinforce that message by directly assessing compliance to those core components.

A UNIQUE BUSINESS ENVIRONMENT

To a very great degree, the business environment in which flight caterers operate has a strong influence on the development of management policies. There is no doubt that the flight caterers serve only one master – the client airline. The fact that their product is actually consumed by a secondary customer – the passenger – is almost incidental. Alpha has no contact with passengers. Customer feedback comes directly through the airline, as do any complaints about the quality of the food. Surveys of customer preferences are carried out by the airline and passed on to the flight caterer.

The front line for Alpha is the aircraft. Their product is delivered to the plane where it is then served to the passengers by the cabin crew. As such, there is a considerable amount of trust that has to develop between the cabin crew as providers and Alpha as their suppliers. The service provided to them has to be 100 per cent because, at 9,000 m (30,000 ft), there is nowhere else for them to go if something goes wrong. It is in Alpha's best interests to make sure that everything is there and that it's all in the right place. Causing problems for the cabin crew will only serve to undermine the total quality of the product. The in-flight meal may be perfectly cooked and beautifully presented, but if it is then simply slapped down in front of the passenger because the cabin steward or stewardess is busy with another problem for which Alpha is responsible, then the whole game is lost. Consequently, Alpha carefully monitors their satisfaction rating with the cabin crews and processes that information back through their control system at regular intervals.

From a marketing perspective, the quality of the in-flight meal can be seen to form an integral part of the passenger's total experience, but from the perspective of the basic mechanics of the flight itself, catering issues are very low on the list. The equipment used to load, store and serve the meals belongs to the airline, not the caterer. The reason for this is a matter of simple economics. The airlines are in the business of transporting passengers from A to B as quickly, efficiently and profitably as possible. In this respect, the design of the galley in which the food will be prepared and served is directly related to the type of aircraft and the distance flown by that aircraft. For the airline, therefore, the food and equipment are simply additional weight and additional fuel to carry that weight. To put this in perspective, Alpha's quality initiatives ultimately come up against the harsh reality of 'this is the amount of space available; we want this type of meal(s); this is the equipment we want it served on; and we want it packed in this way'. Occasionally there is some input on equipment design, but usually the meal specifications are based on the equipment that is already in place.

While these may seem to be excessively strict operating parameters, Alpha has, in practice, chosen to accept the situation and focus on doing their absolute best with the specifications they are given, rather than attempting to introduce new galley styles or new types of equipment. With 'SuperJumbos' carrying 600 or more passengers now appearing on the business horizon, communication between the airlines and their caterers has centred around 'this is the type of equipment you will have, and these are the meals we would like served'. As Gerry Sweeney concludes: 'We deliver the product according to the level of importance that the client airline puts on that process – the more the airline is interested in quality service and in their passengers, the more they talk to us.'

FUTURE QUALITY INITIATIVES

The future direction of Alpha's quality initiatives will centre around two primary object-ives. First, to continue to clearly and methodically standardize their operating processes such that they become the key differentiation factor in why airlines should come to them for their in-flight meals. Consistent high performance both for the product itself and the level of service provided are seen as the means to the maintenance of a significant market advantage. Because they are in the food industry, food hygiene and food safety will remain their primary focus, and absolute guarantees of delivering the best possible food in the safest possible way will continue to be their marketing position. Second, the commitment to an ongoing process of open and honest communication with client airlines on a proactive basis remains paramount. Delivering 'the right product in the right place at the right time with the right attitude' may appear a totally obvious concept, but for Alpha Flight Services, it's what they do best and what they will continue to do best. The flight catering industry may be becoming increasingly competitive, and more closely legislated, but the essential elements remain the same – giving the customers what they want, when they want it.

FOUR

The Cardiff Copthorne: squeezing the most from quality registration

Michael Baker and Peter Cave

It was announced in early September 1995 that Copthorne Hotels had been sold by Aer Lingus to the fast growing Singapore-based hotel group CDL Hotels International. It was reported that CDL had paid £219 million for the group. Peter Taylor, the Chief Executive who will continue in this job under CDL, sees the sale as a positive move for the future of Copthorne. It is CDL's intention to build on the success and achievements of the group. In October 1995, CDL announced a major rebranding exercise for all its hotels portfolio. Copthorne Hotels will join as a subgroup of the newly created Millenium brand and will be known as Millenium Copthorne.

The Cardiff Copthorne, which only opened in 1991, in March 1993 became the first group-owned hotel in the UK to achieve ISO 9000 registration, closely followed by the Scandic Crown in Edinburgh. *Hospitality* reported the general manager as saying that gaining ISO 9000 registration cost more than £35,000 and produced nothing tangible in the way of sales, but was nevertheless worthwhile (McDermid, 1994). How has the Copthorne got a return on its investment?

COPTHORNE HOTELS

Copthorne Hotels is a group of four-star hotels, primarily catering for the business sector. The holding company is Aer Lingus. The hotels are situated across the country, generally in developing locations, and are often new hotels built with grant-aided assistance. There are currently 13 hotels in Great Britain and five in the rest of Europe. Two other hotels are managed by the group: the Santiago in Tenerife and the Atlantic in Banjul, Gambia. The group has plans for further expansion. It employs 2000 people full time and has a turnover of £80 million. Each hotel has a general manager; two of the UK general managers also act as regional managers. The group is decentralized, with general managers in each hotel responsible for managing all aspects of their operation from day-to-day marketing decisions to staffing structures and levels of pay. There are just 25 employees at the head office in Horley, near Gatwick Airport.

MANAGING QUALITY IN COPTHORNE HOTELS

The company places considerable emphasis on keeping the quality it delivers in line with the growing expectations of its business customers and the response of its competitors. Expectations of customers have risen between the mid-1980s and the present, not just in the requirements for additional facilities, such as business centres equipped with fax and phone, etc., but in a more professional and flexible approach to customers' needs, along with an emphasis on value for money.

The company's objective is to achieve and maintain competitive success in the four-star hotel sector. Its strategy is to deliver a consistent standard of service and product; the company's policy and initiatives about quality are in support of this. Leadership in quality is taken by the chief executive, with the two regional general managers, the sales and marketing director, and the director responsible for human resources.

The company has adopted a comprehensive set of minimum standards, set by head office, which are formally incorporated in a quality standards manual. The standards are based on AA/RAC criteria, which are used where applicable. These are physical standards covering such things as the meeting of guests and telephone answering time. This is the basis on which local management, in response to local needs and experience, can develop and build and elaborate. Each department is required to prepare a manual covering the operational aspects of its own part in the hotel operation. The minimum base standards set by head office are related to local circumstances and labour costs. For example, standards can be adapted to take account of menu content, pricing policy, and exploiting individuals' strengths. Employees are consulted in deciding about new procedures; for instance, the waiting staff would be consulted over new procedures for laying up tables in the restaurant. A quality standards meeting is held every three months or so, attended by the chief executive, regional general managers, the finance director, and the human resources director to review the company's quality standards and vary them as necessary. The frequency of the meetings reflect the management's view that expectations of customers are rising rapidly, and standards must keep pace. Standards acceptable in the mid-1980s would not be acceptable in the 1990s.

In a new hotel, the general manager appoints a team with the assistance of the group human resources director. Each task requirement in the departmental manual is discussed with the respective employees and assessed in terms of time and cost. The management of people is seen as the means by which compliance is achieved. In-house training is given to develop new and existing staff and to update skills. Each property has a departmental manual for NVQ (National Vocational Qualification) training. Departmental quality standards are built into NVQs. Specific external training is provided in telephone and selling skills. The general manager holds a daily brief with departmental heads at 9.30 a.m. every morning and there is also a more formal weekly meeting. Departmental meetings, chaired by a department head, are held infrequently or as the business situation dictates. Some proactive departments, e.g. sales, hold monthly meetings with their staff.

As a base standard, the only means of assessing the quality of performance are the number of complaints and the analysis of guest questionnaires, for which the response rate is very low. The company considers that guest questionnaires only show poles of opinion. The company does, however, require full investigation of complaints. Measures of customer satisfaction are obtained by the conference and banqueting departments which undertake telephone follow-up. There is thus little formal measurement of quality specifically required by the company, this being at the discretion of the hotels' general managers.

The achievement of ISO 9000 registration in Cardiff, which proved expensive and time consuming, was a pilot which so far the company has not repeated, although it does provide a checking system and the procedures set up have general value. The company is however giving priority to gaining the Investors in People Award across the group.

COPTHORNE HOTEL CARDIFF

The Copthorne in Cardiff was opened in 1991. The hotel comprises bedrooms, restaurants and bars, together with conference and leisure facilities. During the week most of the customers are on business; but they are primarily leisure customers at weekends. Turnover is about £300,000 per month. The company's view is that the market for four-star hotels like the Cardiff Copthorne is very competitive, but it is one in which this hotel has proved successful.

BSI is approved by the National Accreditation Council for Certification Bodies to register organizations within the Hotel and Catering Industry to BS EN ISO 9000:1994. The ISO 9000 standard is essentially the same as the BS 5750 quality standard which the Copthorne sought in 1992 and 1993. The term ISO 9000 is used throughout the case study to refer to this standard. Registration to the standard requires companies to undergo an initial assessment of a duration appropriate to the size of the organization. The object of this assessment is to establish confidence that the organization is operating to meet the needs of ISO 9000 and its own documented quality system. Once a company is registered, continuing assesssment visits ensure this compliance is monitored and can facilitate quality improvement.

A documented Quality System can be as simple or complex as the company wishes to make it, but it must meet the requirements of ISO 9000. BSI do not develop systems for companies but can give assistance during the route to registration. The development of a system involves time and resource, it has to be appropriate to the needs of the business and be both workable and flexible. Over periods of time, experience shows that systems become more streamlined, focused and user friendly. The very nature of the hotel and catering industry can mean that the development and maintenance of a system is complex. A hotel comprises several process/service areas each with different customer requirements and different methods of delivery.

Benefits from registration to ISO 9000 can include:

1. Tighter control over all aspects of the operation (particularly relevant considering the often chaotic nature of the industry).
2. Repeatability and consistency of product/service/hospitality.
3. Staff are aware of their responsibilities and tasks and are trained to carry out their functions (particularly relevant in an industry where such reliance is placed on people).
4. Greater control over suppliers.

5. Less waste.
6. Inspection and test mechanisms to ensure due diligence. (Downs, 1995)

THE DECISION

In the late autumn of 1991 General Manager, Simon Read (who had joined the company six months earlier) was approached by Laurence Watson, the Group Director of Human Resources, to pilot ISO 9000 for the company at the Cardiff hotel. Watson's view was that ISO 9000 might give a hotel a leading market edge, and one of the hotels in the group should pilot the introduction of the standard, so that possible market advantages would not be missed. Cardiff was chosen because it would be easier to do whilst the hotel was still new, staff were still very keen and the management were 'still fairly flexible to the ideas and thoughts of Copthorne Hotels'.

Another factor was the relative importance placed on registration to ISO 9000 by local businesses. Simon Read is quoted as saying: 'The British Standard is a by-word for quality, particularly here in South Wales, a strong industrial area with a lot to Japanese companies, included Sony and Panasonic, represented.' (McDermid, 1994). South Glamorgan Training and Enterprise Council provided a grant equal to 50 per cent of the costs, and the consultants Dennis Morgan Associates of Swansea were approached. Copthorne Cardiff were keen to make their investment for ISO 9000 in the area and reap the benefits of local experience. They started in the spring of 1992 and, 'maybe naively', the management thought it would only take six months or so to gain registration. It was to take twice as long. Experience elsewhere shows that 12 to 18 months is the usual time scale to achieve this.

SETTING UP THE SYSTEM

Up to the spring of 1992 business had been fairly slack and fitful. The erratic nature of the demand, with many peaks and troughs, made it difficult to forecast future business. However, when the hotel experienced a welcome upturn in business, gaining ISO 9000 registration took a back seat to responding to the day-to-day pressures. Ebbw Vale held its Garden Festival in the early summer of 1992, bringing occupancy rates up from 40–45 per cent to around 70 per cent.

STANDARDS AND PROCEDURES

The biggest hurdle seemed to be getting the quality standards and procedures written. Procedures for ISO 9000 were much more detailed than the existing departmental procedures and required substantial documenting. The time which heads of department had apparently had on their hands to devote to what was turning out to be a terrific amount of paperwork had suddenly disappeared. Simon Read took drastic action. He claims that at one stage he virtually had to lock all the relevant managers into a room one Friday afternoon and tell them they were not going home until the standards of performance and the departmental procedures were written up.

Some parts of the organization found it easier to respond than others. Some departments already had reasonably comprehensive procedures laid down by head office. In other areas, like housekeeping, SOP manuals provided quite detailed standards of performance. Front of house management was used to expecting staff to follow administrative procedures, and also found this aspect easier. But in other areas it was harder. In some cases this had to do with the traditions of the workplace and the style of management being difficult to fit with the formality of ISO 9000. The kitchens and restaurants experienced this difficulty. For example, the restaurant manager commented a year later that if he had known all that he was going to be expected to do when he was offered the post he would not have accepted. He had no problem if he was expected simply to run a restaurant, but all the paperwork was totally unnecessary. Simon Read commented that this was 'perhaps a reflection of the old school that they do find it difficult to have to submit everything in writing'.

Age appeared to Simon Read to affect the willingness of staff to respond – people over 40 believed that they had been successful managers without ISO 9000 and therefore had no need of it. Fortunately for the project the majority of the managers were in their late twenties or early thirties.

Another essentially cultural problem was to do with standards and targets. Managers, who to motivate staff like to set challenging objectives, but accept that performance may fall below this level quite frequently, feel uncomfortable with a focus on standards which represent the minimum acceptable. One specific example of where the hotel got itself into a tight corner was with room service. The restaurant manager, who wanted to deliver a service to the standard appropriate to a four-star hotel, said that for any room service order the tray should be collected within 15 minutes. Wanting to impress the consultant, and knowing it was a good standard, he set out to have the trays collected from the corridors to meet the standard. However, although this was a standard he would have liked to have, it proved impractical as it would have meant having a waiter on every corridor waiting for trays to be pushed from the rooms into the corridor. It took some time for heads of department to realise that they should identify satisfactory performance as what they expected consistently to be able to achieve, not exceptional performance, being what they would like to do and which might be occasionally possible.

Other problems arose through the consultants' inexperience of the hospitality industry. They did not appreciate what was involved and the nature of hotel operations. For example, the consultant felt it would be easy to get the staff all together off site on a Saturday morning, which was clearly impractical. Whereas in manufacturing industry people can be taken away over a weekend for team building, in a hotel environment it was felt at the Copthorne that there was no time when everyone could be got together for a day or two. The development of the system had to be regarded as extra work and it was difficult to keep up the pace. The hotel had no quality executive devoted solely to developing the system until Linda West was appointed in October 1992 and took over responsibility for administration of the system. Linda West was later appointed to the position of personnel and training manager and continues to take full responsibility for monitoring ISO 9000.

To compensate for his lack of experience in hospitality, the consultant had to spend a lot of time in each department listening and seeing what went on, in order to understand what aspects needed documentation. He also had to learn about the wide variety of customers, and how customer requirements consequently differed widely, before he could properly advise the hotel about appropriate controls and procedures. The consultant had not appreciated the varied nature of departments in a hotel, and consequently had not understood the differences in management style, control systems and decision variables between them. Each department had a very different way of working.

Another problem arising from the consultants' lack of experience of the hospitality industry related to the maintenance of a documentary record. It was necessary to maintain at least a three-month history, recording the performance against quality standards, incorporated as part of the quality system. Whereas in a manufacturing industry keeping such documents would have been a matter of course, it was not so in the hospitality industry. This was something the consultants had not made clear. The hotel was almost ready for assessment when this problem arose and the assessment had to be delayed whilst arrangements were made to ensure records were kept. This was a direct result of a difference of culture between manufacturing and the hospitality industry.

An example of detailed recording requirements was in the kitchen. Under the hygiene regulations records had to be kept of the results of food temperature probing. The fridge temperature had to be taken three times a day. Records had to be kept of this and, if the temperature went up or down, what was done about it. Apart from legal requirements, most of the standards are set by the hotel. Under ISO 9000, records of all these measurements had to be kept for three months to meet the requirements of the initial assessment. The hotel did not have sufficient records and the general manager felt they had been 'led up the garden path completely'.

The fact that the consultant did not fully understand hotel operations meant that the system needed to be changed dramatically and this added to cost. The delay did however give a little more time to get things together. The consultants themselves also benefited from gaining a greater insight into hospitality operations.

> Everyone was trail-blazing – when the final assessment came round, even BSI was new to hotels. A major problem, says Mr Read, was that whereas many businesses going for BS 5750 go off on think-tank weekends – the Copthorne, ironically, is a popular venue for this – a hotel's management and staff simply cannot. 'I had to ask staff to perform extra, which, fortunately, they were willing to do, but it's something other hotels considering this course of action should consider very closely.' A personnel and quality administrator is now employed full time. (McDermid, 1994)

As McDermid implies, if the Copthorne was not as prepared as it thought it was for ISO 9000, the British Standards Institute may not have been ready for the hospitality industry. The company felt that BSI's knowledge of hospitality was rudimentary as the hotel knew more about the product and standards than BSI did, and the leaflets and accompanying material that were supplied were very sketchy. This inevitably caused communication difficulties and additional work for the hotel: 'we developed the system rather than they developed the system for us'. Moreover, the consultants' lack of hospitality industry experience affected the design of the systems which were put in place. To eliminate the clumsiness of many of the procedures and to reduce the cost of the operation, the hotel has, since it was registered, revised and streamlined many of the systems. This might also be viewed as part of a programme of continuous quality improvement.

The hotel group understand that the BSI are now adapting to the hospitality industry; when the BSI has undertaken the two most recent follow-up assessments at the hotel, the assessor has been a person with food-industry experience, who understands how the hotel works, which makes the visit more useful.

A VIEW FROM BSI

A representative of BSI informed the authors that, since initial assessment at the Copthorne Hotel, BSI have made a positive commitment to the hospitality industry by employing client managers with hotel and catering backgrounds. This means that BSI client managers understand the peculiarities of the industry and can adopt a more practical approach to assessment. BSI has also undergone a reorganization which has resulted in clients being assigned a one-point contact client manager who not only carries out their assessment but can offer any further assistance they require during the year. BSI has also acknowledged the need for more user-friendly literature to be provided for the hospitality industry and is, at present, rewriting guidelines. In this way BSI hopes it is responding to the needs of its customers.

In the context of the rising expectations of hotel guests, a quality assurance system helps hotels to respond to these expectations by giving clear standards of performance to staff and by ensuring consistency of services, hospitality and food. In respect of record keeping, initial assessments by BSI usually require a minimum of three months' records to demonstrate that the system has been operating consistently over a period of time. However, following this, Clause 4.16 of the standard (Quality Records) requires organizations to identify their quality records and to define their own retention periods, taking into account any legislative requirements (Downs, 1995).

OTHER COMPLICATING CIRCUMSTANCES

Two other changes were in train which complicated the process of setting up the standards and procedures and the subsequent training period. One of these changes was self-imposed. Prior to the assessment in March 1993, the hotel also piloted a new computer system, at the behest of head office. In hindsight this was a system too far. There were numerous problems, particularly in the reception, conference and banqueting areas, adding further extra burdens to staff in the throes of getting ready for the ISO 9000 assessment.

The second change was the national introduction of new hygiene standards relating to the handling and serving of food, which not only had to be implemented but also, under ISO 9000, the hotel had to have records for at least three months. McDermid (1994) quotes Read, recalling the pre-audit visit by the BSI in December 1992 referred to earlier, as saying:

> It was soon clear that we had major problems, mainly because the consultants were not familiar with the service industry but also because we had to conform to additional food and hygiene regulations. We just were not aware that sample temperatures had to be taken from every single dish produced in the kitchen each day. We didn't even have the probe. And when we got it, there was no way of knowing whether the thing was accurate so it had to be sent off to be calibrated.

The new standards had implications for controls and records about suppliers, too:

> And not only did the breakfast sausages have to be checked on arrival at the hotel, as did the van they arrived in and the driver's headgear. In the same way, environmental

health regulations concerning the pH levels in the swimming pool had to be taken into account. Achieving the five AA stars would probably have been easier.

Gaining ISO 9000 registration accreditation involved putting the staff under very heavy pressure.

TRAINING AND BRIEFING

In the first six months the introduction of ISO 9000 was kept under wraps to avoid unsettling new staff. Only when the departmental quality standards had been developed were all the staff informed of the company's intentions. When these standards came out the staff were all required to read them; a briefing was held and training days were arranged. As the assessment day came nearer, means were developed to make sure the staff were aware: for example, 'ten days to assessment' charts were posted, and a quiz was organized with a weekend in Belgium as a prize.

PRE-ASSESSMENT

The hotel was to be assessed in December 1992. The BSI made, as is normal, a pre-assessment visit. Pre-assessment proved to be a discouraging experience, and assessment was postponed for three months. It seemed to the hotel's management that everything was criticized. It was only at this point that many of the problems referred to earlier came to light. It was at this point, too, that the BSI's own inexperience of the hospitality industry may have contributed to the dispiriting nature of the experience; to the management it seemed that aspects which the standard was not supposed to touch, including the layout of the organization chart, were subjected to critical and disapproving examination.

ASSESSMENT

Against a background of growing concern on the part of the group management about the value of the exercise, the increasing costs of consultants, and the length of time and the effort already swallowed up, the Copthorne postponed assessment to mid-March 1993. The management made set to resolve the problems the pre-assessment audit had revealed – building up a history of records and introducing additional standards and procedures where required, and training staff to use them.

After a very harassing three-day assessment the hotel achieved registration in mid-March 1993, one year from the start of the project.

Table 4.1 Critical events in the registration of the Cardiff Copthorne Hotel to ISO 9000

Event	Date
Management team on board	May–July 1991
Hotel Opens	August 1991
Watson approaches Read about ISO 9000	Autumn 1991
South Glamorgan TEC approached	January 1992
Consultants appointed	March 1992
Work commences to achieve ISO 9000 at the Cardiff Copthorne	April 1992
Pre-audit assessment	December 1992
Assessment: Cardiff Copthorne registered to ISO 9000	March 1993

HOW HAS IT CHANGED THINGS?

Systems

The presence of formal systems and controls has had a number of effects. For example, it means that standards cannot slip unnoticed. Heads of departments realize that if they want to change a standard within their operation the change needs to be documented and approved. Three-month quality standards meetings are held attended by heads of department and management to approve changes. Additional meetings are called if the need arises, for example, if there is a danger of standards slipping.

Auditing cycles mean that each department comes under regular scrutiny. Auditing takes at least twenty-four hours by the time all the paperwork and review has taken place. Therefore only two or three departments can be tackled at once in the time available. The audit goes in a cycle and the departments which are due to be inspected in the next cycle can be identified and focused on a little more closely in the intervening six months. It is this process which is seen as providing a unique measure of support for the way quality is delivered in the hotel. The BSI audits bring an outsider in to give an objective and detailed assessment, opening the doors and shining light into every nook and cranny.

There are procedures for departments in a hotel which can go by the way in times of pressure. ISO 9000 ensures that you are working to the latest standards. In contrast, it is not always certain that the personnel and administration manual from head office will always be the latest issue. Checking procedures are applied to suppliers, and frozen food and fresh meat is inspected. Initially delivery vans turned up in a dreadful state, but whether they turned up on time and delivered to order was now documented: 'the supplier is wary of the fact that he is likely to be checked, more so at this hotel than any other hotel'.

The personnel and training manager is the person who drives ISO 9000 on and has been given the full backing of the general manager. If things need to be resolved, a meeting has to be called or authority is required to gain the agreement of members of staff to a particular course of action, the general manager will support her. The backing of the general manager has been, and continues to be, crucial to the whole project. The system is continually being fine-tuned all the time. If this did not happen there would be major problems at the audit.

Morale

As the system settled down heads of department began to recognize the full benefits the ISO 9000 systems bring. The auditing procedures, in particular, were perceived as being valuable in maintaining quality. If ISO 9000 was terminated the general manager believes that the hotel would lose many senior staff. Despite the extra work, as it matures heads of department believe that it is making life easier. The hotel still has most of the senior managers it had at the time. It is also something creditable to have on their CVs. As well as low management turnover, staff turnover, generally, is low for the industry.

Simon Read puts the low staff turnover down to the effect of working in a quality-conscious environment. He says 'why would my head housekeeper want to go and be a housekeeper somewhere else' or perhaps it is an unwillingness to repeat the experience, because once was enough; 'she certainly would not want to go and implement the system somewhere else'. These statements demonstrate an aspect of implementing ISO 9000. It was worth it in the end, but not an experience the staff would wish to repeat too often.

ISO 9000 helped with team building – everyone now knows what everyone should be doing; and the process of achieving the objective has had its effect. Even when the going was tough the consensus of opinion was to carry on, and 'when we passed we all went down the pub and had a few beers'.

The management believe that the existence of ISO 9000 does increase productivity but this primarily depends on maintaining flexible staffing patterns with part-time and casual staff. The standards and procedures provide a means of ensuring these staff are effective, whilst having a wider overall knowledge of the organization. There are a large number of casual staff, particularly in banqueting, who tend not to be aware that they are working to a particular standard, and the respective manager will need to ensure that the standard they should be working to is maintained.

Quality

ISO 9000 does not guarantee improvements of quality, but the Copthorne management in Cardiff believes that the systems and controls have this effect. Auditing, both BSI and internal, provides the opportunity to inspect each department to ensure it is running properly and both the trained internal or BSI auditors will fail departments if they are not performing.

Quarterly quality meetings attended by heads of departments, and *ad hoc* meetings called with the authority of the general manager provide a further opportunity to identify ways of improving performance, and to identify steps needed to maintain quality standards. For example, recently at the end of one month the accountant and general manager were pressurizing some departments to run stocks down, e.g. serviettes or candles. Under the standards maintained under ISO 9000 the hotel cannot afford to run out. It has since been agreed to order as per forecast and not what the head of department feels he might need. A particular example was that instead of replacing the tray papers for room service, serviettes were used instead for five days. Working to the standard, tray papers should have been ordered well in advance and, if these were not available, an improved standard, such as linen napkins, should have been used instead.

The new controls on suppliers provide assurance and a record of performance which can be the basis of decisions about reordering, and choice of suppliers, about hygiene, and also other aspects of service, which can affect costs, such as on-time deliveries. Because the suppliers are aware of the high controls and record keeping at the Copthorne, the general manager thinks that they try a little harder for the hotel than for their other customers.

Attracting business

In many instances in other industries, businesses have gained registration as a marketing tool. Their customers have started to give most of their business to registered suppliers, so acquiring ISO registration is an important market move, to hold existing market share and perhaps take business from firms which do not have registration. But Simon Read has not had this experience. McDermid quotes him as saying:

> I have to say that I'm not aware of it making any difference to our sales. We approached all the local [ISO 9000] companies hoping that being members of the same élitist club would attract them to us for their accommodation requirements. But it didn't help at all. The BSI's local office itself uses another hotel. Coming out of recession, it's all down to price.

On the other hand, the hotel's leisure club has seen an advantage. Alone amongst the departmental heads, the leisure club manager uses ISO 9000 registration as a positive sales and marketing aid against any other hotel. The leisure club is a very profitable operation with 700 members and nets £20,000 every month. The staff point out to customers that specific checks of the pool are carried out to a defined schedule and this and the follow-up action is recorded; this assurance is valued by the customers. The majority of business customers recognize the standard as an indicator of quality. The hotel has put the BSI registered firm logo and its BS registration number on its notepaper and the registration certificate is framed and hung in reception, but few customers seem to recognize the significance.

Perhaps the organization should not have expected such a direct effect on the market. However, it might have hoped that quality would improve and, as a consequence, more customers come and return more frequently. The hotel has little in the way of direct feedback from customers on the delivery of quality as there is a low response rate to comment cards.

Customer satisfaction

Returned comment cards run at about 0.04 per cent to rooms sold. About half of the comments ask for such things as an extra towel in the room, or mention the room was too hot or cold, there was a noisy party in adjoining room, or that the leisure club needs more supervision and so on; the other half are more favourable. Not a great deal can be concluded from this level of response rate and it is well known that business clientele show little interest in responding to comment cards. There is some indication of increased customer satisfaction from the occupancy rates; 1994 occupancy rates were 16 per cent up on 1993 to September and rates for September 1994 itself were 20 per cent up on the previous year. But this is inconclusive; many other factors affect occupancy rates, from the performance of the local and national economy to knowledge of the hotel's existence by business people's secretaries.

Reductions in cost

There is some evidence of ISO 9000's contribution to cost effectiveness. For the example, the hotel in the two years period up to September 1994 had the best food and beverage gross profit percentage in the whole group. The general manager attributes this to ISO 9000's providing a little bit more efficiency. Stock control may also be helped by ISO 9000 as the less there is in store the less there is for the food and beverage manager to count. Food stock holding is 5/6 days and 21 days on liquor, well within the company average. However, another factor which may be relevant is that the new hotel does not in any case have a lot of store rooms. The BSI system does enable the hotel to reduce wastage because of tighter controls and this does affect costs.

HOW MUCH DID IT COST?

The company estimates the cost of implementation to be £30,000 in term of cash outlay, which includes the cost of the consultants, BSI fees, etc. But this excludes the major costs of implementation, which were of management time. The hotel did not keep a record of the hours spent on the implementation by managers and others, but they were considerable. The hotel can identify 20–25 hours a week of the personnel and training manager's time up to October 1992. In October 1992 Linda West was appointed as a part-time Quality Administrator, working 30 hours a week. This is one ongoing cost which can fully be attributed to operating the system. She had formerly been employed in nursing and was consequently comfortable with systems and paperwork such as those associated with ISO 9000. Of course, considerable other management time continues to be devoted to the operation of the system. Another is the ongoing cost of the BSI fee of £550 and £600 for each audit which takes place twice a year.

THE HOTEL'S OWN ASSESSMENT

The present hotels management's own assessment seems to be that it was probably worth the effort. The hotel will not abandon the system now it is in place, but faced with the same situation again, and knowing what is involved, they would not do it again.

The Copthorne Group is proud of its ISO 9000 hotel, but has no plans to introduce the standard elsewhere in the group. Moreover, the group management has been less involved in the process of gaining the standard, and is less inclined to take it as an article of faith that the registered firm logo is worth putting on the group's publicity material. It takes the view that all the costs the local management wishes to include in the annual budget which are in any way discretionary have to be justified. This includes the costs of auditing, training and other costs needed to maintain the system. In the absence of clear evidence of a return to all the cost and effort, local management has to be prepared to support its belief in ISO 9000 through commitments to head office to achieve corresponding higher gross margins.

CONCLUSIONS

The Copthorne Group, exploring different approaches to quality, and recognizing the contribution which quality might play in achieving company objectives in marketing and profitability, decided to gain ISO 9000 registration in the Cardiff Copthorne hotel.

The project was managed by the general manager of the hotel, which achieved registration after about one year. This was a considerable achievement, both personally and for his team. The group supported the endeavour, and has benefited from the PR. The hotel gained considerable coverage in the trade press as a result. Nevertheless, the hotel finds difficulty in identifying any tangible benefits. Although it is one of the most profitable in the group, it is able to attribute little of this success to its ISO 9000 registration, because it is unable to detect cause and effect. Broadly, the local management's assessment is that ISO 9000 is worth its ongoing maintenance, but may not have been worth the investment of time and money setting it up.

The group has never done a formal evaluation but the Company still happily refers to ISO 9000 registration in Company brochures and literature. Simon Read doubts, however, that the Copthorne group, or indeed the industry as a whole, will ever wholeheartedly embrace ISO 9000.

REFERENCES

Downs, V. (1995) Correspondence with the authors, May. West Region, BSI Quality Assurance.

McDermid, K. (1994) *Copthorne Hotel, Cardiff: a powerful but worthwhile process. Hospitality*, February, p.18.

FIVE

Country Club Hotel Group

Andrew Ghillyer

In early August 1995, it was announced that Whitbread had bought Scott's Hotels including the master franchise and development rights for Marriott Hotels in the UK. In November 1995, it was announced that Whitbread would be dropping the Country Club name in favour of Marriott at ten of its resort properties. The group will now be known as the Whitbread Hotel Group. The Country Club Resorts will retain their individual names but with Marriott inserted at the beginning, such as the Marriott St Pierre Hotel and Country Club. The Travel Inn brand, however, will be maintained.

As recently as 1991, Whitbread's hotel division was one of the poorest performers in its portfolio. With a 25-year history as the Whitbread Group of Hotels, the division was characterized by operating margins well below industry norms, an underperforming management team and a track record of poor capital investment. The recession of the late 1980s appeared to mark the moment of decline for the division, and the only future seemed to be a departure from the hotel business altogether.

In terms of the parent company's long-range strategy, however, the hotel division formed an integral part of a development programme that focused on the attainment of a level of progressive synergy between divisions – brewing, pubs, off-licences, restaurants, and hotels. For this programme to succeed, it was obvious that the hotel division needed to be rebuilt almost from the ground up. A new managing director was appointed – Alan Parker, formerly responsible for Holiday Inn's European, Middle Eastern, and African operations – with the remit of transforming the fortunes of the Whitbread Group of Hotels. The extent of that transformation has been remarkable. With 4,700 rooms, the newly rebranded Country Club Hotel Group (CCHG) now stands as the fifth largest hotel company in the UK (up from tenth in 1994–95), and with a major capital commitment to an expansion of the Travel Inn brand (managed by CCHG as the internal franchisor). CCHG is also currently the fastest growing hotel company in the UK. The story behind the transformation is one of a 100 per cent commitment to quality of product and quality of service, and of the willingness to take whatever painful steps were necessary to achieve those objectives.

A QUALITY TRANSFORMATION

In 1991, the Whitbread Group of Hotels was comprised primarily of 45 three-star Lansbury hotels (which had been operated as Coaching Inns until the autumn of 1989), and eleven Country Club hotels. An extensive strategy review of operations determined that the Lansbury and Country Club properties were not being run to their full potential – they were run as completely separate companies, with an inefficient cost base, underperformance in sales, and poor awareness of customer service levels. With the hotel industry at the bottom of its cycle in the recession of the late 1980s, there were already too many bargain properties on the market; attempting to unload the whole portfolio was not a viable option. The decision was taken to adopt a two-step Performance Change Plan – first, to rationalize the size and structure of the division and, second, to carry out a dramatic change in both the operational and management policies of the division by means of an ambitious Quality Service Plan.

'CAMELOT'

The first stage of the plan – the rationalization of the division – was given the code-name 'Camelot'. Its implementation removed three regional offices, achieved a 30 per cent labour reduction, and cut payroll costs by over £1 million. In addition, 27 of the original 45 Lansbury hotels were divested over a six-month period, either through lease agreements or outright sale, and all at prices more than book value. Considerable overhead savings were achieved by integrating the support management and marketing of the Country Club and Lansbury divisions, and by introducing one central reservation system that, in turn, promotes cross-referrals between hotels.

The success of the rationalization programme has allowed CCHG to undertake a significant investment programme in their Country Club Resort hotels to provide new business centres, refurbished bedrooms and upgraded golf courses. This is in anticipation of a strong recovery in the conference business and an upturn in the golf and leisure markets. The first stage of this investment is nearing completion at the St Pierre Hotel in South Wales, where a total of £3.5 million has been spent. In its new format the Country Club Hotel Group is intended to represent a corporate image of quality rather than a specific brand identity. By extending the good reputation of the Country Club properties to encompass the group as a whole, it was hoped that a more dynamic image could be presented. The use of the name Whitbread Group of Hotels had not carried the same impact and had seemed to give the misleading impression of the company simply being the hotel division of a brewery company.

The Travel Inn brand, which is managed as a stand-alone component within the group, currently has 65 units in operation, with a total of 200 planned by the year 2000. Originally designed to compete with Forte's 'Travelodge' brand, the first Travel Inns were built on the surplus land bank of Whitbread's Beefeater restaurants as rooms-only operations. The flexible design format allows units to range in size from 40 to 120 rooms. The cost of developing a 40-bedroom Travel Inn has been reduced from £960,000 eighteen months ago, to £800,000 today.

Following an agreement with BAA, two larger than average sites opened in 1994 at Glasgow and Gatwick airports, and the first Travel Inn to be sited next to a TGI Friday's has opened in Coventry. With an anticipated growth rate of two units per month, any new units that are not sited next door to an existing Whitbread restaurant will provide both accommodation and integrated bar and restaurant facilities. The first of these opened in Hemel Hempstead in February 1994.

The Country Club Hotel Group is now positioned as Britain's leading leisure-based conference and hotel operator, incorporating a total of 29 properties in the UK and one in Hamburg, Germany. Within the group there are 12 Country Club Resorts, ten of which feature 18-hole golf courses. With the Dalmahoy Hotel near Edinburgh, the St Pierre Hotel in South Wales, and the Forest of Arden Hotel in Warwickshire all rated as championship golf venues, CCHG is now the largest European golf hotel operator. Each of those hotels has hosted a European tour tournament in 1994, and the St Pierre will also be the venue for the Solheim Cup in 1996.

The 18 remaining properties represent the survivors of the extensive rationalization of the original 45 Lansbury hotels. The name Lansbury has now been phased out completely, and the properties are now marketed as individual hotels within the group on the basis of their unique locations and facilities. In contrast to the Country Club Resorts that are generally situated around elegant, historical, former country houses, the hotels are much smaller, with a maximum of 60 bedrooms, and are all different in character – some are of historical interest, others are new. Located in town centres, suburbs and rural settings with good access to major roads and motorways, the hotels are packaged as offering an individual style but a national standard in terms of restaurant, conference and leisure facilities.

The second stage of the plan involved a dramatic change in operational and management policies. Its objectives were to develop the company's operating practices beyond the industry norms, and to bring about a culture change within the organization such that everyone would focus on satisfying the needs of the customer. A kick-start approach was taken to this redevelopment of the company's operating outlook – the position of quality service manager was created to coordinate an extensive series of training initiatives; a new sales team was developed to totally redesign the CCHG sales programme; and a state-of-the-art labour scheduling system was introduced to optimize performance levels. The transformation of the corporate culture to focus directly on the quality of customer care was undertaken through the Quality Service Plan.

QUALITY SERVICE PLAN

'Camelot' enabled the organization to start with as clean a slate as was physically and commercially possible, given their current operating environment. By divesting themselves of the properties and management team members that no longer fitted with the new corporate profile, a clear statement was made as to how sincere this commitment to the provision of a quality product and quality service to customers was to be.

The company's original commitment to quality had been via the typical 'flavour of the month' customer-care programmes. Under this new initiative, the perspective taken was that the journey from mediocre performance to world-class service delivery could not be made based on simplistic add-on programmes. What was needed was a detailed examination of the fundamentals of the product which CCHG provided to their customers, and an identification of the critical success factors which had to be achieved. In practice, this required an accurate analysis of customer perceptions and expectations, the measurement of conformance to those expectations, a meticulous inspection of the hotels themselves, and a total redefinition of training procedures.

STARS

Accurate measurement of performance is fundamental to the role of the general manager. At CCHG this is achieved by means of a customer satisfaction tracking system known as STARS (Satisfaction Tracking And Research System). Every calendar quarter, over 7,000 guests from the previous quarter complete a detailed questionnaire which examines every service area of the hotel in which they stayed, from check-in, through room cleanliness, food and beverage quality, leisure club facilities and staff contact. A percentage rating is achieved, which is then used as a benchmark for future perform-ance goals. To date, eight waves of questionnaires have been issued, with an average response rate of 40 per cent. The initial performance rating achieved was 80 per cent, and the base target rate is 85 per cent. The questionnaire itself is modified every quarter. The current version includes questions which ask customers to rate CCHG against their competitors. This allows the company to derive both internal and external ratings of how well they are doing.

For the unit managers, the STARS programme offers considerable financial motiva-tion, since the successful achievement of a target rating forms an integral part of their year-end performance bonus. The programme is very much in its early stages, but it has allowed CCHG to identify where they stand at the moment, and also where the effort has to be focused to achieve their goal of becoming a world-class service organization. As Angie Risley, the Human Resources Director, explains: 'When we began this programme, we were miles off our goal ... now we are certainly matching the industry average, if not exceeding it slightly, and with our ongoing commitment to these quality initiatives, we will eventually be much further ahead'.

QUALITY SERVICE AND CLEANLINESS (QS&C)

CCHG's commitment to the quality of their 'product' is shown in the operation of the Quality, Service and Cleanliness (QS&C) programme. Every six months, each hotel receives an unannounced incognito visit from an Automobile Association hotel inspector, sent at the request of the company, to inspect the property and assess the personnel in relation to predetermined service delivery standards. (Travel Inns use a mystery guest programme rather than hotel inspectors.) The hotels then receive a percentage performance rating (in addition to their STARS rating), which is then used as a base rate for future performance targets. As with STARS, the QS&C rating forms an integral part of the unit management bonus scheme. The current average perform-ance rating is 78 per cent, with an immediate goal of lifting that above the 80 per cent mark.

GOLD STANDARDS

The service delivery criteria that form the basis of the QS&C programme are derived from the company-wide Gold Standard programme, introduced during 1993/94, which sets the minimum service standards across all operational areas within Country Club Resorts and Hotels. Developed as a joint project between the training department, the operations team, and the quality service manager, Gold Standard represents the means by which every CCHG employee, from head office down to the unit front line, is brought together towards the achievement of a common goal. As the CCHG mission statement declares: 'At the Country Club Hotel Group, we aim to be Britain's leading hotel and leisure company by serving our customers better than our competitors. To do this we will provide *our best for every guest.*'

The role that Gold Standard plays in this provision of 'our best for every guest' is simply to focus on the fundamental service elements that every employee must follow and integrate into their own work performance. Employees have their own personal record of achievement to monitor their progress against Gold Standard, and after successful completion of a test (85 per cent pass rate required), they receive a certificate and a badge. The company has a stated goal that by the end of the 1995 financial year, 85 per cent of all CCHG employees will be Gold Standard trained.

There is nothing revolutionary in any of the specified minimum service standards, as the 'ten service signals' show:

- Zap the Phone
- Pleased to See You
- Use that Name
- Know it All
- Give It Five (offer a helping hand)
- Right First Time
- You're on Stage
- Work Clean – Work Tidy
- Magic Moments
- Add a Bit More

However, the underlying message is one of total commitment to responsive customer service and 100 per cent guest satisfaction. The extent to which this culture has been taken on board by the employees is best demonstrated in two 'moments of magic':

- A stranded delegate attending a course at the Edgwarebury Hotel was rescued by part-time secretary Dee Kidd. The guest telephoned to say she had broken down and would be late, but Dee jumped into her own car and collected the guest on the roadside.
- When their daughter needed to be rushed to the hospital in the middle of the night, a couple at the Honiley Court Hotel wanted to follow behind the ambulance. Panic set in when their car would not start, but the night porter, Roland Swift, turned their moment of misery into a moment of magic by unhesitatingly giving up the keys to his brand new Ford Escort.

The Gold Standard criteria are seen to apply as equally to the head office operations in Leagrave as they do to the front-line units. All calls that come into head office must be returned within three hours, whether that call is from an employee or a customer –

for a customer call you are expected to break a meeting if necessary. In addition, a programme called At the Sharp End is now in place, in which once a year (usually in January) every head office employee, from Managing Director, Alan Parker, downwards, spends a couple of days working in a hotel to gain front-line experience – for some this is a completely new experience, and for others it represents something of a refresher course. The overall objective of the programme is to bring everyone within the organization closer together as an operating team.

To promote the idea of cross-training across departments, it is possible to achieve a Double Gold by qualifying for Gold Standard in more than one department. This idea is being augmented in the food and beverage department with a project to recruit multi-skilled employees who would be able to work in the bar, restaurant and kitchen if needed. This represents quite a step forward from the current employment procedures where employees are recruited for one department only.

PRIDE

In 1993, the company undertook a Quality of Working Life Survey of their employees (achieving an excellent 71 per cent response rate from permanent employees) to try to find out the level of commitment to the objectives of the Performance Change Plan, and to derive some indication of the continued response to their ongoing quality initiatives. The most significant piece of data that came out of that survey was that maintaining the momentum of the programmes would require offering the employees more than just the satisfaction of 'getting it right'. What the survey suggested was that the employees wanted an incentive programme in place to provide some form of recognition and motivation over and above the certificate and badge they received for completing their Gold Standard training.

In early 1994, the company responded to that request with an incentive programme called PRIDE – Professionalism, Respect, Initiative, Dedication, Efficiency – which was designed to reward employees directly for achieving targets and for improving the service provided to guests. The system is based on the achievement of reward points awarded according to the employee's work status – either Category A (for staff who work an average of 25 or more hours per week each month) or Category B (for staff who work an average of eight to twenty-four hours per week each month). To be eligible to participate in the PRIDE programme, employees must have achieved their Gold Standard. There are two ways of achieving reward points – either by monthly sales target, or by quarterly STARS score:

Monthly sales target

The premise of this is simply that 'if your guests enjoy good service, they are likely to spend more on meals and extras during their stay and will plan to return in the future'. The monthly sales target that the general manager sets for his/her hotel then becomes the sales target for PRIDE. If that target is achieved, every member of staff in that unit receives a reward points pay-out which can then be used to buy from a selection of prize items in a special PRIDE catalogue. There is a consolation points pay-out for achieving 95–99 per cent of the target, but the size of the pay-out increases considerably between 100–104 per cent, 105–109 per cent, and 110 per cent +.

Quarterly STARS score

Every member of staff receives PRIDE points for achieving Gold Standard. If their hotel then improves upon its STARS rating from one quarter to the next, the employees receive an additional points pay-out. At the moment, the base level for participation in the STARS reward is a score of 85 per cent. Over time this level is likely to rise as the company continues to raise its performance standards.

Employee response to the programme has been tremendous, with the element of recognition appearing to be as attractive as the reward points themselves. The Honiley Court Hotel, for instance, coordinated an intensive programme of three Gold Standard training sessions per week. The result was that 30 of their employees could pass their Gold Standard questionnaire more or less on the same day, which, in turn, qualified them to participate in the PRIDE points bonus for achieving 123 per cent of their sales target for August 1994.

The PRIDE points are paid out on a monthly basis. Within seven working days of the month end, every employee receives a personal statement that shows the number of reward points he/she has earned. The employee then has the choice of using them straight away or accumulating them for a larger prize item. The PRIDE catalogue offers a range of items that would be the envy of any department store, with everything from an electric toothbrush (2520 points) to a 29-inch stereo colour television (88,540 points).

When explaining the decision to use an incentive programme to motivate their employees, Angie Risley concludes:

> We felt that 'what you reward you get', and we firmly believe that PRIDE has given a focus to what we are trying to achieve. It has proved to our employees that we are serious about this new relationship. The decision to follow this quality line may have been made at corporate level, but we can't do it without our employees. PRIDE gives us a means of providing a pretty immediate response to their efforts. It gives them the message that – 'you do your part of this and we will do ours'.

EXTERIOR QUALITY INITIATIVES

To a large extent, the CCHG quality initiatives remain insular in nature. The high level of response to their STARS questionnaires provides the company with more than enough quantitative data to work on in improving the quality of their product and the level of their customer care. The tremendous amount of energy that the PRIDE programme appears to generate keeps everyone focused on the goal of providing 'our best for every guest'. As an increasingly valued member of the Whitbread organization, CCHG has access to a wide range of resource and training initiatives should they choose to benchmark other ideas. Whitbread itself has a stated strategic objective of serving its customers better than its competitors, and its primary brands – Beefeater, Pizza Hut, and TGI Fridays – are all market leaders. This, in turn, provides CCHG with a substantial source of ideas for improvement.

BS 5750

The decision not to pursue the British Standards accreditation was made on the basis of a belief that it would not be of any direct use in helping the company achieve their objectives. As Angie Risley explains: 'Our programmes are about service delivery and contact with the customer. We felt (rightly or wrongly) that BS 5750 was too process-oriented. It's great for manufacturing operations – our beer company has it – but we couldn't see that it would help us in driving our business forward from a quality point of view'.

Investors In People (IIP)

In contrast, the IIP programme has been taken on board as a means of putting a framework around the many initiatives that are now in place within the organization. The company is currently at the point of having presented a letter of intent to participate within the programme – the expectation is that participation will be a relatively straightforward exercise since many of the individual elements of IIP were already in place before the commitment was made. The idea of external recognition is regarded as being secondary to the idea of setting up a system that will help to produce 'the right candidate for the right position'.

One key element that has arisen from the strategic review, the Performance Change Plan, and the ongoing feedback from the STARS questionnaires, is that the new corporate philosophy created under the CCHG banner now needs a different type of employee – one who is more aware of the need to satisfy the needs of the customer over the long-term. With a stated goal of becoming a world-class service organization, the company needs to achieve a high degree of behavioural change within their operations. It is hoped that IIP will help to prepare their people to 'step up a gear' and flourish in this new quality environment.

The development of Business Improvement Teams (BITs) – a form of Quality Circle – is one example of the apparent willingness of the CCHG to rise to the new challenges being offered to them. There are currently BITs in operation to examine food procurement and logistics issues (a team of chefs, food and beverage managers, and restaurant managers), service guarantees (general managers and front-line service employees), and the ramifications of the new operating systems which are being introduced (representatives from each department).

A QUALITY CULTURE

As to their long-range strategies, CCHG see themselves as only being in year two of a five-year programme for complete transformation of the company and its operating culture. While everyone is proud, and rightly so, of the tremendous advances made so far, they all remain conscious of the hard work ahead on the road to becoming a world-class service organization.

Profits tripled (from a relatively low base) in a flat sales market during the first year of the Performance Change Plan, and the Quality Service Plan is seen as playing a very significant part in that achievement. Ensuring that the energy and enthusiasm that these programmes appear to have released within the CCHG workforce remain channelled towards those long-term objectives requires a different approach. With STARS, QS&C, PRIDE, and the Gold Standard, there are already enough quality initiatives, programmes and acronyms in place to see the company through the next decade. What is needed now is a system to ensure that this new culture becomes embedded in every level of the organization – the initial momentum may have come from senior management, but the long-term survival of the culture will be decided on the front line. For CCHG, the key to the survival of quality is the performance of their general managers.

Through STARS, the company is now listening far more closely to their customers, and through PRIDE and the Gold Standard, they are now getting the commitment of their employees in responding to the needs of those customers. To ensure that the right unit management team is in place to oversee this very upbeat environment, CCHG has sought the advice of the Hay Management Group in developing a detailed profile of the type of general manager they needed to maintain the momentum of their quality initiatives and to move the organization on to the next stage of development. That profile has been developed not on identifiable competencies as such, but on their impact skills – what they as individuals are going to be able to contribute to the organization as unit managers and as team leaders of staff within those units.

The inherent complexity of the task of finding the 'right people for the right position' has prompted the company to examine not only the recruitment procedures to find those people, but also the remuneration policies needed to keep the best people within the organization. A bonus system in direct relation to achieved STARS and QS&C ratings is already in operation, and the logical evolution of this is seen to be a pay structure in which individuals can have even more influence over what their annual salary is going to be.

The form to be taken by this new pay structure is not the typical performance related pay scheme championed by most quality programmes, but rather a definitive pay matrix with identifiable high and low salary ranges for different job descriptions in direct relation to the abilities of the individual in that position – the idea being that employees can anticipate the financial reward that increased training and experience will bring. To that end, the corporate structure will be based on five employee grades between operations director and kitchen porter.

FUTURE QUALITY INITIATIVES

Having achieved their initial goal of putting the fundamental infrastructure in place to provide a quality product and quality service to their customers, the company's immediate objective is simply to continue raising performance standards through the consistent improvement of the unit STARS and QS&C ratings. The information derived from the STARS questionnaires will continue to reveal (it is hoped) what their customers expect from them, and by participating in Investors In People, the company aims to have the necessary framework in place to make sure that they recruit and train the right people to meet those customer expectations.

CCHG remains committed to the belief that their employees will ultimately decide the success of their corporate transformation, and they intend to continue with their annual employee surveys to find out what their employees think and feel about how the company is evolving. The result of the 1993 survey was the introduction of PRIDE. The latest survey has just been completed – the results will no doubt make interesting reading.

SIX

English Lakes Hotels

Andrew Ghillyer

The English Lakes Hotel Group is a privately-owned, family-run hotel company based primarily, as the name suggests, in the Lake District. The company is a member of the Best Western marketing consortium, which gives them access to a national marketing and advertising programme, and to international markets. The property portfolio currently consists of five hotels and an extensive Watersports Centre on Lake Windermere.

ENGLISH LAKES HOTELS

The Low Wood Hotel

In 1952, Norman Buckley, MBE, a solicitor from Manchester, and uncle of the current Chairman and Managing Director, Michael Berry, bought the Low Wood – then a 36-room seasonal hotel in Windermere. The property was developed and expanded through the 1950s and 1960s, ending in the early 1970s as a 148-room seasonal hotel. In July 1988, by which time the hotel was operating year round, a complete redevelopment of the property was undertaken. This was a £5.5 million project and included the total refurbishment of the main hotel, a new 300-delegate conference centre, a £1.5 million leisure club with swimming pool, sauna, steam room, gymnasium and two squash courts. In addition, 18 new executive bedrooms and a new 42-room staff lodge were constructed. The hotel now has 99 rooms.

The Low Wood Water Sports Centre

Built in 1983–84, the centre originally offered only boat storage and ski lessons. The property has since been developed and now also offers scuba diving, windsurfing, canoeing, archery, fishing, yachting and yachting tuition.

The Wild Boar Hotel

A smaller three-star property in the village of Crook near Windermere with 36 rooms. The property began as a farmhouse and was later extended to offer accommodation facilities. The hotel restaurant was built around a large rock face, part of which forms a natural interior wall in the dining area.

The Waterhead Hotel

The smallest of the five hotels, this two-star property in Ambleside has 26 rooms.

The Royal Hotel

This is a two-star, 29 room property in Bowness operated as a bed and breakfast establishment.

The Lancaster House

The flagship of the group, this is a relatively new four-star, 80-room property in Lancaster next to Lancaster University. Opened on 12 July 1991, the hotel offers conference facilities for up to 150 delegates, and a Management Development Centre, owned by the University, where up to 180 delegates have access to the most up-to-date computer and electronic communication systems. In addition, The Sandpiper Club leisure complex offers a swimming pool, fitness studio, sauna and steam room.

The issue of star classification systems generates some confusion within the group. The Lancaster House Hotel carries a four-star rating under the RAC motoring organization grading system and currently holds a '5 Crowns' under the English Tourist Board rating system. Best Western, however, uses the AA classification system, which only awards the Lancaster House a three-star rating. To achieve a four-star rating, the company discovered that they would need to upgrade the armchairs in the bedrooms to a larger size (this was considered too expensive). Involvement with the AA system is currently under review.

COMMITMENT TO QUALITY

The Company is run by a management board comprised of three family and three non-family members. Quality initiatives within the organization are essentially 'top-down', with the Board committing resources to those initiatives and deciding what form and direction they should take. The issues of quality service and consistency of performance are implicit in the corporate mission statement (Table 6.1), and the long-term objective for the organization is to incorporate the quality message into every aspect of the day-to-day operation of the business.

Table 6.1 Mission statement of the English Lakes Hotels

- To surpass our guest expectations by providing a quality service experience through attention to detail.
- To encourage our employees to reach their full potential through training and motivation.
- To be innovative and creative in all we do.

Quality through people

The operational philosophy on which the company is run is that 90 per cent of the success of the operation is based on the people in the organization. The product itself is seen to account for only 10 per cent of that success – the money spent on the properties may look good in the brochure, but it is the effectiveness of the staff that will ultimately determine whether or not a guest has a satisfactory stay at an English Lakes hotel.

An integral part of this people orientation is the management's commitment to nurturing high levels of motivation among their employees. A staff magazine is produced three or four times a year to facilitate two-way communication with staff members; customer care awards are in place for each hotel offering 'employee of the month' bonuses and certificates; and long-service financial incentives are awarded for each year of service.

Alongside this reward structure is an equally strong commitment to training across the board, to enable the staff to achieve the high levels of performance that the quality programmes demand of them. The company is an active member of the Lakeland Hotel Training Group, which is comprised of some 15 to 20 hotels which cooperate in the coordination of National Vocational Qualifications (NVQs) programmes in the area. The Lancaster House Hotel also operates a training facility as a joint venture with Lancaster University.

ISO 9000

The development of plans to build a conference and business hotel in Lancaster in the late 1980s coincided with the growing interest in ISO 9000 as an accreditation tool for quality in the hospitality industry. As a greenfield site, the Lancaster House offered an ideal opportunity to develop a quality system base for the operation from scratch. It was felt that simply opening the doors of a brand new property would not guarantee success, nor would transferring staff from the older hotels into this new four-star environment promote the consistent performance levels that the new operation would need. The decision was taken, therefore, to pursue ISO 9000 as a means of establishing a firm quality standard from the outset.

In commenting on that decision, Douglas Dale, director of the new hotel, explained: 'We had to set policies and procedures for the new hotel anyway, so we decided to introduce quality management from day one. Leading companies in business and industry are ISO 9000 registered; they understand it and will be attracted to hotels that are registered as such'. In practice, the approach remained essentially operational in focus throughout the accreditation process – the idea of using the 'kudos of the Kitemark' as a marketing tool became a secondary issue.

Accreditation was achieved on 16 December 1992, 18 months after it was agreed as a main Board objective. When the hotel first opened on 12th July 1991, it was believed (rather naïvely as the management team now readily admits) that the process would only take about 12 months. With low occupancy levels anticipated for the first few months of operation, it was felt that there would be plenty of time available to handle the paper-work for the accreditation process. In addition, with Board-approved funding for consul-tants to guide the management team through to completion, ISO 9000 was seen as something of a formality. The reality was very different.

The consultancy company recruited to help the English Lakes management team to achieve accreditation was Manchester-based Oranvale Consultants, a firm that had risen to prominence by guiding the Avant Hotel in Oldham (also a new hotel) to becoming the first hotel to achieve ISO 9000. (The Avant Hotel later became a victim of the recession and lost its registration when it fell into receivership). With a work force of less than 500, English Lakes qualified for a grant of between 50 to 66 per cent of the cost of a consultant for a maximum of 15 days, under a Department of Trade and Industry Enterprise Initiative.

The involvement of a consultant did little to change the casual approach to ISO 9000. The management team's own presentation on the programme failed to get the message across about what was actually involved in documenting every aspect of the hotel's busi-ness operations. As a result, in the initial stages, no indication was given of the 'finer details' of the accreditation process, and for the first couple of months everyone remained convinced that they would achieve the quality standard within one year of opening. A progress check after three months proved to be a severe culture shock for the management team. The prevailing attitude of 'we'll do that tomorrow' had resulted in no major forward movement being achieved in the first quarter, and so the team was forced to start from scratch again.

The responsibility for the accreditation process had originally been given to the personnel and training manager, but it was now transferred to Edward Hart, Accommodation Services Manager, on the basis that he was more involved in the general operation of the hotel. The personnel and training manager had not been familiar with the operating procedures in the bar or housekeeping departments, for example, and so Edward Hart became the unofficial 'quality assurance manager' with the responsibility for restarting and maintaining the momentum of the programme. This ranged from enthusiastic pep talks to 'hitting people on the head' when they failed to carry out the documentation required in the accreditation process.

At the second attempt, the senior staff in each department became more aware of the considerable work and commitment that would be involved – a documented procedure had to be written for every element of the duties and tasks their staff performed. Once every one realized where they were going and how they were going to get there, every-thing began to fall into place. The anticipated slack period in the first few months of operation did materialize, and this gave the heads of department (HoDs) some free time to work on the procedures and paperwork. However, the senior staff members were still busy supervising the practical training programmes and, as a result, about 50 per cent of the overall workload had to be completed in their own spare time (for which they received no additional salary payment).

Consultants' visits were scheduled for every two weeks or so to provide guidance and encouragement where needed, and it became the responsibility of the new quality assur-ance manager to ensure that things ran smoothly between those visits. This primarily involved monitoring the consistency of the working procedures that were being written up. With each member of a department approaching the duty differently, it became necessary for one person to oversee the document as a whole and to decide on the one correct way for the task to be performed.

During this time, the company was fortunate enough to have a very low rate of staff turnover, and this helped to both increase the consistency of performance and to maintain the momentum of the programme. The extra work put in by the HoDs in their spare time sent the message to their staff that the commitment to ISO 9000 was a serious one, and the involvement of every staff member in the documentation process underlined the message that the achievement of the quality standard was to be a concerted group effort.

COSTS AND BENEFITS OF ISO 9000

Given that around 50 per cent of the paperwork was done in the HoD's spare time, it is difficult to arrive at a true labour cost figure for the achievement of ISO 9000. Ean Scott, the General Manager, estimates that at least £13,000 was spent in direct labour costs in the on-duty work which was performed during the quiet periods. Consultant costs amounted to £6075, of which the hotel paid 50 per cent (the balance being met by the DTI Enterprise Initiative). In addition, the initial accreditation fee of £6,000, and other miscellaneous administrative start-up costs produced an approximate grand-total cost of around £30,000. There is an ongoing cost for twice-yearly audits undertaken by the Associated Offices Quality Company (AOQC) which amount to £450 per visit. Determining the perceived value and financial viability of the quality standard is even more difficult than estimating the total cost of the process itself. The management team has taken the position that there are both external and internal benefits to being ISO 9000 registered.

External

The Kitemark is prominently featured on the hotel's conference brochure and letterhead, but that is about as far as its utilization as a marketing device goes. As Ean Scott explains: 'There is this general idea that ISO 9000 is a great marketing tool, but we never set out with that objective in mind – we wanted it to help us get the hotel up and running with the consistency of performance to be expected of a four-star establishment'. In this respect, the hotel's advertising campaign still centres around the business and leisure facilities that the property has to offer.

If anything, the Kitemark has proven to be something of a double-edged sword for the hotel's public perspective. As Edward Hart notes:

> We've had comments from guests saying that it is obvious that we have achieved ISO 9000 because we are so consistent in our service delivery; and we've also had comments which question whether we should be a part of the ISO 9000 programme because we didn't deliver on what we promised!

Such negative comments are treated as clear examples of system failure, and the review procedures set out under the quality guidelines are used to identify the problem and to take immediate corrective action.

Internal

The Lancaster House was fortunate to have a stable team of HoDs in place throughout the implementation of the ISO 9000 operating guidelines, but the biggest benefit of the programme is the high level of consistency that will be maintained when those HoDs have moved on. The use of a teamworking approach from the outset has encouraged cooperation and discipline – if one department fails, then the whole hotel is seen to fail, and so there is a strong psychological wish to not let your colleagues down. This 'togetherness' is seen to provide a stronger sense of self-worth in the work environment, and over the past two years it has helped to keep staff turnover low.

Ean Scott believes that it is the consistency of performance rather than the quality aspect of ISO 9000 that has been of the greatest benefit to the hotel: 'I would estimate that the sense of disciplined performance that the quality standard has installed within our operation, and the repeat business that, in turn, has generated, has given us anywhere from a 10–20 fold return on our original £30,000 investment'.

THE FUTURE FOR ISO 9000

ISO 9000 remains very much a live document for the management team, and it is constantly being updated. There are regular management reviews, and the hotel conducts its own annual review in addition to the six-month external AOQC audits. The procedure manuals, which were written with the direct input of the staff members themselves, are seen to represent what day-to-day quality means for the Lancaster House, and they are still used to train staff from day one.

There are, however, no plans to roll out ISO 9000 to the other four properties in the group. In retrospect, the whole experience is regarded as something of a unique situation. Setting up training and procedural systems from scratch in a new hotel was an ideal environment in which to establish quality standards via the ISO 9000 accreditation process. In addition, it saved the management team from having to focus on changing the three-star mentality that had become ingrained over the previous decade.

The primary drawbacks are the time requirement and the amount of paperwork involved. As Ean Scott admits: 'When there was no systems foundation in place, and we were starting fresh in a relatively quiet period, then ISO 9000 was ideal – but to do it now in a fully functional property, we would have to employ an extra person in each department just to handle the paperwork'. In general terms, the lessons learned from ISO 9000, and the operational policies that the quality standard advocates, are still being passed on to the rest of the group, but for their company-wide quality initiative, English Lakes chose to pursue accreditation through another external programme – Investors In People.

INVESTORS IN PEOPLE (IIP)

The decision to join the government scheme to become recognized as an 'Investors In People' employer was announced by the Management Board in December 1992. After an initial pre-assessment in November 1994, their final assessment was carried out on

24 and 25 February 1995. Final accreditation was achieved on 13 March 1995, giving a total investment of over 26 months in the IIP accreditation process. As Ean Scott explains: 'Pursuing ISO 9000 at Lancaster House put us in a position where we already had a lot of the IIP procedures in place, but we had to wait for the other properties to catch us up so that we could proceed as a group'.

The primary objective in taking IIP on board has been to develop a more formal framework for the personnel and training initiatives for the organization as a whole. While the corporate mission statement (Table 6.1) proclaims the organization's belief in the need to nurture the potential of their workforce, before the commitment to IIP, the company's approach to personnel issues had lacked a defined policy, and there were very few personnel procedures in place.

'Investors In People' is fundamentally personnel-based and people-oriented. For English Lakes, it is seen as following through on their commitment to the achievement of a quality product through the consistently high performance of their staff. By enabling the group to identify training needs and to quantify the cost of those needs, IIP aligns itself very closely to two specific corporate objectives:

1. To provide good working conditions and to maintain effective communication at all levels; to develop better understanding within the company; to develop training programmes, thereby helping staff in developing their own skills.
2. To support managers and other staff in using personal incentives to improve the quality of operation; in developing a pride in the company and the recognition of the importance of genuine respect for all the individuals who comprise each employee team.

With a relatively small catchment area from which to attract staff, the issues of employee retention and labour turnover have become crucial to the success of the English Lakes quality initiatives. The commitment to IIP has helped to underline the importance of the staff contribution to the achievement of the companys' goals.

As to the day-to-day mechanics of the programme, the implementation process has been somewhat problematic. Many employees found the IIP procedures to be very 'jargonistic', and it took over a month simply to reach a point of understanding as to how the initial training portfolio should be put together. Fortunately, the company has been able to work closely with their local Training and Enterprise Council (TEC) in setting up their training initiatives, such that the programme as a whole remained on track, and there was no need for the culture shock which was necessary to kick-start the ISO 9000 programme.

THE FUTURE FOR ENGLISH LAKES HOTELS

After making a considerable capital investment in the group properties during the late 1980s and early 1990s – the construction of the Lancaster House and the expansion of the Low Wood – the short-term goals of the organization remain focused on the continuous improvement of the product and services offered within those properties. In line with the corporate philosophy that 90 per cent of the success of the operation is based on the people in the organization, the primary emphasis of the English Lakes quality initiative is likely to remain on training.

Through their commitment to ISO 9000 and IIP, the company feels that they have made a strong statement about the importance of their people in providing a quality guest experience. IIP has raised the profile of the training programme, and the managers feel that they are well on the way to developing a true 'training culture' within the organization. Training initiatives now cover a wide spectrum from experience-based to formal external courses. Specific areas covered include customer service (the Cumbria Tourist Board undertakes customer care training), telephone skills, telephone selling, listening skills, psychology of selling, and complaint handling. In addition, the necessary health and safety training is given in such areas as food hygiene, fire training, and first aid. Courses vary in length from two hours to four days.

Deriving a precise evaluation of the benefits arising from either ISO 9000 or IIP has been difficult. In general terms, the company has been seen to follow through on their commitment to a people-oriented quality programme by being prepared to sanction the expense of both ISO 9000 and the necessary training courses needed to enable their staff to provide the best possible service to their customers. This represents a long-term approach, in contrast to the more convenient TQM package initiatives adopted by many companies, and the full benefits of that approach have yet to materialize. However, by being prepared to 'walk the talk' in this way, a strong statement has been made, and judging by the response to the available training courses, the staff are starting to rise to the challenge.

SEVEN

The Gleneagles Hotel

Andrew Ghillyer

The Gleneagles Hotel at Auchterarder, Perthshire, Scotland, was built in 1924 as the flagship hotel property of the Caledonian Railway Company and was originally designed as a summer golfing resort. It was to remain the most famous property in the British Rail-owned British Transport Hotels Group until 1981, when it was transferred to the private sector.

The Estate currently amounts to some 304 hectares (750 acres) (including its own railway station), and is considered by many to be one of the finest resort properties of its kind in the world. Since 1982, more than £25 million has been invested in transforming Gleneagles from a summer resort into a year-round luxury '5 Red Star' resort, and it is now one of *The Leading Hotels of the World*. In 1988, the Gleneagles Mark Phillips' Equestrian Centre was added at a cost of three million pounds; a further four million pounds was spent during 1989, as part of a continuous programme of further improvements. In 1990, a £1.35 million extension to the Country Club was opened to provide spa facilities.

In addition to the Country Club and the Equestrian Centre, the extensive amenities now available to guests include three world-class 18-hole golf courses, the Jackie Stewart Shooting School and the British School of Falconry. The £5.9 million Monarch's Course, designed by Jack Nicklaus, was opened in 1993; in 1994, £800,000 was invested in refurbishing 34 fourth-floor bedrooms in a contemporary style. An ongoing refurbishment programme, focusing on upgrading single rooms to doubles, has reduced the total number of rooms from 249 to 234.

Acquired by Guinness as part of the hotel portfolio of Arthur Bell & Sons in a £370-million takeover in 1985, Gleneagles survived the sell-off of its sister properties, including the North British (now the Balmoral) and the Caledonian in Edinburgh. Plans to develop a global network of Gleneagles Resorts in the late 1980s never progressed beyond the contract stage. To date, the only corporate operation outside Perthshire is the Equinox Resort in Vermont, USA.

As the only hotel in the Guinness business portfolio, Gleneagles is the subject of scrutiny and frequent speculation as to the exact nature of its role within its parent company's plans. The current state of ownership affairs seems that while Gleneagles' 1993 turnover of around £20 million represented a very small contribution to the over five billion pound turnover of its parent company, the property is still a prestigious jewel in the Guinness crown. Rumours of selling prices of anywhere from £50 to £100 million surface almost daily. Those pundits seeking to find the inside track even interpreted the absence of the Gleneagles brand on the front cover of the Guinness annual report for 1992 as a sign that the hotel remained out of favour!

More recently, media attention has focused on the day-to-day operation of Gleneagles – specifically the structural and operational changes being introduced under the leadership of Peter Lederer, Managing Director. Stories of 'a new approach to management' and 'attacks on the sacred cows of hotelkeeping' are now attracting as much attention as the sale rumours.

THE NEW GLENEAGLES CULTURE

The eponymous phrase 'new culture' is about as far as anyone at Gleneagles will go in putting a name to the metamorphosis currently taking place. In simple terms, the entire organization is being put through a process of reorientation. The perspective being taken is that too much time and too many resources are lost in the preservation of bureaucratic functions and the maintenance of interdepartmental barriers. The result of this inefficiency will be an organization that is out of touch with the market in which it is operating, and is too slow to respond to the expectations and complaints of its customers. If the stated goal of the organization is to provide guests with the highest quality service, then, it is argued, the most important people in that organization are the members of staff who deal directly with the guests on a day-to-day basis.

So far so good. The trade press has been inundated with the public proclamations of many companies promising to treat their front-line people as 'their most important asset'. What makes Gleneagles any different? As Peter Lederer admits:

> It's more a recognition that what I had been doing for the last 20 years didn't work
> ... The biggest failure managers of my generation have made is in seeing people as
> a cost rather than a resource or asset – my biggest strategic assets are my people.
> My generation always saw them as 34 per cent.

In recent years the usual response to this realization has been the figurative inversion of the pyramid of a traditional management hierarchy to put the front-line employees at the top and the senior management at the bottom. Typically, this inversion has been accompanied by a removal of one or more layers of middle management, as companies have sought to be more responsive to the needs of their customers.

For Gleneagles, the perspective has been markedly different. Rather than simply inverting the pyramid, it has been completely disassembled and rebuilt to focus on both external and internal customers, and to undermine the traditional departmental barriers in a hotel operation. Thus, increased responsiveness has been sought not through the shortening of the vertical communication chain, but through the creation of a more efficient interdepartmental communication process.

A HORIZONTAL MANAGEMENT STRUCTURE

The day-to-day operation of the hotel is now divided into three distinct areas: Today's Guest, Tomorrow's Guest and the Internal Customer. Thirty-five teams are divided between these three areas, under the leadership of three senior managers.

Today's guest

Under the guidance of Deputy General Manager, Kevin Poulter, this 'division' is responsible for the customer contact areas of all in-house guests – reception, leisure, food and beverage, concierge and retail outlets. In line with the Gleneagles culture, the primary remit of this area is to ensure that the needs of the guest are met quickly and efficiently. In operational terms, these are the front-line teams where the stated goal of 100 per cent guest satisfaction will ultimately be achieved.

Tomorrow's guest

As the name suggests, the objective of this division, under the guidance of Sales and Marketing Director, Neil Woodcock, is to concentrate on the future business of the hotel through resort sales, marketing, and public relations.

The internal customer

This area focuses on the 'back-of-house' support functions – kitchen, housekeeping, maintenance, accounts, and personnel. While not regarded as front-line, it is these teams, under the guidance of Deputy General Manager, George Graham, which form the key to the objective of increased responsiveness. By focusing on the relationships between the guest contact departments and their support departments – i.e., the restaurants and the kitchen, or reception and housekeeping – Gleneagles has moved beyond the preoccupation with the front-line to encompass the idea that everyone in the hotel forms an integral part of the total guest experience. As Resort Operations Analyst, Terry Waldron explains, 'It may take a while for the kitchen to recognize that the waiters are their customers, but the chefs wouldn't accept being yelled at by their suppliers, so why should they (traditionally) be allowed to scream abuse at the waiters over the hotplate?'

While the management at Gleneagles would fully support any programme that places the front-line employees at the head of the organization (such as America's Malcolm Baldridge Quality Award), every effort is made to ensure that the company does not simply jump on the quality bandwagon. The phrase 'total responsibility' is used to suggest the importance of providing the best possible service to your customers, whether those customers are paying guests in the hotel, or other departments of the business. Any other acknowledgements to the acronyms and phraseology of the Quality Movement are avoided on the premise that when a policy is labelled as 'the latest thing', a time frame is put on it. In the minds of the employees it will soon be replaced by the 'next latest thing', and so full commitment to the concept is withheld in anticipation of the next version. Consequently, Gleneagles has avoided pursuing BS 5750 (now called BS EN ISO 9000) as a public demonstration of their commitment to quality service. While the kudos of the kitemark may be good for public relations, management's greatest fear lies in what comes after – once you have the certificate on the wall, what are you going to follow it up with? As Peter Lederer concludes: 'I would rather go through the hoops that the customer wants than the hoops dictated by BS 5750. We will look at programmes to see if they can be of use to what we are trying to do, but there will be no blind adoption'.

One programme that has been of use is Investors In People (IIP). In particular the use of regular Impact Reviews has ensured that team leaders sit down with every member of their team on a regular basis to analyse past performance and future goals and objectives. By focusing on the Impact Reviews in this way, Gleneagles has chosen to mould the programme to their needs by cherry-picking the elements that specifically suit their objectives rather than attempting to mould the organization according to the demands of a programme manual to achieve an exterior accreditation.

'BREAKTHROUGH'

An integral part of the focus on interdepartmental communication has been the management's decision to put every member of staff through an intensive training programme on communication called 'Breakthrough', run by Tim Seaton, Canadian management consultant. After witnessing the success of the programme in other Guinness divisions, Peter Lederer put the Gleneagles management staff through the programme in January 1994, with the intention of allowing them to spread the word to their people. Upon completion of the course, however, it was realized that the energy and ideas generated within the course would best be shared by allowing the staff to experience the programme themselves firsthand rather than through the fervent exhortations of their managers. The considerable expense involved is indicative of Peter Lederer's commitment to the breakdown of departmental barriers as the key to service quality.

The immediate response to the programme has been overwhelming. In the follow-up sessions, employees were asked to develop their ideas of what Gleneagles would be like in the year 2000. Of the hundreds of ideas generated, many are already being carried out, and others are taking management in directions that had never been considered before. As Peter Lederer comments:

> If each person in this organization came up with one idea per year, that's over 500 improvements in one year. In the old system only the managers had the ideas – how many will come out of that? It is a misperception that managers must come up with ideas – it is management's job to encourage, collect and support the creative input of his people.

The ultimate success of 'Breakthrough' will depend on the ability of the senior managers to move beyond the energy and hype of brainstorming sessions for the year 2000. The long-term commitment to 'walking the talk' and carrying through on promises made has only just begun. Creating the horizontal management structure and putting every member of staff through the 'Breakthrough' programme has certainly succeeded in focusing everyone's attention on the idea of breaking down interdepartmental barriers. What the senior managers now recognize is that for the momentum of the programme to continue, their task must be to make sure that the team leaders and their team members receive whatever support and encouragement they may need in delivering a first-class service to the guest.

The most convincing practical demonstration of this belief that staff should be treated with the respect they deserve has been the substantial financial commitment to the refurbishment of the live-in staff quarters. In 1992, more than two million pounds was invested in upgrading the adjoining Whitemuir House to provide five-star staff accommodation (including a shop and social club). Lederer's philosophy on this is quite simple: 'It is essential that we look after our own people ... because we rely on them to look after our guests.'

The mission statement for Gleneagles simply states that:

> We are all here to ensure that
> Gleneagles is the
> Hallmark of Excellence
> amongst luxury golf resorts.

Beneath the simplicity of that statement lies a much stronger message. Every member of staff at Gleneagles is now regarded as totally responsible for ensuring that each and every guest leaves the hotel 100 per cent delighted with their stay. As Peter Lederer explains:

> London Business School did a detailed study for us in 1993, and we now know that it costs us 11 times more to go and find a new guest than whatever it costs to look after the one we've got. Simple logic tells me that we've got to do whatever it takes to stop a dissatisfied guest from leaving the hotel with a negative experience, and we've got to reduce the money spent on finding new guests.

Each of the 35 teams is now self-directing in the achievement of that objective. What this means in practice is that the senior managers, having taken on the responsibility of creating the vision of how Gleneagles should look and operate, are now looking to the experience of their employees in their respective fields, for the solutions to the achievement of that vision, rather than simply passing down directives from above. The standard operating procedure (SOP) manuals are being completely rewritten by the corresponding departmental team. As Waldron explains:

> Some of the manuals are very old and quite insulting in places – they treat the issue of staff training almost as if they were training chimpanzees. Our staff don't need me to tell them how to do their jobs. What we are doing is agreeing on the level of service which best exemplifies the quality that our guests expect from Gleneagles.

STARS

Perhaps the finest example of Gleneagles' commitment to the participation of all their people rather than just management is the STARS programme – the acronym stands for Service Targets and Resource Survey. Each of the 35 teams, for the first time, is now putting together a zero-based budget for 1995. Rather than being simply presented with a budget (if, indeed many companies even show their front-line people a budget), the employees themselves are now in the position to develop their own budgets, staffing levels, equipment needs, and service benchmarks, and to identify plans and developments for their own department.

As well as increasing their workload considerably, the management is passing on a very strong message that there is a price to be paid for the independence that is being offered to them. In this respect, ideas are not simply taken in and then worked on by management teams. Each idea is considered and then presented back to the employees for their continued involvement to the point of completion – the role of the team leader and, if necessary, the senior manager is to be there as a support resource. In this way, it is argued, the employees feel true ownership of the project and can therefore share the full benefit of seeing it through to completion, rather than simply dropping a note in a suggestion box, never to be seen or heard about again.

As Country Club Manager, Sean Spillane adds:

> For the first time in a long time we are asking ourselves some very basic questions about the service we provide to our guests and members. For too long we have built on rocky foundations with regards to some of the approaches we have taken to service. Now what we are doing is stripping them down and analysing them in far more detail than we've ever done before. Rather than simply modifying service systems that are in place, we are moving away from the perspective that 'we've always done it that way', and ending up with a totally revamped approach to service.

To evaluate the grass roots response to this grand vision for Gleneagles, we looked at the performance of two departments within the hotel – The Drawing Room (lounge), and the Gleneagles Country Club.

THE DRAWING ROOM

The staff in the Drawing Room are structured in a self-directed team of 12 people when fully staffed. (At the time this case study was undertaken there were, because of seasonal turnover, only eight regular members of staff, with the shortfall being covered from banqueting and casual staff.) There is no manager in this department. When the previous manager left, the staff were given the option of finding a replacement. It was their decision to try to operate the Drawing Room without one. As Team Leader, Greg Black put it:

> We were managing very well without a manager and we didn't really want to give up the responsibility and go back to taking a back seat. Instead of one person thinking about the department, we now have eight (and eventually 12) people thinking about how to improve it. We don't think of it as a cost-cutting measure for the hotel – we feel that the burden of reporting to a manager has been taken off us. We all have a say in what goes on in the department now, rather than doing the bidding of one manager.

As a designated Team Leader, Greg Black does not regard himself as simply a 'manager-without-a-title'. 'I do have to do a lot of managerial things like paperwork and preparing the rotas, but I think that, once we are fully staffed, we will be able to delegate most of that so that everyone can be involved in running the department.' Three members of the team, including Black, act as team leaders to ensure that there is always someone on duty to act as a point of reference for the other team members. Greg Black continues:

Our system is running very well. We work as a team now rather than as a group under the direction of one person. Everyone pulls together – if one station is really busy the other team members will help out rather than let that one person struggle on their own.

At present, besides the day-to day operation of the Drawing Room, the team is compiling their own SOP manual. With the support of Terry Waldron, every aspect of the operation is being looked at, even down to producing 'time-and-motion' profiles for serving tea or coffee, to ensure that the department is working at peak performance levels. Response to this increased responsibility has been very positive. As Greg Black explains, 'We have asked Kevin Poulter about learning more about our financial information in this department. We haven't had access to it in the past, and we would like to see just how well we are doing as a team'.

THE COUNTRY CLUB

In January 1994, Sean Spillane was transferred from the position of conference manager to become the new manager of the Gleneagles Country Club. Since joining the company straight from university, Spillane had worked primarily in the conference department – he had no experience of leisure club management at all. Traditional managers would regard this as heresy, if not lunacy – 'a manager can't tell people to do something that he can't do himself'. Whilst admitting to a few qualms himself, Spillane chose to regard the transfer as a sign of Peter Lederer's confidence in the people in the Country Club who would be working with him. They had the experience and ability to do the job. As Sean Spillane comments: 'What they need in me is someone to give direction, someone to build the team, allocate resources, provide guidance and leadership.'

The initial response of the Country Club staff was equally uncertain. Spillane's predecessor had been an experienced leisure club manager, and so they were faced with a complete change in management style from the more traditional 'knows how everything works and can stand in anywhere if needed' approach, to a manager who openly admitted that he didn't know how the plant room operated and had no intention of spending all his time learning how it operated. As Club Assistant, Fiona Hay, admits: 'Initially we were very concerned, but once Sean communicated to people the fact that he trusted us and wasn't wanting to know how everything worked, I think everyone relaxed a bit more'. Receptionist, Elenor Ramos, agrees:

We all went through a period of real anxiety at first, but we all knew what we were doing and I think we have more respect for him for admitting that he didn't know all the answers and was coming to us for help and support. Sean's experience in other areas of the hotel gives him a different perspective on the Country Club as a business rather than as just a pool to be maintained, a restaurant to be run, a reception desk to be staffed, and the like.

As a self-directed team, there are no supervisory positions between the employees and the Club Manager, a situation that Sean Spillane is perfectly happy with:

I don't think I've ever been as frustrated as I was when I had to work through two supervisors who had been there for four or five years. I was managing by checklist and banging my head against the wall. Now I am able to meet regularly with the people who deal directly with our guests every day, and I can get their views and opinions first hand. I have a lot more one-to-one discussions than the old management style ever allowed – there's much more sincere communication. Of course, this all takes time each day, but it's worth it.

Rather than just becoming involved in the day-to-day running of the Club and its disparate parts, the team is also actively involved in the longer-term objectives of budgeting and personnel. Prospective new team members, for instance, are invited to work for one full shift to make sure that they would enjoy working in this new arrangement. The team members conduct the interviews and pass on their recommendation to the Club manager.

Plans are currently being developed for a complete refurbishment of the Country Club, and the team members are directly involved in the grand-scale decisions, such as whether a training pool should be built, whether the restaurant should be expanded or a second one built, whether a wet bar should be built in the middle of the large pool, etc. It is this demonstration of trust and the obvious respect the management has for the opinions and experience of their staff that generates the tremendous levels of energy and enthusiasm among the team members.

This high level of positive response has not been matched in every department of the hotel – yet. Many remaining middle managers, after seeing their positions disappear in other departments as the self-directed teams were introduced, are very unsure of the whole system. This, in turn, makes the delegation of responsibility to the teams that much more difficult for them, as they try to maintain their position within the organization. As Sean Spillane comments: 'Some people are insecure in the fact that they are no longer the centre of attention and that they are no longer constantly being looked for.'

For the new team leaders, the transition from the more traditional role of supervisor to a less well-defined position as coordinator is a difficult one to make. Trusting in the abilities and experience of your fellow team members to solve any problems that may come up, rather than expecting them to turn to you automatically is a change in operational style which may take a lot of time for many to assimilate.

One other area of concern which still has to be addressed is the question of promotion and career advancement within this newly flattened organization. If the pyramid has been redesigned and the traditional management hierarchy replaced, what has happened to the promotion ladder? The significance of this question has become apparent in one department that has yet to adopt the self-directed team concept as fully as those we have seen.

GOLF OPERATIONS

The reputation and quality of the golf operations at Gleneagles are crucial to the success of the property as a whole. It is estimated that at least 30 per cent of guests are there specifically for the golf facilities. Given the external location of the department, the barrier between the staff of Golf Operations and the rest of the hotel staff has been one of the most difficult to remove. The hotel people think the golf staff ride around in golf carts all day, and the golf people think the hotel staff (particularly in the colder weather) do nothing but swan around in a nice warm hotel! There is a serious side to these caricature stereotypes – overcoming the problem of insularity has been a major concern. Until the movement towards the new culture was undertaken, the golf staff were given very little training and information about the other facilities the hotel had to offer, and the only hotel staff who were fully aware of the golf operations were the receptionists who were responsible for booking tee-times.

Now that the hotel has moved into an environment in which each employee is totally responsible for guest satisfaction, a question or complaint about any department cannot be automatically passed over to that department. The employee must now take ownership of that question or complaint, and this means that he/she must now be far more aware of what goes on elsewhere in the hotel and in the external operations, if a solution is to be found.

For the staff of Golf Operations, participating in the 'Breakthrough' programme along with all the other Gleneagles staff helped to underline the need for open communication and the involvement of everyone in providing guest satisfaction. This is particularly important for this department because the new horizontal management structure has yet to generate the same level of enthusiastic response as other departments in the hotel. To some degree, this is due to the greater rigidity of the career ladder in this area. As Greens Assistant Keith Haslam, explains:

> There is a great deal of concern that if we have this horizontal structure where everyone is responsible, where is there for you to go in the future? On the greenskeeping side, you have to put your time in as an assistant, a first assistant, and then as a deputy head greenskeeper, before you can become a head greenskeeper. They're concerned that if all you have are greenskeepers and one head greenskeeper, they won't be able to get the experience as a recognized deputy to then move on to a head greenskeeper position somewhere else. People are very wary of this new structure – it's almost as though we're being encouraged to move on in order to be promoted.

This issue of reduced promotion prospects has been addressed to some degree by an increased commitment to cross-training within the organization. By encouraging staff to spend short periods working in other departments, Gleneagles is achieving a double objective. First, this exposure generates a greater knowledge and awareness of the respective work pressures of each department. Second, the work opportunity encourages the employees to broaden their horizons beyond the career ladder of their immediate position – a ladder that the horizontal management structure appears, at first glance, to have taken away.

The example of Sean Spillane's move into the Country Club with no leisure experience has prompted many members of staff to reconsider their future direction within the organization. Country Club Receptionist, Elenor Ramos, for instance, recently completed an extensive training programme within the sales department, during which time she was given responsibility for familiarization trips for visiting group travel agents. In her words:

> That kind of opportunity wouldn't come under the traditional job description of a Leisure Club Receptionist! It has given me a great deal of confidence in dealing with people who have a lot of buying power and could be very important customers to the hotel. I took the offer as a sign of the company's confidence in my abilities, and everyone was so helpful and gave me so much support, that what started out as a scary and daunting proposition turned out to be a fantastic experience for me.

As a result of the introduction of the horizontal management structure and the creation of self-directed teams within the organization, there are many people who are finding themselves in uncharted waters. For those who find this new environment too different from what they are used to, there are plenty of other organizations that have not yet realized the potential of this style of operation. For those that choose to remain, Gleneagles is prepared to invest the time and resources in offering whatever training that individual may feel he/she needs to cope with the new operating parameters.

TRAINING NEEDS

Although the Training Department has no guest contact and deals with a captive market of 550 employees, this department has also been aligned to the new Gleneagles culture. As Training Manager, Annie McLeish, explains:

> We regard ourselves as service providers, and we treat our colleagues – our internal customers – as people coming in to buy our service. OK no money changes hands, but we have to provide a top-notch service – we can't get by selling secondhand goods just because we're selling to our own people – there's no room for excuses any more.

Traditionally, the training manager decides what type of training material will be made available and the choice is then presented to the employees to make their selection. For Gleneagles, this situation no longer applies – even the term 'training' is open to debate. Animals are 'trained', not people. 'Training' conjures up thoughts of exercise and physical fitness – the term preferred by McLeish and her team is 'education', since the learning process aligns itself with the role of change agents in which they now see themselves.

The identification of training needs is now made based on a detailed analysis of the Impact Reviews. By focusing on the individual targets of the employees and the future objectives of the self-directed teams, a Resource Guide is produced which offers a whole range of opportunities including CD Interactive, Linguaphone, Open Courses, books, tapes, and videos. A programme of evening courses has also been made available in such subjects as wine-tasting, basket-weaving, flower-arranging, and painting, where the employees themselves pass on their skills and experience (gained professionally or as a hobby) to their colleagues. The objective of this programme is obviously to improve morale, but it also offers the opportunity to develop the staff to feel better about themselves and to allow them to interact with guests on a wider range of subjects.

The one-off purchase of these materials in order to develop a Resource Centre of training programmes and facilities within the hotel has prompted McLeish to overspend a budget that had already been increased from £75,000 to £110,000 in response to the 150 per cent increase in demand when the Resource Guide was first published. Encouraged by the tremendous response to the new facility (Greens Assistant Keith Haslam is learning Spanish, for instance), the senior managers have been happy to approve the overspend – although there is by no means a blank cheque. As McLeish concludes:

> Historically, our budget has been treated as a black hole with nothing in place to evaluate what we do. That is wrong because we are a part of a money-making machine. We are now looking at measurements. Each request must be proven – how are you going to improve and how will your team and the company benefit from your taking

this course. We are now looking for a return on investment in terms of both skills and awareness which must ultimately relate to how the guest is going to benefit.

THE FUTURE FOR GLENEAGLES

The introduction of the horizontal management structure, the creation of self-directed teams, and the demonstration of commitment and support through the Resource Centre, 'Breakthrough', and the STARS programme, have all succeeded in unleashing a tremendous amount of enthusiasm and energy within the organization. Everyone we spoke to seems willing to take on the responsibility of 100 per cent guest satisfaction, and everyone seems to feel confident that the company will be there as a support resource should the need arise. How much of this is initial euphoria, and how much is previously untapped creativity and commitment remains to be seen.

What can be said is that great care must be taken if Gleneagles is to avoid simply grabbing a tiger by the tail. 'Breakthrough' was openly introduced as an experiment rather than a corporate directive, and everyone seems committed to making it work. However, despite the perspective of making the employees more responsible and self-reliant, the continued success of the programme must rest with the managers continuing to 'walk the talk' and following through on promises made. Without that, the new Gleneagles culture will alienate the very people it seems to cherish the most.

There are still bridges to be crossed. The questions of promotion prospects and career development within the organization still have to be examined in great detail. Also, the question of remuneration for this increased responsibility still has to be dealt with. Ideas about profit-sharing plans and performance-related pay feature strongly in our interviews. Performance-related pay is being looked at for introduction in April 1995 in conjunction with the periodic Impact Reviews.

Does this system work? The final word comes from Sean Spillane:

> The response has been incredible. People that I had pigeonholed, people whom I wondered 'how did they ever get a job at Gleneagles?' – their performance has been transformed in a matter of weeks. We went through an unfortunate time when a 'flu bug hit the hotel, and there was a member of staff (who I hadn't really given a lot of time to) who turned around and essentially took control – he reorganized rosters, brought people in from outside, worked double shifts and on his days off. When I saw that, it brought it home to me that this change in structure and the concept of self-directed teams is exactly what we should be doing, and we should be doing more of it.

EIGHT

Haven Leisure

Andrew Ghillyer

Haven Leisure is the UK's largest holiday park operator, offering a total of 54,250 self-catering beds and 3,500 catered beds in 50 parks (1995 figures). This capacity places them slightly ahead of Forte in bed-space. Their customer base is generally divided into two types: holidaymakers (of which they have 1.3 million per year) to whom they provide self-catering and catered holidays in caravans and chalets, and private caravan owners to whom they sell caravans that are then kept on site at Haven parks (13,000 units). In addition, the company has a rapidly expanding European operation, with a total of 56 small parks in France, Spain and Italy, providing self-catering accommodation, (in caravans or tents) to 120,000 holidaymakers per year.

At its present size and capacity, Haven Leisure achieves a 15 per cent market share. Its sister company Butlins holds an equal 15 per cent share, with the closest two contenders – Pontins and Center Parcs – each holding a 7 per cent share (1994 figures). By far the biggest share is held by independent park operators who currently account for 46 per cent of the market.

GROWING PAINS

The path that Haven has followed in reaching this joint-pole position has been far from straightforward.

In 1972, the Rank Organization, as part of a diversification programme funded by the substantial profits generated by their investment in Rank Xerox, purchased (among other things) the Butlins company, which was operating seven holiday centres at the time. Following their initial success with this new division, the decision was taken to acquire a few smaller holiday centres, and in 1980 Rank purchased a company called Leisure Caravan Parks, which sold caravans on ten parks in the UK. In 1986, by which time the operation had increased to 16 parks, Rank purchased Haven Holidays that also had sixteen parks (and a small operation in France), and so the company doubled in size virtually overnight. The new company – Haven Leisure – was now in a new market, since Haven

Holidays did not sell caravans, and so the company moved from selling caravans, that also happened to be available for rent, to being a professional caravan holiday operator.

In 1990 Rank bought the Mecca organization that had within it a company called Warner – a holiday park operator with 28 parks. Thus the division virtually doubled again to form a new company – Haven Warner – with a total of 62 parks in the UK. In 1993, Warner was divided off as a separate holiday centre company, with a core of six centres (now built up to eight), featuring a new Warner adult product. Haven Warner became Haven Leisure again, and after divesting the few parks that did not fit the overall corporate profile (including the transfer of two parks to sister company Shearing's), the company now operates a total of 50 parks in the UK.

The parks are classified into three separate categories in relation to the range of amenities provided.

All-action centres

As the name implies, these parks offer the widest range of facilities for visiting holiday-makers, including fun pools, leisure complexes, food courts, bars and bistros, shops and family entertainment centres. Eleven of the 50 parks fall under this category, and they are, by definition, the largest parks in the group.

Family parks

While the emphasis is still placed on the range of facilities available, these slightly smaller parks focus on high standards of accommodation in a more relaxed atmosphere.

Character villages

Chosen for their 'exceptionally attractive and unique settings', these locations emphasize a more sedate environment with access to outdoor pursuits such as riding, sailing and fishing. Holidaymakers at these parks are typically looking for a relaxing atmosphere and a base from which to explore the surrounding area.

The European operation has continued to grow apace, with an expansion rate of ten parks per year over the last three years and a goal of growing from 56 to 100 parks over the next three years. Haven Europe provides holidays in their own units of accommodation – either caravans or tents – on spaces that are primarily leased from third-party campsite owners. Of the 56 sites, two are owned by Haven, and the company would like to increase that to five over the next five years. However, with the aggressive financial criteria that Rank places on potential acquisitions, and the complexities of the French taxation system, it has proven very difficult to put together outright purchase deals in France.

AN OLD-FASHIONED BUSINESS

Given the size and complexity of the Haven organization, one might expect a collection of grand quality initiatives and verbose mission statements to grace the corporate operations manuals. The reality is quite different. In serving over 1.3 million holiday-makers every year, the senior management team appear to maintain a clear and concise view of precisely who their customers are and what they expect from their Haven holiday. The company considers itself a holiday provider rather than exclusively an accommodation or catering provider. The social demographic breakdown shows a customer profile of 42 per cent ABC1, and 58 per cent C2DE, but if you ask any of the Haven employees what the company is all about, you will get the much simpler answer of 'providing fun family holidays in a wide choice of locations which offer top-class accommodation, facilities and entertainment'.

In this respect, the extent to which the holidaymakers use the parks and their facilities is very clearly defined. The strongest asset each park has to offer is its location, and a large proportion of the brochure information on the park is devoted to the attractions that can be found in the surrounding area. Characteristically, Haven holidaymakers spend three to four days of the average seven-day holiday visiting off-park attractions, returning to their caravans or chalets in the evenings and making use of the centre's night-time entertainment facilities.

The traditionally unreliable British weather makes this situation a little more compli-cated for Haven. If the weather is fine, the parks are empty during the day as everyone is off at the beach or exploring the local area. If it is cold or raining, everyone stays in and looks to the park facilities to keep them entertained. Thus, Haven is faced with the prospect of large capital investments in providing on-site facilities, while being dependent on the weather for the eventual use of those facilities – the summer of 1994, for instance, was particularly good and this tended to lower the average spend within the park. Close dependence on the weather, however, is only one of many specific operating parameters with which Haven must come to terms in delivering a quality product.

SPECIFIC OPERATING PARAMETERS

Seasonal opening

All but five of the parks open to the public on a seasonal basis – from 1 March to 31 October each year. The parks at Caister, Mill Rythe, Duporth, Harcourt Sands, and Lyme Bay are all catered holiday villages that predominantly offer chalet accommodation rather than caravans – they are more indicative of the Warner product that the company took on board in 1990 – and they remain open almost year round, offering 'mini-breaks' in the off season. For the other 45 parks, being closed for four months out of the year appears to offer several benefits.

The off-season downtime offers the perfect opportunity for a thorough deep-clean of the entire park. Caravans, which are renewed about every four to five years depending on usage, can be replaced and any major construction work can be undertaken without incon-veniencing the customers in any way. In addition, scheduled refurbishment can take place to ensure that the park always looks fresh when the season opens. Thus, Haven appears to have something of an advantage over its year-round competitors in the provision of a quality substructure within the park environment.

Seasonal labour

Operating on this basis requires only a seasonal labour force, and this can present many problems for maintaining consistent performance levels. With only 2000 full-time staff and a peak season complement of 8000 temporary staff, recruitment and training issues remain paramount in the delivery of a quality product and service to the customer.

DELIVERING QUALITY

A quality product

With 50 highly individual locations throughout the UK, the delivery of a quality product is achieved through attention to the standard of accommodation provided and the range of facilities available. UK Operations Director, Brian Wetherall, maintains a clear viewpoint on this issue:

> There's nothing we have which can stop people from taking a holiday abroad, but if they have decided to holiday at home, then there are certain issues which we have to deal with – the most important of which is the misperception of what a caravan is. People still think of it as a metal box with a bucket underneath, with communal toilet and shower blocks and running up and down in your dressing gown. People will stay in a chalet first because of this perception of a caravan, but when they arrive on site, they are disappointed because they are in a chalet which, despite being refurbished regularly, was probably built somewhere between the late 1950s and early 1970s, whereas our caravans are changed every four to five years. If you go into one of our modern luxury caravans, they are at least equal in furnishings and equipment to our chalets. We are striving all the time to educate the public on what a caravan has to offer.

Despite the superiority of the caravans, it is unlikely that Haven will move over to 100 per cent caravan holidays. As Brian Wetherall concludes:

> We feel that there is a market out there that would never actually stay in a caravan, because they wouldn't like to tell their neighbours that they had been on a caravan holiday – they prefer to say that they've stayed in a chalet in a holiday 'village' rather than a caravan park.

For this reason, the company is committed to an ongoing programme of redevelopment of their chalet facilities to bring them up to par with their luxury caravans.

The second element of the Haven quality product is the range of facilities available, and in this area the company is currently responding to a marked swing in customer preferences. Where its male customers used to be happy to drink 'ten pints a night', in the last five years spending profiles have changed dramatically. Beer sales are now falling in the evenings, and that revenue is now appearing in an increased spend on family activities during the day. In response to this, Haven is now actively looking to provide alternate sales generators by adding more family-based facilities such as golf driving ranges, toboggan runs, dry ski slopes and bolingo (half-size bowling alleys).

The harsher economic climate of recent years has also brought about a greater consumer awareness of perceived value – people are wanting to see more for their money both during and at the end of their holiday. In this respect, there has been a marked increase in retail souvenir purchases (T-shirts, gifts, etc.), to which Haven is responding by improving their on-site retail facilities.

A quality service

Clean caravans and modern facilities may be crucial to the first impression gained by the customer, but during the seven-day average stay, it is the interaction with the Haven staff that will ultimately determine whether that customer will have a good time at a Haven park. The key people that the customers encounter are the entertainment staff (Haven Mates), lifeguards, and the bar, catering and retail staff. Having the right people in place in each of those departments to make sure that every Haven holidaymaker has a good time is therefore a primary objective in the provision of a quality service.

Those front-line positions are filled by seasonal labour and, of the 8000 staff recruited each year, only 25 per cent are likely to return from one season to the next, usually as a result of a change in personal circumstances – finding full-time employment or, for the student portion of the labour force, graduation and direct career-based employment. What this means for Haven is that each season they face the prospect of retraining 75 per cent of their labour force. Responsibility for that retraining comes under the remit of UK Personnel and Training Executive Alan Reid and he is the first to admit that Haven's approach to this problem of seasonal labour has not been always a proactive one:

> When I joined Haven seven years ago, we were literally doing *nothing* in terms of training, management development, succession planning, appraisals or performance reviews. We had some very backward methods of recruiting staff – to some extent that was due to the speed with which things were happening at the time. In the last seven years, we have taken over the Warner business and lost it again, we've reorganized the corporate management structure on at least three occasions, and we've extended our European business dramatically.

Over that seven-year period, the personnel and training functions have been developed almost from scratch. The old-fashioned personnel department which dealt primarily with employee welfare issues has now been completely redesigned to a point where Haven now has a well-equipped human resources department. The 'backward' recruitment methods have been replaced by detailed job descriptions and specifications, assessment centres, panel interviews, and personality questionnaires – all designed with the specific objective of recruiting the right person into the right job. Skills training programmes are now in place for every area of the business – operations, management, sales, telesales and reservations.

In building a fully-fledged human resources department in such a short time, Haven has sought the input of outside training providers in assessing the needs of their business and the needs of the individuals within that business. As Alan Reid explains:

> We are currently working with the Dunchurch Management Centre up in Rugby, who are helping us put together a commercial management training programme for our senior general managers and executives. The first programme started in December 1994, but we had actually been working with Dunchurch since July 1993 to put the programme together. There is a considerable financial investment in this programme, and if we're going to do it, then we're prepared to take the time to do it properly and very carefully.

SEASONAL TRAINING ISSUES

The easiest solution to the characteristic problems associated with a seasonal labour force – low morale, poor consistency of performance – would be to open all the parks year-round and to make the commitment to training a new permanent work force. Since Haven has no plans to do that, the seasonal training issues must be addressed by a different approach. In this instance, that approach has simply been to treat the staff as professionals – they may only be with the company for a short time (as little as 12 weeks), but by making the effort to expend time, energy, and resources in the areas of training and certification, it is hoped that the word will spread that Haven appreciates good people. Alan Reid, again:

> We know for a fact that a lot of our seasonal staff have been with other companies and have not been treated terribly well – they may get a higher rate of pay, but they're not properly trained, not given uniforms, their accommodation is poor, and they usually leave very quickly. We know our rate of pay isn't marvellous (£2.97 an hour less £20 per week for accommodation), but we treat our staff very well and we feel that the labour turnover among our seasonal staff isn't excessive and we have generally good morale across the board.
>
> We have ongoing and intensive training programmes for our seasonal staff, and each and every year we tweak them a little to make them more user-friendly and more interesting. This year, for example, we have introduced Gold Badge Awards in which every member of staff who goes through a specific training programme receives a certificate and a little gold badge to acknowledge their completion of the programme.

Maintaining this level of professionalism with their seasonal staff is starting to pay dividends for the company. At present, of the permanent vacancies which arise within Haven, as many as nine out of ten are filled by ex-seasonal staff.

QUALITY LINE MANAGEMENT

Much of the responsibility for the intensive training of the seasonal staff rests with the general managers within each park. The only staff members who receive group training are the Haven Mates, who are put through a rigorous training programme at a central facility for one week in late March. For the remainder of the park staff, training begins when the season begins, on the assumption that the first few weeks of the season are quiet enough to accommodate some intensive training exercises.

The reliance on line management is simply a matter of logistics. With 50 individual parks, it is not possible for the human resources department to be everywhere at once. Instead, the issue is dealt with by 'managing upwards' by means of area meetings to pass on any new training initiatives, and by using designated HR trainers to undertake personnel and training audits of the individual parks.

Leaving the training to the general managers and their heads of department (with suitable training and development support from head office) places a great deal of responsibility on the line management in delivering quality standards on the front-line. Performance bonuses offer a financial incentive to achieve those standards through monitoring customer complaints and departmental sales levels, but Haven has gone one step further by identifying the current heads of department – Clubs, Accommodation, Retail, Sales – as a key area for training on their career paths as future general managers. A two-year career and personal development programme (CAPD) has been developed to give them the skills, knowledge, and experience necessary to handle the position of general manager of a Haven Holiday Centre. In this way, the company is prepared to take a more long-term perspective towards quality by committing training resources to the future managers as well as the existing management teams.

PERFORMANCE MEASUREMENT

Monitoring the success of these initiatives in producing satisfied Haven customers is achieved by means of two performance measures – the percentage of customers who book a holiday for the following year (currently around 25 per cent), and the number of complaint letters received. Customer satisfaction questionnaires are placed in almost every unit – one in three for the large parks, one in each for the smaller ones – which currently generate a 25 to 30 per cent response rate. The questionnaire focuses on every aspect of the park and its staff, but the primary objective is to determine whether the customer's holiday was worse/as good as/better than expected, and whether that customer is more or less likely to book another holiday with Haven next year.

Since the holidays are booked through a brochure, everyone at Haven is very conscious of the need to live up to expectations. It is very easy to make the parks look fabulous in the brochure, but it is the performance when the customer is on site that finally counts. At present, Haven receives an average of one complaint letter for every 200 holidays – a dissatisfaction rate of about 0.5 per cent. The ongoing commitment to improving performance has reduced that rate from 0.73 per cent in 1991 to 0.47 per cent in 1994. In the early 1980s, when the Company was still coming to terms with the transition from caravan sales to caravan holidays, that figure had been as high as 1.7 per cent – almost four complaint letters for every 200 holidays.

One of the main advantages to closing the parks down for four months of the year is that the company can take the information gathered from the questionnaires and the complaint letters and analyse them in detail, both centrally and at unit level, before the next season begins. As Brian Wetherall explains:

> The complaint letters tend to be fairly detailed because our customers seem to feel that for their complaint to be acknowledged there has to be 'plenty of meat on the bone'. We divide those complaints into two categories – those which were avoidable, and those which were unavoidable.
>
> If somebody stays in one of our caravans, and they've never stayed in one before, and they only see eight inches of space between the bed and the wall in the bedroom, they are going to complain about not having enough room to get dressed. In the long-term we can look at changing the design of our caravans, but for that day of that week, there is nothing you can do but apologize – we show the floor plans of the caravans in the brochure. On the other hand, if the caravan is dirty on arrival, that is very avoidable, and all our efforts are focused on making sure that such avoidable events don't happen.

Managing Director John Murphy concurs:

> We can always anticipate a certain type of complaint at a certain point in the year – for example, at Easter it can be fairly cold and wet, particularly on the east coast, and so we can anticipate complaint letters at that time. We can only do certain things to combat that – better drainage at our parks, and better insulation for our caravans – but, in general, where we see specific problems arising at specific parks, then to the extent that we can take action, we do so. Over the longer term we are committing around £20 million a year in refurbishments and new facilities, in direct response to the information we receive from the questionnaires and complaint letters.
>
> If we feel that there is a genuine case for complaint, then we have a series of responses in place. The first level is a simple 'thanks for letting us know – we're sorry'. Often the fact that they get a letter back showing a certain amount of concern and sympathy and a promise that we'll do something about it, covers 50 to 75 per cent of their anger to a great extent. At the other extreme, we'll give them 100 per cent of their money back but that is *very* rare because it's generally not necessary. It doesn't cost us a great deal to give away short breaks at certain times of the year – there's really only the incremental cost of cleaning the caravan – nor does it cost us much to issue vouchers to redeem against future Haven holidays. Our objective is to make sure that the customer is completely satisfied, so I think if anything we are slightly more than generous in those respects.

EXTERNAL QUALITY INITIATIVES

Given the transformation of the Haven market from caravan sales to caravan holidays, they could be forgiven for rushing out and buying every add-on quality programme relating to their new business. This has not been the case, however. Haven considers itself to have a specific set of operating parameters that precludes the use of prepackaged quality initiatives. The change in emphasis from retail caravan sales to caravan holidays has been a gradual one over the last decade, and it has taken place incrementally with each new business purchase. To some degree, Haven's current management philosophies have originated through a process of learning as they went along. As Brian Wetherall explains:

> In our takeover of Warner, they were far more advanced on the issues of customer care than we were at the time. We thought we had it right and that we were doing well, but Warner's systems, though quite simple and basic, were far more experienced than ours, and we learnt a lot from that. The same applies with the Haven purchase – we suddenly had a team of sixteen park managers who thought only of customer care in their parks and nothing about selling caravans, and we learnt from them too. Even when we buy individual parks now and again we can walk in and pick up something from the private owners which can be applied to the rest of our organization.

BS 5750

There are no plans to introduce this British Standards quality accreditation into the company. As John Murphy explains:

A couple of years ago, BS 5750 was a great thing in the Rank Organization. We looked at it, but to us it appeared to be more for manufacturing industries, and in particular technological manufacturing industries, than for our situation. We tend to remain sceptical of these techniques and concepts because they sometimes overtake the purpose for which they are there.

Investors In People (IIP)

The corporate approach to IIP, in the face of many requests by Training and Enterprise Councils (TECs) around the country, has been to undertake a pilot scheme at Harcourt Sands on the Isle of Wight. The programme started in March 1994 and is currently work in progress. Response to the programme has been mixed. As Alan Reid, Personnel and Training Executive, explains:

What we are finding is that whilst the general manager and the management team are very committed to it, they are finding it very hard work. The amount of paperwork required is difficult in relation to the resources of the park – the paper mountain is proving to be a very difficult obstacle to overcome.

My impression is that at the end of the day it will have been a very useful exercise, but I'm not sure whether we would wish to pursue it further once the pilot scheme has been completed. There's no way it could be rolled out to all our other parks, because we have some very small parks which are almost one-man-band operations – the level of management staff on some of these small sites probably couldn't cope with the mountain of paperwork. The parks where it should work are those where they are open for 12 months of the year – i.e. the catered ex-Warner parks – if it is rolled out, I suspect it will only be on those five.

DEVON CLIFFS

Having examined the head office policies on quality, it is worth considering just how much of the customer-care message filters down to the front line. With only an area manager (a total of five in all) between a general manager and the senior directors at head office, Haven believes in a lean and responsive operating structure, and defines the role of head office as that of a support service to the individual parks. But how much of this apparent commitment to quality and customer service actually survives in the heat of battle?

With a total of over 2000 unit pitches (500 corporate units, 1200 private units – of which 250 are rented by Haven for the owners – and 350 touring caravan sites), the Devon Cliffs park in Exmouth is Haven's premier holiday centre. It is classified as an 'All-Action Centre', with a private beach, three swimming pools, a fun fair, an indoor fun palace, a go-kart track, its own shopping precinct, a food court, and several restaurants, pubs and clubs. At peak season (July and August) there are, on average, around 11,500 holidaymakers on site.

Devon Cliffs has been run for the past eight years by Mrs Joan Thomas (referred to by everyone in the Company as 'Mrs T.'), who is one of only three female general managers in the organization. With 23 years of experience in this sector of the industry,

Mrs T. has long since developed her own ideas of what it takes to run a park of the size of Devon Cliffs. Nevertheless, her approach to the programmes and initiatives generated by head office remains totally positive:

> We have a very good relationship with head office – as long as you are turning in the performance they expect from you, you don't get that much trouble from them. They are fair and they listen to you. If they come out with a system that I don't think will work, I'll say so, but I will try it out. They need their systems and we need ours, but I think there's room for us to come together a bit and find something that suits us all – especially with the accounting side of the business. They have to report back to Rank according to specific procedures, and so they do things a little differently than we do it here – we do our accounting on a daily basis, whereas they do it monthly, and we always have a problem with the cut-off dates which their system places on our figures.

As Haven's premier holiday centre, Devon Cliffs is the subject of constant refurbishment and capital investment during the off season. With a 25 per cent repeat business rate, there is an inherent market expectation of new facilities, and it does not hurt to put something new in the brochure every year. The old chalet accommodation has just been torn down and replaced by a new idea – 18 mobile homes on permanent sites offered as 'lodges'. For the 1997 season, an all-weather centre is being built on the site of the outdoor fairground, the reception centre is being moved from the entrance into the centre of the park (to be equally accessible from all areas of the park), and there are even plans for a toboggan run!

New projects and refurbishments can provide exciting times, but the key to good performance lies in the day-to-day management of the park, and Mrs T. has her own views there also:

> I've been able to develop a strong team around me over the years – no matter how good you are as a GM, you have to have good staff in the key positions – Clubs, Catering, Shops, Sales, Accommodation – half of my management team have been with me for eight years now – three have moved on to become GMs in other parks, and I have three members of staff with me now who are in line for their own parks.
>
> We get about a 50 per cent return rate on our seasonal staff. We have an intensive training programme on the park in which we bring the designated supervisors (who are usually returning from last year) in for two weeks before we open. We focus on their people and service skills, and when the new people arrive, it then becomes their responsibility to train them (they receive a pay differential as supervisors). Customer service isn't that difficult – it doesn't cost us anything to say 'please' or 'thank you' or 'sir' or 'madam', or simply to have a smile on your face – it's part of our business.
>
> We aim to give good value for money – our customers have come to our holiday park to have a good family holiday and it's our responsibility to make sure that they get that. We do get a lot of training support from head office – much more than we used to – and I think that by training the staff in the way we are now, we have a far better success rate. Obviously, with 350 staff here in the summer, the odd one does fall through, but we don't automatically dismiss that person for a lack of people skills – we may look into transferring him/her to a what we call 'behind-the-doors' position.

By virtue of its size, some operating procedures at Devon Cliffs are run a little differently from the company standard – particularly in the area of housekeeping. With an average stay of seven days, Saturday can bring a turnaround of anything up to one 1000 units in only five and a half hours (from 10.30 a.m. check out to 4 p.m. check in). In this context, following quality standards in the face of impatient customers waiting for their caravans becomes a very difficult problem. As Mrs T. explains:

> On the invoice it says that customers cannot have their keys until four o'clock, but with 2000 sites that just can't happen. We tried it once and succeeded in blocking traffic in Exmouth, so we had to find an alternative. Now if someone comes in for their caravan and it's not ready, we simply reassign them to another clean unit -we have so many of the same style anyway. If a guest is unhappy with their unit, for whatever reason, we move them as quickly as possible to another unit, because whatever we could try to do to that unit to satisfy that guest, it would never be enough.

With a dependable management team, and the necessary training support from head office, Mrs T. appears to have all the right mechanisms in place to ensure that Devon Cliffs will continue to be Haven's premier holiday centre, but there is one issue that she would still like to change:

> I've always been an operator, and I enjoy my work outside the office, but I've found over the last few years that I haven't had the customer contact and the opportunity to research new ideas in the park because of the daily paperwork I have to attend to. If I had another assistant manager (there is currently only one assistant manager on the park) to take over this daily work, I would be able to get out there more and research exactly what our customers want from us.

THE FUTURE FOR HAVEN LEISURE

Haven's commitment to quality has arisen more out of a gradual development over the years through inheritance and assimilation, than from any conscious decision from head office to run out and pick up the latest TQM system or quality technique. Quality has tended to come from the purchase of existing corporate systems; from an experienced GM who has a good system in operation; and from the ongoing experience of running the business on a day-to-day basis.

There is no identifiable 'quality manual' in the organization as such, but there is a series of specific performance manuals that, as part of the training perspective, are designed to improve the overall quality of the product. As John Murphy comments:

> I don't think there should be too many manuals out there, because it's very difficult to relate a nebulous concept of 'quality of service' by means of a manual – there are a whole series of elements which go into it – one of which is *what* you do, and another of which is how you *approach* what you do.

For Haven, the greatest strides have been made in the transformation of its personnel and training department into a fully-functional human resources department. Having succeeded in developing the HR function virtually from scratch in a very short time, it is only now finding itself in a position where the quality aspects of personnel, training and management development can be considered.

There is still considerable ground to be covered. The issue of cross-training has yet to be examined in depth. As Alan Reid concludes:

> We have always run a traditional business -almost to the point of taking a straight-jacket approach. Our bar staff are our bar staff, and our Haven Mates are our Haven Mates. We haven't really encouraged the concept of everybody taking a broader view of how the company operates, and I think that is to the detriment of some of our customer service situations – there is definitely room for improvement in that area of the business.

For the company as a whole, the idea of an ongoing refinement of existing management policies appears the key to future development. To some extent Haven's business strategy is defined by what it is allowed to do by its parent company, and since that parent company also happens to own Haven's biggest competitor – Butlins – the situation does present several restrictions. It is unlikely that Haven would be allowed to bid for any other holiday companies because of the likely interest from the Monopolies and Mergers Commission.

In this respect, future purchases are likely to be individual family-owned parks (two are under consideration at the moment). There are marked geographical holes in the Haven operation – it is not featured in the Blackpool area or in Scotland – and filling those holes remains a key objective. For a whole host of reasons, that objective may prove difficult to achieve – a park may not exist in the area in which they are looking; it may be too expensive; it may not be acceptable to Haven's high standards; or it may not even be for sale.

With a £20 million commitment to refurbishment and capital investment each year, the quality of the Haven product will continue to grow from strength to strength. The quality of the services provided in each Haven holiday centre is likely to remain dependent upon an equally strong commitment to both the development of a top-class management base via the CAPD, and the creation of a stable and reliable seasonal labour pool via a professional programme of intensive training and certification. This may be an old-fashioned business, but it needs a considerable investment in capital and training resources to stay out in front.

NINE

My Kinda Town Restaurants

Andrew Ghillyer

Launched as My Kinda Town plc in May 1994, the My Kinda Town Group is one of Europe's leading independent American theme restaurant groups, operating six distinctive concepts – 'The Chicago Pizza Pie Factory', 'Henry J. Bean's', 'The Chicago Rib Shack', 'Chicago Meatpackers', 'Tacos', and 'Salsa!' – in 19 cities throughout the world. With a current total of 33 units, the group's themes are represented through subsidiaries and franchises in the UK, France, Germany, Ireland, Spain, Belgium, Thailand, Argentina, Israel, Cyprus and Lebanon.

The history of the group dates from the 1977 opening of 'The Chicago Pizza Pie Factory' in London by Bob Payton, the late American restaurateur and hotelier. As one of the first restaurants in Europe to sell Chicago-style deep-dish pizza, the restaurant was a huge success and in 1979 it moved to its current larger premises in Hanover Square, London. Over the next nine years, further 'Chicago Pizza Pie Factory' restaurants were opened in Barcelona and Paris. In addition, new concepts were created: 'The Chicago Rib Shack', one of Europe's first American barbecue restaurants, opened in Knightsbridge, London, in 1982, and 'Henry J. Bean's', an American neighbourhood bar, opened in Kensington, London in 1983. The first franchise agreement was entered into in 1985 with the opening of a 'Henry J. Bean's' in Aberdeen, Scotland.

Further concepts have been added and expansion has continued with company-owned and franchised outlets. 'Chicago Meatpackers', an American family restaurant, was launched in 1987 to coincide with the 150th anniversary of the incorporation of the City of Chicago, and now has outlets in the UK, France and Germany. The UK recession of the late 1980s prompted the group to begin operating in Germany in 1989, and they now operate in Cologne, Dusseldorf, Hanover and Bonn through three concepts: 'Chicago Meatpackers', 'Henry J. Bean's' and 'Tacos' (a Mexican theme restaurant). In 1993, 'Salsa!', a Latin American bar with live music, was opened in Soho, London.

The traditional American holidays of Thanksgiving and Valentine's Day are focal points in the My Kinda Town calendar for new restaurant openings, and on Thanksgiving Day 1994 three new restaurants were launched – a 'Chicago Meatpackers' in Frankfurt (corporate), a 'Henry J. Bean's' in Cologne (corporate) and a 'Henry J. Bean's' in York (franchise).

THE PURSUIT OF QUALITY

The quality perspective at My Kinda Town is that the key to success lies in looking after the fundamentals. The general managers' primary objective is to ensure that their customers come to them for good food, good service, and a fun atmosphere, and that they leave having had a good time. As Group Managing Director Peter Webber explains: 'At the end of the day this isn't space technology ... It is essentially a very simple business ... You serve the hot food hot, the cold food cold, and everybody smiles.'

In this respect there are no grand visions of quality and no embellished mission statements designed to inspire the workforce. The traditional hierarchical pyramid has not been inverted, and the front-line employees are not prized above all others. There are no identifiable total quality management (TQM) programmes, quality circles, self-directed teams or empowered employees. The only benchmarking that has taken place has been the adaptation of the American themes themselves.

What is in place is a very tightly controlled operating system that has been created over 17 years to monitor concepts that, for 'The Chicago Pizza Pie Factory', 'The Chicago Rib Shack' and 'Henry J. Bean's', are fast becoming mature product packages. Rather than seeking inspiration from the latest management techniques, the group has chosen to focus on a process of continuous improvement of what it does best. In practice, many of its management policies can be related to specific TQM techniques, but their origins lie more in a proven track record of success than in the decision to take on any external quality initiatives.

The Ritz-Carlton Hotel Group, for instance, has made much of their policy of empowerment with a stated philosophy of 'Ladies and Gentlemen serving Ladies and Gentlemen'. For My Kinda Town, the approach has been the same, but without the explicit title of 'empowerment'. It recognizes the crucial role played by its staff in providing a quality service product to its customers and it treats them accordingly. Much time and energy are devoted to the recruitment of new employees. Once recruited, an equal amount of effort is expended in providing them with the necessary guidance, via rules and regulations, to ensure that they are fully aware of what is expected of them. From then on, the employment relationship remains simply one of doing what is asked of you to ensure that the customers are kept happy at all times. There is no quality jargon of serving 'on the front line' or of being 'empowered to do whatever it takes'. The focus is solely on the provision of detailed guidance and the expectation of consistently high performance.

A LEAN OPERATION

Between Group Managing Director Peter Webber and the unit managers there is only one layer of middle management. It consists of three directors: Simon Kossoff (responsible for UK and Ireland), Andrew Bassadone (France and Germany), and Douglas Smillie (Group Franchise Operations). The reason for this is not any public commitment to the TQM policy of a flattened pyramid or a horizontal management structure, but to simple common sense. As Webber explains:

> I worked for Grand Metropolitan for fourteen years under Sir Maxwell Joseph, and he always said, 'Head offices don't make money, they spend it, and every time you

appoint someone to a head-office position there may come a time when you will have
to sack them, which is far more painful,' and I fervently believe that. When I joined
My Kinda Town in 1986 we had a training manager, a personnel manager, and a food
and beverage services manager. They were all super-efficient people and all very well
paid, but they are no longer with us. Of course, our directors now have a lot more
work to do, but there's nothing like busy people to give more work to!

Much of the operating policies of My Kinda Town can be attributed directly to Peter
Webber's management philosophies, but this was not always the case. The founder of
My Kinda Town, Bob Payton, was just as passionate about his vision of what constituted good service, but his approach was very different. Renowned for his 'high involvement' management style, Payton revelled in cycling to and from 'The Chicago Pizza Pie
Factory' and 'The Chicago Rib Shack' (and, for a short while 'Payton Plaice') and maintaining a very 'hands on' approach. His ideas of employee motivation included dancing
with the staff, often making them laugh, and making them cry – sometimes all at the
same time. The staff went along with this partly in recognition of Payton's fervent
commitment to giving his customers a good time, and partly because, with 6000
customers a week, they were too busy to do otherwise.

As a successful marketing executive in the USA, Payton created the original restaurants simply to have some fun with them, and they were run the way he wanted them
run. He did not drink coffee, for example, and so the restaurants did not serve coffee;
and when they did start serving it, you could not get a second cup because that meant
you were staying too long at the table. The rules and regulations were very tight and
never to be questioned. A sign over the pizza station in 'The Chicago Pizza Pie Factory'
warned you that failure to weigh every item would result in a £25 fine. Similarly, a sign
in the kitchen of 'The Chicago Rib Shack' warned that if you were caught picking at the
food you would be instantly dismissed.

In 1986 Bob Payton began to turn his attention towards a new venture – a country hotel
called Stapleford Park, which opened in 1987. His relationship with My Kinda Town was
to continue for several more years. He became Chairman in 1987, and was a board director
from 1989 to 1993. Payton's presence remains with the company to this day and probably
always will, much as the presence of Walt Disney still permeates the Disney corporation.
Peter Webber himself still quotes 'Bobisms' which reflect the spirit of My Kinda Town.

Peter Webber joined the company in 1986. With a more traditional background of executive experience with Grand Metropolitan and the Imperial Group, Webber's approach to
management is very different to that of Payton. The warning signs were removed as the
first stage of a shakeup that eventually saw almost one third of the rules and regulations
removed or replaced. Payton never really envisioned the company growing beyond the two
or three restaurants he had started as 'something to have fun with', and it was to be
Webber's remit to oversee the careful expansion of the original concepts that Payton had
created.

Webber sees his role as simply making sure that his customers have a good time. As
he explains:

> Everything we do is aimed at that. I don't see myself as the 'Keeper of the Holy Grail'
> or the 'Carrier of the Torch' or anything like that. I just make sure that we have the
> right tools in place to achieve that objective. We have a number of things that we do,
> and we have a number of sets of rules and regulations of how we do it. I wouldn't say
> we regard it as a quality mission *per se* – it's more of a business lifestyle – this is how
> we recruit, how we train, this is what we do, this is our philosophy.

FRANCHISED OPERATIONS

The first franchise was granted in 1985 for a 'Henry J. Bean's' in Aberdeen. Since then, the Group has expanded to 13 franchise units based on two of the six concepts – 'Henry J. Bean's' and 'The Chicago Pizza Pie Factory'. The franchise contracts are typically granted for ten to twenty years and require a monthly royalty payment of between 5 and 7 per cent of sales. Franchisees to date include Scandinavian Airline Services and the Amari Group (a Thai hotel chain).

Despite a management policy of restricting the number of franchised units to only one third of total operations, My Kinda Town nevertheless needed a fully systemized set of operating policies if the consistency of the product was to be maintained worldwide. Therefore attention has been directed towards the development of specific performance criteria rather than any explicit TQM initiatives. A customer in the 'Henry J. Bean's' in Madrid must receive the same quality of service as a customer in Brussels or Barcelona or Manchester, and the company's operating manuals have been developed over the years specifically to ensure that is the case.

In this respect, My Kinda Town has followed the lead of its American counterparts by going to great lengths to put everything down on paper. The guiding phrase is 'If it can't be written down, it can't be measured, and if it can't be measured, it can't be controlled.' After nine years in the franchise business, there are now manuals for everything – everything you have to do before you open the property, everything you have to do during the opening period, and everything you have to do from then onwards. Each department also has its own manual, and your job in that department will require that you learn that manual. Consider for example, the induction process for a waitress:

> You come into Head Office on Monday morning and spend from 9–9.30 reading the company newspaper which tells you all about My Kinda Town and its corporate philosophy. You then get to see two short newsreels about the company of about 10 minutes each, and then you get to chat to somebody senior in the organisation (whoever happens to be in the office that day). You are then assigned to a unit to begin your training. To indicate your status, you do not wear a bow tie, but a badge which says 'Trainee'. As a trainee you spend a morning in the kitchen, a morning working with a busboy, and so on. You are also given a manual which has to be read and fully understood since you will be given a practical test on it in 7 days. If you pass all the tests, you are signed off for that portion of the manual and you can then wear the bow tie with pride.

The emphasis is on the practical application of proven techniques. There are no motivational speeches or enthusiastic exhortations to take on a corporate mission of 'bringing the world a better deep-dish pizza'. After 17 years, the My Kinda Town Group feels that it knows what type of person works well in its organization, and it has developed a very detailed training course to make sure that each person understands what his/her job will entail. One of the earliest Bobisms, which still holds true today, was that 'We employ the kind of people that their mothers would be proud of'. In practice, this means the general managers aim to recruit the kind of people who will provide the same kind of fun experience that they would like to have themselves when they go out.

There are specific rules about dress and appearance – men are not allowed to have ponytails or to wear earrings; women are not allowed pierced noses or more than one earring on each ear. The service encounter is scripted, but not to the point of a recital. The manual lists the information that must be covered, but not the way in which it is said. The managers recognize that it would be difficult to talk to a group of 20-year-olds in the same way as a group of 50-year-olds and so they focus on the recruitment of the right personalities and trust their abilities to adjust their presentations accordingly. Many observers would consider this policy to be an example of empowerment, but for My Kinda Town it is simply a matter of recognizing the dynamics of the personalities involved, and the interplay between those personalities.

A QUALITY LEADER

My Kinda Town was one of the first restaurant companies in the UK to achieve the BS 5750 quality standard. It was prompted into doing so by the tremendous success of its product concepts and the growing interest from potential franchisees. Showing the franchisees' restaurants filled to capacity was simple enough, but it needed proof that the product could be recreated anywhere in the world and operated with the same level of consistency. It was felt that the external accreditation of the BS 5750 standard would provide that proof. As Webber argues:

> We took it on because it was the only vehicle that allowed us to tell people we were professional in any other way than our saying 'come and eat in the restaurant' or 'come and look at our accounts' ... It was another means of telling interested non-trade people that we have standards and that we follow those standards ... We may look like a flip bunch of people, but underneath there is a very serious business going on!
>
> BS 5750 is not perfect by any means but it's all there is. Some of the forms are gobbledegook and it has all the worst characteristics of a government quango. The enforcement agencies are dealing with restaurateurs one day and widget-makers the next, so they can't be as helpful as you might want them to be. I'd like to see it become more sympathetic and industry-specific rather than presenting everything in this rounded consultancy terminology.

The achievement of BS 5750 proved to be relatively straightforward. With such detailed operating manuals in place, there were no major adjustments to be made, other than writing down policies that everyone had taken for granted. The six-month follow-up inspections have been 'absolutely painless', and the Group now looks upon BS 5750 as a means of spot-checking their performance every six months.

INVESTING IN PEOPLE

With the BS 5750 standard already in place to add credibility to the successful track record of its franchise operations, My Kinda Town is now in the process of achieving the Investors In People (IIP) award. In this instance, however, the external accreditation of IIP is not the primary objective, and the award is being sought for the benefit of the organization as a whole rather than simply to facilitate the development of its franchise operations.

IIP is being sought as a means of coming to terms with the growing maturity of the company. The management structure has changed fundamentally over the last eight years under Peter Webber's directorship, with the result that the majority of employee training is now handled at unit level by the general managers rather than through training or personnel departments. If the commitment to a lean head-office operation is to be maintained, then the general managers must be given the best tools to undertake training at the unit level. It is felt that IIP will give the company those tools. As Peter Webber concludes:

> Training used to be about 'take these two pills and you'll get better'. I don't swallow those pills. Our role is to continue to employ young, uncynical people, and I think that we're constantly trying to train that first level in. We were already doing about 70 per cent of what IIP requires, and we have had to change the way we do some things, but overall we have found IIP much easier to work with than BS 5750. It's still bureaucratic, but we think that, warts and all, it will bring tremendous benefits to our organization.
>
> When we had 6000 people a week going through the 'Rib Shack', all we really needed was someone who could make sure the food was served properly and that the place was kept clean. Now that the place is 12 years old, you have to manage your business that much more tightly ... A mature business is far more difficult to manage.

Even with Peter Webber's wholehearted support and endorsement, IIP has not been taken on as a blind adoption of a prepackaged training programme. From the outset the approach has been to integrate the key elements of the programme into an already proven operating system. The objective behind the pursuit of IIP was not to fix what was there already but to adapt to the training needs of a changing workforce.

In the early days of My Kinda Town, the average tenure of employees was very brief – they tended to burn out very quickly, either because of overwork or of Bob Payton's draconian management style. Over the last eight years, staff turnover has been reduced considerably and, as a result, the focus of the training programmes has moved away from simply teaching the fundamentals to a constant flow of new recruits, to a new teaching environment in which the longer-term development of the individual is considered. The need to teach the basics will always be there, and the frequent usage of those manuals in the setup of new franchise operations will ensure that they remain current. In general terms, however, My Kinda Town now has a larger proportion of its workforce that has grown up with the company, and their training needs now have to be considered. It is felt that Investors In People will provide the solution.

NON-TQM INITIATIVES

Despite the absence of any explicit TQM programmes within the group's management philosophies, the success of My Kinda Town can still be attributed to operating policies that contain the essential elements of a total quality initiative. On the surface, the company does give the impression of carrying on regardless of the latest techniques in the industry, as if it is all of no interest to them. In reality, the situation is quite the opposite. As Peter Webber explains:

> If we're not making sure that 90 per cent of our conversations are about better serving the customer, then we're not doing our jobs. I constantly try and bring things back to

'what's in it for the guys who bring in the money to pay the bills?' ... The systems,
if we're not careful, can start to obscure what you're trying to do.

In practice, many common features of a TQM programme – quality circles, lean management structures, responsive communication systems – have been in place for several years without an explicit quality label.

Meetings

Meetings are held on an informal basis rather than through a specific team structure. Peter Webber himself attends My Kinda Town meetings at least once a year in all the units. The objective of these meetings is to keep him in touch with every member of staff in the organization, but as the company has grown, it has become difficult to avoid the suggestion of an annual 'royal tour'.

For the directors, meetings with their unit management teams take place according to a more structured calendar to respond to training schedules and unit performance figures. At unit level, session meetings take place before the lunch and dinner service periods to ensure that everyone is kept up to date with menu alterations or immediate policy changes. Management team meetings take place in each unit at 4 p.m. every Monday. The minutes of each meeting are then faxed through to the responsible director for any further action. Departmental meetings within individual units are held regularly to encourage ideas for improving the quality of services provided to the customer. (An earlier experiment with suggestion boxes was unsuccessful.)

Customer feedback

Service quality is monitored by secret/mystery diners for every unit in the organization. These 'invisible visitors' fill out a six-page questionnaire to assess how well each unit has measured up to the predetermined performance criteria. The reports are produced monthly for head-office analysis, with an immediate response for any unit that fails to meet the required standard. In addition, comment cards are periodically placed on every table, with an equally rapid response for any comments about poor service quality or food quality.

PROSPECTS FOR THE FUTURE

With improved prospects for the UK economy, the My Kinda Town Group is ready to consider expansion at home rather than focusing solely on business opportunities abroad. The strong reputation of the franchise units continues to generate enquiries and direct approaches from potential franchisees, and continued growth is anticipated in this area, particularly in the Far East – Singapore, Hong Kong, Kuala Lumpur.

With the fundamentals of their operation so closely refined, the focus appears to be on the optimization of profits from the existing concepts rather than an aggressive expansion into other sectors of the market. The introduction of new concept ideas will always be a possibility, but given the current level of interest from potential franchisees for the existing concepts, it is likely that the process of continuous improvement of the fundamentals will continue.

FUTURE QUALITY INITIATIVES

In addition to the 100 per cent commitment to the process of ongoing improvement of the fundamentals of the operation, the primary focus of My Kinda Town's quality initiative is on the achievement of the Investors In People award. Once in place, it is hoped that the formalized training programmes will provide a firm foundation for continued expansion over the next three to five years.

The continuation of these expansion plans, after a period of relative consolidation in the mid-to-late 1980s, has helped to relieve the pressure that many advocates of a lean head office are now experiencing – namely the pressure to provide career advancement opportunities for 33 unit managers when there are only three operating director positions to work towards. The creation of master franchises in other countries does offer the possibility of regional management positions becoming available in the future, but for the corporate units, Peter Webber's commitment to a lean operation restricts career advancement possibilities to bigger or different units. Over the longer term, of course, increased numbers of units will bring area management positions on line. Considering the company's policy of promotion from within, this should provide enough opportunities for the high-flyers within the general management team.

The apparent clarity of focus of My Kinda Town about what its objectives are, and what its proven methods for achieving those objectives are, offers a strong insulation from the faddish nature of many TQM techniques. After 17 years of careful refinement, there appears very little that any so-called new quality initiative can offer which is not already in place in one form or another. To quote Peter Webber:

> I believe that the fundamentals that we have in place are really sound and will stand us in good stead. The concepts may be superficial, but the real difference that separates the men from the boys is how you run your business on a daily basis. That may be old-fashioned, but this is really a very old-fashioned business.

TEN

Rombalds of Ilkley: The Stepping Stones and The Moor

Michael Baker and Peter Cave

THE CHIEF EXECUTIVE'S STORY

In 1981 Ian Guthrie left the engineering company where he was managing director. During the previous 20 years he had stayed in hotels all over the world, spending over 100 nights a year in hotels. He had a lot of experience of hotels from the customer's point of view! He also had a life-time hobby of cooking. With this experience he thought that he might be able to run a hotel. Jill Guthrie's previous career was as a nurse, midwife and health visitor. She was an extremely accomplished 'domestic' cook and was prepared to risk her luck running a hotel.

When they bought the hotel it was extremely run down. It had no bathrooms en suite, most of the furniture was junk or broken, the carpets were threadbare, the garden was waist high in weeds, broken window-boxes hung off the window sills and the whole place looked half derelict. Full of optimism they bought it and completely rebuilt the hotel from inside out, creating 22 bedrooms with en suite bathrooms. Rombalds opened on the 12 July 1982, and the Lord Mayor of Bradford, Joan Lightband, performed the official opening ceremony on the 29 October 1982.

Things started well. In the first year occupancy levels reached the average for the Bradford district, and without any advertising the restaurant, which was never intended to be the main part of the business, became very busy. Sometimes the Guthries got to bed at 4 a.m., only to have to get up again at 6.30 a.m. ready to serve breakfast. Ian cooked breakfast and Jill served it; then, still wearing his apron, he went out to the reception desk to do the guests' bills and take their money and Jill went upstairs to make the beds and do the rooms. In the afternoon Jill would do all the daily food shopping and then commence the dinner preparation. At 5.30 p.m. she would begin cooking dinner simultaneously looking after reception, telephone calls and chance arrivals even with her hands covered in pastry. At dinner-time Ian took orders and served in the restaurant.

When the restaurant business grew further, Ian took responsibility for this side of the business; when they found chefs unwilling to stay longer than seven days he hired four City and Guilds graduates from Bradford College and started to make a team. With perseverance and trial and error things grew still more. In 1986, Rombalds won the 'Restaurant of the Year' award from the Yorkshire Evening-Post, then it won 'Yorkshire's Best Hotel' and 'The Best Breakfast in Yorkshire'. Other recognition came from *Michelin*, *The Good Food Guide*, *Johansen's Guide* and then all the major guides followed.

In 1987 Ian Guthrie relinquished control in the kitchen to the team which he had formed from raw recruits, who by now could run the kitchen on their own. He turned his attention to the service out front, where quality was inadequate. Improvement proved much more difficult to achieve than it had been in the kitchen. Jill and Ian were managers, supervisors, operators, trainers and heads of all departments. Using their own training programme, slowly, with patience, incredibly hard work, much heartache, they got the team together and started to produce results. By 1988 it had started to feel like a professional operation. In 1989 Rombalds completed their Coach House project, a conference/presentation studio with modern audio-visual facilities, which seats fifty. It won yet another award. Rombalds now had a first-class team, operating a first-class product.

Ian and Jill Guthrie's training programme was highly developed, one which companies many times this size would be proud to have. They were dedicated to continuous improvement by the application of the best employment practices possible. Only four members of their current staff had been with them less than one year. They believed it was realistic to imagine that in ten years they could reach the very top, recognized for their quality in service throughout Britain

THE ESTATE AGENT'S STORY

Set well back from Wealds Road with pretty gardens in between, Rombalds forms part of an elegant terrace and is believed to date from the 1830s. Records suggest that it has been a hotel for at least one hundred years during which time its position on high ground has provided far reaching views over famous Ilkley Moor. Nowadays, the business is operated as a top-class country-house style hotel that caters for an up-market clientele drawn from both commercial and tourist sectors.

Location and Sources of Business
Close to the centre of this delightful Spa Town on the River Wharfe, Rombalds has a beautiful trading position on the very edge of the moor and the boundary of the Yorkshire Dales National Park. This makes it a perfect base for short breaks spent walking and exploring the unspoilt moors and fells, as well as Brontë country and heritage attractions such as Bolton Abbey. This peaceful setting has enabled the hotel to draw lucrative expense account trade from easily accessible Guiseley and Harrogate as well as other commercial and industrial centres along the Wharfe Valley.

Recent History
Acquired by Mr and Mrs Ian Guthrie in 1981, Rombalds has subsequently been restored and refurbished in comprehensive fashion. A most notable improvement was the introduction in 1989 of an award-winning conference/presentation studio with state of the art audio–visual facilities that added a new dimension to the hotel's more traditional services. Although Rombalds has given them considerable pleasure over the years, the proprietors believe the time is right to move on to a fresh challenge, and hence the sale.

(From the Particulars of Sale for Rombalds published by Robert Barry & Co, Chartered Surveyors of Harrogate, in 1994).

IAN GUTHRIE'S STORY

Ian Guthrie's experience was increasingly a feature of the 1980s. Fired by a belief that they could be successful hoteliers, but with no more knowledge of the trade than that obtained by staying in hotels and eating meals in them, many people left the employment in which they had been all their working lives and invested their savings, their inheritance or their redundancy money in small hotels, usually those described as 'country-house style'. Ian and Jill Guthrie started on this path earlier than most. They thus had a longer period of relatively benign economic conditions than many in which to learn their trade. This and their determination not to accept second best in anything had turned Rombalds into an award-winning success as the 1980s turned into the 1990s. Believers in training, the Guthries had by the late 1980s introduced training regimes in all departments, which should have ensured that the constant presence of the boss on the shop floor was no longer necessary to ensure continued delivery of the quality which had won Rombalds awards across Yorkshire.

By 1994, however, the time of this case study, Ian Guthrie was expressing disappointment with the results of many of the training initiatives which he had initiated. Between 1991 and 1993 turnover had dropped from £575,000 to £550,000 and the Guthries expected no more than £470,000 in the year ending October 1994. Rombalds was up for sale and the owners were moving on. What lessons about quality can be learned from the Rombald story?

ROMBALDS: SOME DETAILS

Rombalds has fifteen letting bedrooms, two double, five twin, three single, one family and four suites, all with private facilities en suite. The four suites each have a sitting room, double bedroom and a bathroom. All the rooms are fully equipped with telephones, television, etc. (This excludes the owner's accommodation and a bedroom normally used for resident staff.) The public rooms include a lounge and cocktail bar, a restaurant usually set for thirty-six, a drawing room which can be divided to provide a separate syndicate buffet area, and the conference meeting room. This room, designed for fifty delegates (theatre style), takes the form of a presentation studio with a video system, projector slides, overhead projection and other equipment suitable for conference presentation activities. All well-known guides feature Rombalds.

> **Guide Entries**
> * AA Two Star and Red Rosette
> AMEX
> Egon Ronay
> Which Hotel Guide
> Johansen's Recommended Hotels
> RAC Merit
> Michelin
> Martell

The hotel employs 34 people (equivalent to 17 full-time staff). The organization chart is shown in Figure 10.1.

The turnover of about £500,000 is divided as shown in Table 10.1.

Table 10.1 Distribution of income

Food	54%
Accommodation	26%
Bar	14%
Conference	2%
Other	4%

The Guthrie's philosophy is expressed in the Rombald's Mission Statement, a copy of which is issued to every employee on joining the hotel on a plastic covered card which can be carried at all times.

Mission Statement: The Rombalds Way

In our business, our aim is to give customers friendly, efficient service and value for money second to none. We believe that by giving excellent customer service we will earn their loyalty and word of mouth recommendation to others. This is the only way to secure our future, and so looking after the customer must be our number one priority at all times, and we really do expect all in our partnership to give above average service.

The Rombald's Way also believes that work should be rewarded, enjoyable, satisfying, stimulating and fun.

We believe that most of this stems from self-confidence. We believe that this confidence comes from the secure knowledge of a job well done with total competence in the doing. We believe that if people enjoy what they do they will do a better job. We believe in aiming to be the best at all times.

This means that we expect and demand superior performance from our partnership with quality of service, attention to detail in everything we do. We believe that customer satisfaction is the most important thing we can achieve, for from this our security and long-term fulfilment will naturally follow.

(N.B. There is no formal profit sharing arrangement beyond the message that Ian Guthrie has tried to inspire in the staff that if the business does well everyone does well; a belief that all staff are a team and 'all in this together'.)

To achieve superior performance in quality of service and consequently the customer satisfaction which the hotel aims to achieve, a number of means are employed:

A heavy investment in staff training.
A chain of command with conventional means of motivation and sanctions.
Regular departmental meetings for formal review.
A deliberate policy of informal communication.

TRAINING

A number of strands of the hotel's policy on training can be identified: first, the company has a comprehensive and formal induction process; second, there is an exten-

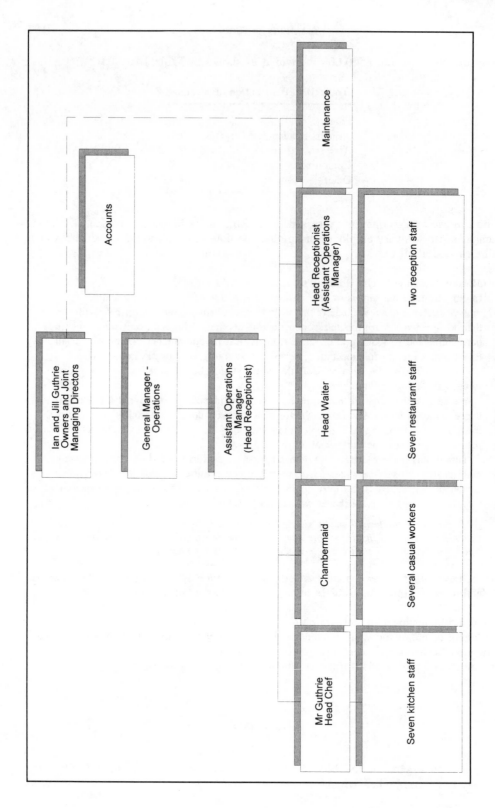

Figure 10.1 Rombalds: staffing structure

sive programme of ongoing training for each staff member. Supervisors have attended external courses, mainly those run by the Hotel and Catering Training Company (HCTC), such as on how to manage staff to ensure they give of their best. On reflection, Ian Guthrie told our researcher that, looking back, he now considered that more could have been done on supervisory training, most supervisors having been trained on the shop floor in order to acquire the necessary craft skills. A programme of in-house training seminars focuses on those areas where a weakness has been identified by the supervisory team. The general manager is responsible for this. Finally, there is an implicit assumption of team-building training.

The General Manager, has, however, learnt a great deal from the supervisor's training courses she has attended and ideas generated from these courses have been incorporated into training sessions. An underlying problem here, which helps to explain many of the difficulties Rombalds has faced over the years, is that despite considerable efforts, Ian Guthrie has not been able to imbue a sense of working together as a team of equally motivated people. Although Ian Guthrie did not want a hierarchical structure of management, the staff seemed to expect this. An instance of this is that although he had encouraged staff to call him Ian they insisted in calling him 'Mr Guthrie' and the supervisors reinforced this, discouraging any familiarity from junior staff.

This is also reflected in staff attitudes to training. The Guthries had found that training was only accepted if it was formalized and structured; staff resented being corrected whilst they were doing the job.

INDUCTION PROGRAMME

There is an induction programme for full-time staff spread over a period of four days (with a shorter process for part-timers). Further induction also takes place in the department in which the employee is going to work. The whole induction process, which is monitored, has taken up to 12 weeks, which Ian Guthrie admits is longer than intended.

On the first day a new member of staff is put in the charge of an inductor who is responsible for conducting a formalized induction process, and then a further period is spent in the department in which the employee is going to work. The training is formalized against a checklist and employees are asked to sign that they have completed a particular training session. This has proved to be useful when employees claim they have not been told about a certain procedure, e.g. relating to health and safety matters. Someone is asked to look after the new recruit during this period and acts as mentor to the new member of staff. The induction programme covers such things as clocking in, completing personnel and starting forms, and learning about rates of pay and holiday entitlements; learning about the policies of the hotel on such questions as training, health and safety, hygiene, and equal opportunities; contracts of employment and handbook; and learning about hotel layout, for example the location of the staff room, the staff entrance, the stores, and so on.

The new recruits learn the fire drill and meet their own head of department, who will tell them about the absence and holiday procedures. They also learn grievance procedures and procedures relating to uniforms, such as how to get them laundered; they are allocated a locker key, shown the changing area, and are instructed in first aid and how to report an accident. The new employees are also, at this stage, introduced to the departmental induction process. Departmental induction is usually done by the head of department, or occasionally by a senior colleague. This induction covers departmental working procedures not covered already and health and safety and hygiene training messages are reinforced.

The new recruits will spend an hour or two in the departments in which they are not going to work, shadowing people. In this way they are better able to work with those departments when called to do so in the course of their duties. Also, during the third day, the new recruits meet Mr and Mrs Guthrie for an informal chat, in the course of which they will receive vouchers to cover a novel feature of the Rombald's induction procedures – an opportunity to give staff the experience of what it is like to be at the receiving end.

All new staff from the kitchen porter to the general manager are given vouchers for each product on offer to the public. They may bring a guest for an overnight stay, breakfast, lunch, dinner, plus Sunday lunch and Sunday dinner. Staff are therefore given an opportunity to sample all six products on offer to the public. Wine and drinks are included. In return the member of staff is required to prepare, within four weeks, a written report of the experience, in which he or she is asked to consider whether Rombalds is an inviting place at which to eat or stay. Feedback varies from the banal to the highly perceptive and intelligent. These reports are circulated to all supervisory staff.

Ian Guthrie told our researcher that he felt that, regrettably, some staff wrote their reports from their own viewpoint rather than considering the quality of service as experienced as a customer. He also thought that sometimes the vouchers were seen as something of a 'free jolly' and not as part of the training exercise; on occasions staff had chosen to use their vouchers to celebrate a birthday. The idea behind the scheme was that the staff members' comments should relate to their own ability to do something about the deficiencies they observed but the reports tended to highlight deficiencies with the physical stock rather than the service standards. (Ian Guthrie commented that clearly staff were not offered the best rooms.) However, as the receptionist's and the headwaiter's stories show, the opportunity to see things from a customer's point of view is instructive, despite what might be seen as drawbacks. Moreover, the (admittedly small) numbers of reports submitted by members of staff after the visits and reviewed by our researcher showed that, despite the fact that the members of staff concerned were usually unfamiliar with the experience of being customers at an establishment as expensive as Rombalds, the reports, although varying in perceptiveness, gave a balanced all round view of the experience.

In the course of the induction process new full-time staff are issued with a number of documents, falling into three categories. First:

> Documents issued to take home, once explained.
> Documents to read through making sure they are completely understood.
> Forms to fill in for staff records.

Documents which fit into the second category include:

> Cost of poor health and safety at work.
> Health and safety information.
> Personal hygiene.
> Reporting procedures.

The third category includes the employee handbook, which includes the background history, a code of conduct, time keeping, payment of wages, meal times and holiday entitlements. The induction schedule is issued to each staff member with every item in the induction programme enumerated, and at the end of the period the member of staff is asked to sign to confirm that all these items have been covered.

During the process of induction, the new member of staff is introduced to the 'Rombalds Way' – a summary of the mission statement printed on small plastic cards; these are the five 'Stepping Stones' of the Rombalds Way.

The Rombalds Way Stepping Stones
1. To provide second-to-none service and value for money for all our customers.
2. To provide ourselves with secure, well-paid jobs in a stimulating, interesting and satisfying equal opportunities environment.
3. To be profitable to ensure long-term growth and survival so that we can achieve 1 and 2.
4. To create a partnership amongst us all in which each individual is encouraged to develop their skills for the complete satisfaction of their own potential.
5. To have every job at Rombalds occupied by someone who is fully trained to do it, is comfortable in it, is achieving total satisfaction in performing it, and knows that all the partners appreciate their contribution in full.

Ian Guthrie expects the highest standards from staff and requires them to maintain the right image of Rombalds at all times. For example, staff who smoke whilst on duty or make private telephone calls on hotel lines can expect to be dismissed. Members of staff are at no time expected to be seated in the presence of a guest, except at the reception desk when they are working out bills. Staff are not allowed to 'chat or gossip' to a colleague in the presence of guests and are not expected to initiate conversations with guests. Staff are encouraged to watch the guests' 'body language' to obtain clues to customers' satisfaction. They are discouraged from becoming over-familiar with guests and from interrupting those who are engrossed in conversation over business for example. Underlying the Rombalds Way is a philosophy which attempts to foster universal responsibility. For example, if a light bulb fails the first person that spots it should take action to replace it.

Quality audit

Each month a different member of staff takes responsibility for undertaking a quality audit. This involves noting any deficiencies in either the physical stock of the building or in service. The staff are responsible for noting those areas which can be dealt with immediately, such as a broken bulb, and for making observations on the standards of service. The idea is to instil a sense of responsibility, and for emphasizing that everyone is responsible for managing quality. In addition serious shortcomings are raised at the departmental heads' meeting and training seminars may be arranged to correct deficiencies.

Ongoing training

Training is carried out mainly on the job, with each member of staff's departmental head responsible for overseeing his or her training. As referred to earlier, formal training seminars are arranged in response to particular needs which have been identified by the management team. The general manager and departmental heads decide what these should be, often prompted by Ian Guthrie. Examples of subjects covered in these formal sessions include layout of tables, cheese service and wine. One drawback with this approach was that the most recent training seminar tended to be 'flavour of the month' and this aspect of service would be done very well for a period and then lapses would occur again when something new was being addressed.

Training records are kept for each staff member. These document the trainee, date of training, trainer and refresher training. Six weeks after commencement of employment, the new recruit is given an appraisal which comprises a fifty-question test, to be completed in forty minutes, covering aspects of health and safety, general hotel operations and responses to hypothetical situations. Records of this test are placed on the trainee's file and further training needs are identified.

Culturally everyone in the organization is a 'trainee' in the sense of an underpinning belief in 'lifetime learning'. New recruits are not specifically referred to as 'trainees' as they may already be 'qualified' prior to joining. However recruits with little previous experience are given a badge indicating that they are a trainee. Some inexperienced staff have the word 'trainee' in their job title.

It was recognized that training messages need to be constantly re-enforced. In some things, staff could maintain a good performance for a few days but might not sustain this for longer. For example, our researcher was told of the examples while records revealed serious errors of service; this was referred to the supervisor. Staff were tackled about these and the response was 'I forgot' without the least hint of remorse or regret.

Ian Guthrie felt that training manuals were no substitute for on the job corrective action. Staff and indeed supervisors resented this as they felt such direct intervention, frequently by Ian Guthrie himself, constituted a 'bollocking'. Staff favoured formalized training sessions. Ian Guthrie maintains that investment in training is no substitute for occasional on the job 'knuckle-rapping'. It was often therefore necessary to drive the training lessons home by creating situations which illustrated the consequences of failure, or, ultimately, by threatening disciplinary action.

One waitress, despite being reminded on several occasions by Ian Guthrie to provide fish knives and forks when fish was served to customers, seemed not to be able to grasp the requirement. Ian Guthrie, eating in the restaurant, ordered fish and when the right cutlery did not arrive he didn't start his meal. The waitress passed his table a number of times before enquiring whether anything was wrong and still failed to bring fish knives and forks. Eventually the meal was wasted but Ian Guthrie believes the message finally got through.

Ian Guthrie told our researcher that he and his first-line supervisors differed in their views about how much training could be done during the normal course of the working day. He said that the staff felt that training should only be undertaken in specific designated training sessions. He gave the following example to illustrate the way in which staff were not receptive to the idea of shop floor training. He had taken a young waitress to one side and showed her how to lay out the coffee tray. A few moments later this person was in tears in the kitchen being consoled by staff members. The complaint had been that she was 'being shouted at'. Staff were distracted from their job looking after the waitress rather than the customers. He had tried to distinguish between disciplinary action and training on the shop floor by coining the mnemonic 'TINABET' (this is not a bollocking, it is training) but the staff still felt that such shop-floor training was inappropriate.

Training is given a high priority and Ian Guthrie emphasized that 10 per cent of the manpower budget was spent on training, a not inconsiderable percentage for a small company.

The receptionist's story

The receptionist had been with the hotel for about six months when our researcher asked her about her induction. She recalled that she was told about the hotel's history, the main objectives of Rombalds and 'what they call the Rombalds Way'. She had been introduced to everyone when she joined, which had enabled good working relationships to be established, and she recalls the induction process as being relaxed. The induction process had covered the management structure, fire procedure and the basic legal framework. She had been given a handbook and a contract and her induction schedule had been marked off as various stages were completed. Similarly her training record was signed off as stages of the training was completed; training was an ongoing process and training times were given in the induction period.

She felt that a benefit of the induction process was that staff were not bombarded with information and so could absorb things gradually. A few new topics were covered each day. 'There was more a sense of belonging; it was not all rushed; it sinks in a lot more easily than if you were hit with all the information at once'. The induction process provided information on things that you would not normally expect to pick up during the normal course of work and after six months it was still helpful to have that information. It was mainly of interest to her, although on occasions it helped her answer questions which the guests might raise.

As yet, she had not used her voucher to come to the hotel as a guest and have dinner and stay the night but she knew from other members of staff that the vouchers enabled staff to notice things from a customer perspective and help to draw attention to practices that staff might unwittingly engage in, for example, being noisy with cutlery, making a noise from the kitchen, waiting too long or not long enough before serving the next course and not making sure the food was cooked to the customer's liking. It helped staff members to see how staff served the customers and this helped to 'correct things that are not that good'. 'It is mainly about customer satisfaction; whether you meet the standard that *you* expect when you go out, and fulfil everything that the customer wants.' Although being served by your friends puts you in a difficult position, when they came to use their voucher staff did tend to be critical in their reports.

> When staff come as guests you tend to be more attentive; it puts you in a bit of an uncomfortable position as well, because you know they are looking for any mistakes that you make; they are doing a report on you. If you are busy you tend to treat them like any other customer, but if things are quieter you are likely to go and talk to them.

She felt that the induction encourages team working. Her induction was with one of the chefs and this established a good line of communications with the kitchens which are often very separate. She thought that in an organization as small as Rombalds you had to work as a team. 'You are introduced to people as you are shown around the hotel. It is not a formal induction, very relaxed, one-to-one.' She admitted that she could not now recite the five steps of the 'Rombald's Way'. But 'It is all filed away and not used every day but you need to know it'. It was something the staff were aware of. 'The stepping stones, as on Ilkley Moor; you don't use it every day; you feel at home; it's in the back of your mind.' She thought the staff manual, which is given to all staff during the induction, was very useful and summarized all the essential information which staff needed to know.

The headwaiter's story

The headwaiter had been with Rombalds for 15 or 16 months. He had been made redundant from his previous post and had not worked in the catering industry before. He had originally come to Rombalds for four months on one of the Government's training-for-work schemes, spending one day a week at college in Leeds on an NVQ training course organized by the Hotel and Catering Training Company. The training at the college had been very basic and he had found that he learnt a lot more at Rombalds. Rombalds had then offered him permanent employment. The induction process had been 'a fantastic help' to him because of his lack of experience in the hospitality industry. The induction provided a 'back to basics introduction'. Everything was pre-planned – what he would be doing on certain days. The various styles of service and food were set out. The induction was tailored to his lack of experience in service at table or in the bar. When a function was coming up, he would go through the procedures for that function and there would be a follow-up session when it was over. 'The fact that it was so structured and pre-planned was excellent as I was so inexperienced. I did not feel at a loss and that I was being thrown in at the deep end. I was given the assistance that I needed.'

There were some things that staff would come across very rarely but were shown as part of the induction on the training sheets. He was now in a position in which he was hiring staff in the restaurant himself. He was using the induction process himself, explaining the same things, some of which he may well not have done himself more than once. There is also the refresher system. From time to time a particular matter is gone over again with all the staff. This is another important part of the process.

Induction and training procedures are modified periodically. This is done mainly by the General Manager, but other supervisors have an influence. Early in his time with Rombalds, the headwaiter had become concerned that certain parts of the hotel were tatty and needed re-furbishing. He wished funds were available to do something and remembered thinking that customers were noticing. When he came to use the experience vouchers as a guest, he realized that these were things he took no notice of. The vouchers were valuable to see how systems were working, to get the feel of how the customer sees what staff were doing, and to modify what they did so as to overcome any negative impressions. 'For example, if someone is sitting in the lounge, the conversation between someone behind the bar and someone taking orders is perfectly audible to all the guests, especially if it is quiet. You don't realize this when you are working.'

He said that when the staff stayed overnight they often mentioned the décor in the rooms but this was something that could not be acted on immediately. If something was highlighted which could be acted on quickly and economically changes were made, but if it needed finance then it had to be planned. When a member of staff on an experience voucher had been served with stale bread, the procedures, for checking the bread and ensuring the right amount was taken out of the freezer or ordered in fresh from the baker, were reinforced. Other examples were making sure that salt and pepper pots were full, water was offered with lunches and wine was topped up.

These were things that tend to get forgotten and that customers may not mention. Customers don't like to complain unless there is something drastically wrong. He explained that staff were told that they should approach the table and top up the glasses but they were reluctant to do this. As a result of this reluctance, a role-playing exercise had been introduced into the training. This had given staff more confidence to topup the glasses and get over their reluctance to approach the table and appear to interrupt.

Training needs were highlighted through the appraisal system; difficulties between supervisor and staff, for example. After six to eight weeks the supervisor will sit down with the new staff member and go through areas which they might be unsure about. For him this covered the service of liqueur coffees and knowledge of wines. From this discussion particular training needs were identified. There are no specific team-building exercises, but Ian Guthrie considers that the whole process from induction, staff meetings, consultation meetings and appraisals all reinforced the team-building approach. The whole process was a team-building one.

NVQs

Ian Guthrie admits that his experience of NVQs was one of unmitigated disaster. His training costs average about 10 per cent of his total manpower budget in 1990. Smaller operations needed more generalized training; many of the operational NVQs were too specialized and were only suitable for larger companies. The problems for smaller companies needed to be addressed. There is a critical mass below which NVQs could not operate. For example, a vast range of interpretation exists as to what evidence is required for assessment. The managing director had assumed that if an individual had proved a competence over several cycles of operation he could 'sign this off'. In fact, the requirement is that when the operator is competent, then a certain period of formal assessment needs to be set aside. It is not possible in a working kitchen to set aside a block of time for one operator to make egg-based dishes, for example, in order to monitor what he did and how he went about it. A task such as that would not be started as a continuous operation. Initially he would make the pastry and in the meantime he would make the filling for tarts. When the quiche was baking, and it could not go in the oven until 11.45 a.m., he would be preparing sandwiches for lunches. It is not practical to set whole sections aside for one process.

Although some of these more practical problems have since been sorted out, Ian Guthrie feels that the trainees who are now recruited regard the hotel as 'school'. The last two NVQ candidates who went through NVQs from start to finish left within two days of acquiring their NVQ certificates. Ian Guthrie had found that bringing people up to NVQ Levels One and Two in the context of his operation was not a cost-effective way of using training time. 'They regarded it as only coming to Rombalds to learn. Once they got their NVQ Level 2 Certificate, it was, "we've learnt that, now we'll go and get a proper job".' There was still a culture against training in the small business environment. Candidates were only prepared to go through the assessment procedures if these were undertaken in paid working time. Despite the fact that the qualification would give them better earning potential, they felt it was something they were doing for Rombalds. As they wanted payment during assessments it became an extremely expensive process.

Reflecting upon these experiences Ian Guthrie felt that he embarked on NVQs too early, before the support structure was in place with the training providers and the awarding bodies. Ian Guthrie was involved in the development of the NVQ structure itself and feels that this may have encouraged him to be over-enthusiastic. He tried to graft it onto Rombalds' existing system, without realizing that the existing system was probably more advanced. He raised staff's expectations, but was unable to sell the concept of in-house assessment. The assessors who were trained left within days of completing the Assessors' Course D32. The process itself he felt was too paper-driven, time consuming and bureaucratic.

Recently there has been a revolution in attitude with a greater recognition of and commitment to training compared with ten years ago. Ian Guthrie made it clear that he could no longer afford to pay and at the time of our research Rombalds has five NVQ candidates all of whom were prepared to pay registration and assessment fees at the rate of about £13.70. per week. Ironically, having agreed this with the staff, the Hotel and Catering Training Company provided the money from government funds.

ACHIEVING RESULTS THROUGH THE CHAIN OF COMMAND

Ian Guthrie believes that leadership is vital in a small operation and the lead needs to be set from the top. As Managing Director, Ian Guthrie provides the culture of the organization by 'setting the tone'. Constant reinforcement of the quality message is necessary.

Figure 10.1 (the organization chart) shows that the five departmental heads report through the Head Receptionist/Assistant Operations Manager and the General Manager (Operations) to Ian and Jill Guthrie, the owners and Joint Managing Directors. The accounts department reports directly to them. Another interesting feature is that Ian Guthrie has taken on the role of Head Chef, and in that role he reports to himself (in the role of Managing Director) through the General Manager.

Staff's own perceptions of the management structure lead to a hierarchical management structure. Ian Guthrie has advocated a 'flat management' style but has found it difficult to break down traditional barriers. There have been numerous instances where junior waiters have known the product to be wrong but have been unwilling to question what has been prepared by a more senior employee.

On a recent occasion a customer had asked for well-done duck. Ian Guthrie considers that every employee should know that this means 'no pink'. Before the duck reached the customer's table a senior member of staff noted that the ticket said the duck was supposed to be well done. The junior waiter was asked why he had not reminded the chef that it was supposed to be 'well done'. The response was that 'it was nothing to do with me'. Another example occurred when a smoked salmon sandwich had been produced for a customer on the wrong type of bread. When Mr Guthrie questioned the waiter on why he had served it, the response again that it was not for him to question the chef. Ian Guthrie had not succeeded in breaking down these barriers.

He told our researcher that all the staff should have ownership of quality but he had found this hard to achieve. Ownership needed to be handed over to the staff; quality could not be achieved by asking the staff to read standard operating manuals. For example, the Food Safety Act provided standards of inspection for cleaning of equipment, etc. but this needed constant reinforcement by instructing staff that they were responsible.

Disciplinary measures were used if staff failed to stick to the quality standards. For example, two waitresses, who had failed to set up tables to the set restaurant standards, when challenged had said they knew it was wrong but one said she 'wanted to get off' and the other said 'she was feeling a bit tired'. They were given a formal warning and left the company soon afterwards. They acknowledged that they could not meet the standards which had been set. On another occasion staff in the kitchens had been told innumerable times that they should not place the chrome-plated parts of cafetiéres in the dishwasher. The staff response was that they 'could not see the point' and, in this case, threats of disciplinary action if the instruction was not routinely observed were required. As noted above constant reinforcement of the quality message was required.

INFORMAL COMMUNICATION
THROUGH MANAGEMENT BY WALKING ABOUT

The hotel is a small organization; although there is a formal chain of command and lines for communications, Ian Guthrie believes in keeping a personal eye on all aspects of the operation, and keeping lines of communication open with every member of the staff. Through this means he can communicate up-to-date information to the staff, keep his finger on the pulse of staff morale, and ensure that everyone understands what is required not only of themselves, but their colleagues.

Ian Guthrie firmly believes that it is necessary to have credible sanctions, including dismissal, to support the delivery of high performance and constant reinforcement of the training message is necessary. He is strongly of the opinion that 'direct supervisory controls could not be replaced by manuals'. He did concur with the view, however, that the expectations which he had of his staff were perhaps unrealistic as he expected employees to think as he did.

Reviews through departmental meetings

Ian Guthrie tries to hold a formal meeting every month which is attended by departmental heads. At this meeting he communicates strategy and other issues are discussed, depending on the events of the previous month. Timetables and agendas for departmental meetings are agreed.

Departmental meetings, of which Ian Guthrie attends around 50 per cent, are conducted by the departmental head and attended by the general manager. The kitchen, housekeeping, reception, and food service (including bar) departments hold their meetings twice a year. Meetings are arranged one year in advance. Staff are encouraged to attend meetings outside their own department, but in practice only reception and food service staff attend the other meetings; to facilitate this the two departments hold meetings to follow one another.

Several formats have been tried for the departmental meetings. The general manager has realized that the format of talking at the staff does not work so an interactive approach has been used to put the staff in the driving seat. This has meant encouraging the junior members of the group to come up with ideas and to get suggestions from the rest of the team. Ian Guthrie describes this as sometimes like milking a stone. He told our researcher that he found dealing with the wide range of intelligence, educational attainment, and quickness to grasp problems exhibited by the staff particularly difficult. He said that he found the process of trying to communicate with some of the more junior staff frustrating and he got irritable if he was not understood. He found that if he used words or expressions that were not easily understood, the staff would not ask what they meant if they were unsure.

The departmental meetings are used to:

- Identify quality problems which may indicate a training need (departmental or for an individual).
- Marketing – to assess customer feedback.
- Policy – e.g. communications.

THE INVESTORS IN PEOPLE STORY

Investors In People was seen as a process of imbuing a culture into a company with a style of good people practice. The consultant who assessed Rombalds, as part of the process to introduce the standards for IIP, stated that there was little that needed doing to meet the standards. Staff consultation processes were formalized with two meetings a year with an agenda and minutes. The appraisal process was also formalized. In addition self-appraisals were devised, although this is not a formal requirement of IIP. Ian Guthrie felt that self-appraisal helped to give a more accurate picture. The appraisal contained 60 statements which employees were asked to agree or disagree with using a 5-point scale. People were more accurate about themselves. In fact in one case an employee realized that she was not meeting the required standards and left on the basis of her conclusion! Rombalds were one of the first restaurant businesses in the country to get IIP as nearly all the standards were in place. However, Ian Guthrie realized that the benefits from IIP were not from winning the award, but from going through the process. As they had already largely gone through the process, they had reaped the benefits already

Ian Guthrie feels that IIP does not mean a great deal to customers, although he does believe that, regrettably, the initial blaze of publicity did help to advertise the staff to potential employers. On reflection Ian Guthrie felt he should have adopted a much lower profile on getting IIP. However, it still has a motivating factor for the staff.

THE CHIEF EXECUTIVE'S VIEW

Ian Guthrie has found that if he took charge of a part of the organization and ran it personally, in the role of a first line supervisor, he could achieve the quality he sought. This had been his experience in the kitchen. Having trained a successful team in one area, he was able to move to another area, and devote time to that. He had believed that staff who were trained in what to do and how to do it should have little need of direction to do their jobs properly, given that there were adequate systems in place. He had therefore, through a process of personal leadership and high expenditure on training, tried to drive up quality standards. He had thought, on reflection, optimistically, that once the quality machine was in place, it would continue to run and produce a quality service. His experience has been, however, that without constant personal pressure, the quality performance falls off.

One problem was the high labour turnover in the industry. No sooner was a good team fully trained and capable of working effectively, than the most talented members would leave for more pay. The second problem has been motivation. He has found that without his personal supervision, the staff are insufficiently motivated to achieve his high standards. 'Direct supervisory controls cannot be replaced by manuals.' He had hoped that once the systems were in place, he could to some extent leave the hotel to run itself; he and his wife have been disappointed. 'We backed off and tried to replace ourselves with systems; standards are now lower.' Mrs Guthrie, daunted by the poor response of the staff to maintaining quality standards, relinquished her day-to-day management role.

As the report of the NEDC Working Party on competitiveness in the tourism industry pointed out a combination of comparatively low pay rates and a mediocre level of productivity has enabled the industry to stay competitive on price, but not on quality, with our continental competitors.

Rombalds hotel had built up a considerable reputation for training by 1990. The consequence of this was that it advertised to every hotel in Yorkshire the excellent quality of the staff employed in Rombalds. Ian Guthrie estimates that his training costs averaged about 10 per cent of his total manpower budget, but every one of the staff who left went for a less than 10 per cent increase in their total salary. Staff in fact departed to an environment that was likely to be less critical, where the standards were not as high and as rigorously enforced as they were at Rombalds. Ian Guthrie feels that a major failure was that he was unable to build loyalty into the system.

Ian Guthrie believes that most people have little perception of what is really involved in the hospitality industry. Teachers on placement, from two days to two weeks, initially perceive the unsociable nature of the job with low pay and long hours. However, by the end of the placement they tend to see the industry as exciting, a challenge and with lots of opportunities.

CONCLUSIONS

Through personal drive, a fanatical personal attention to service quality, and substantial financial investment, Ian and Jill Guthrie built Rombalds into an establishment renowned for its high service. But, after ten years, they had not managed to convert the high investment in training into a highly motivated team of staff, with effective control systems, which would continue to deliver high quality without constant supervision from the proprietors. Continued high labour turnover meant that Rombalds was acting as an unpaid training school for its competitors. The Guthries knew that if the hotel was to continue achieving high standards under their management, it would require further investment of time and money, and no opportunity to ease up and take a back seat. They had already decided it was time to think to the future when our researcher made his first visit.

Ironically, there is a final twist to this story. When Ian and his wife decided to lead less from the front and did not get so involved with matters of detail, almost simultaneously levels of staff satisfaction, judged by the appraisal system, shot up. However, Ian feels that this has been a mixed blessing as he notices a marked deterioration in what he would perceive as acceptable standards. A dead fly lying on the landing was unnoticed for three days before he finally felt compelled to mention it to a staff member. Cobwebs remain in some recesses. However, Ian Guthrie admits that since he stood down from hands-on management, customers' complaints have not generally increased.

In fact, the hotel found itself in financial difficulties and is now being sold to a new owner. Ian Guthrie sees the single most important cause of the growing financial problem as the proportion of his manpower budget devoted to training. As he himself observed, most small businesses do not bother about training and the staff failed to appreciate the value of the training they obtained free at Rombalds, except in the sense that the accolades which the hotel obtained through its pursuit of excellence made these same staff more marketable elsewhere.

REFERENCES

NEDO (1992) *UK Tourism: Competing for Growth* London: NEDO.

ELEVEN

Scott's Hotels Ltd.

Andrew Ghillyer

In early August 1995, it was announced that Whitbread plc had bought Scott's Hotels including the master franchise and development rights for Marriott Hotels in the UK. In November 1995, it was announced that Whitbread would be dropping the Country Club name in favour of Marriott at ten of its resort properties. The group will now be known as the Whitbread Hotel Group. The new group has a commitment to adding another 2,000 Marriott bedrooms over the next ten years.

Scott's Hotels Ltd. (Scott's) is a wholly owned subsidiary of Canadian conglomerate Scott's Hospitality Incorporated – a corporation that has interests in fast food and transportation in Canada. The UK operations include Perfect Pizza.

In January 1992, Scott's Hotels gave up the Holiday Inn franchise they had held since the early 1970s to become the sole Marriott franchisee in the UK. In signing this Master Franchise agreement (Marriott's first outside the US), Scott's committed themselves to a brief twenty-four-week conversion period, to meet an operational date of 15 July 1992. In the words of Jan Hubrecht, Managing Director: 'On 14 July, Scott's customers went to sleep in a Holiday Inn and woke up in a Marriott hotel. This was achieved without closing the business and without using external consultants.'

The transformation of their fifteen hotels from Holiday Inns to Marriott core brand and Courtyard by Marriott properties was undertaken based on direct employee involvement. Using a nine-person corporate task force to coordinate the physical conversion and cross-departmental teams within each hotel unit to prepare for the overnight transition, the logistical nightmare of replacing every piece of Holiday Inn equipment – signs, stationery, uniforms, soaps and shampoos, cutlery, etc. – was to prove to be a textbook exercise in communication and teamwork. Marriott International felt that Scott's operating philosophies, and in particular their commitment to the support and development of their front-line employees as the key to customer responsiveness, echoed Marriott's own corporate philosophies, and was prepared to give Scott's the sole franchise rights to the Marriott and Courtyard by Marriott brands in the UK.

The Scott's–Marriott partnership continues to go from strength to strength. Scott's now operates sixteen properties under the franchise agreement – in twelve Marriotts and four Courtyards. In 1993/1994 Marriott was recognized as the Hotel Brand of the Year; in the 1993 British Hotel Guest Survey, the company received the First Direct/*Daily Telegraph* Customer First Award for the provision of outstanding levels of customer service; and in March 1994 the Bristol Marriott was voted 'Best Hotel in the UK' by the Institute of Travel Managers.

To examine the reasons behind the success of this partnership, it is necessary to explore the history of Scott's commitment to quality:

THE SCOTT'S QUALITY STORY

The initial momentum for Scott's quality initiatives came from Jan Hubrecht, Managing Director, who, in the mid 1980s, began to realize the need for a company-wide commitment to quality as the key to the achievement of a sustainable competitive advantage in the marketplace. To quote the company profile:

> Firstly, there were new concepts and new companies entering the UK marketplace, creating a significant shift in the competitive environment. Secondly, existing hotels were changing hands and being upgraded constantly. Thirdly, our customers were becoming increasingly more demanding, they knew exactly what they wanted and how much they were prepared to pay for it.
>
> We also knew that if we didn't change some of our work practices, not only would we lose some of our customers to the competition but our staff as well. A quality product and service offered in a quality environment were critical keys to business success, if we were to maintain our competitive advantage.

The first quality initiative took a 'suggestion involvement' format when the company adopted a 'together we care' programme in 1985. Using a variant of the quality circle known as a 'service chain', Scott's endeavoured to develop a competitive campaign of employee suggestions in return for incentive prizes. Unfortunately, the use of slogans and hype created nothing but indifference among the employees, and the programme failed. The lack of response to 'together we care' forced the company to go back and examine how the philosophy of total quality management (TQM) could be utilized to ensure that the commitment to quality at the top of the organization could be passed down to the employees at unit level, and how the energy and enthusiasm of those employees could be harnessed for the future development of the organization as a whole.

Beginning with a strategic conference of the company's senior managers in September 1989, Scott's movement towards TQM was launched with the creation of a corporate Total Quality Steering Group (comprised of Hubrecht and his senior management team), and the introduction of a quality circles pilot exercise in three hotels – Glasgow, Cardiff, and Slough – in November 1989. By October 1990, quality circles had been set up in all eleven properties in operation at that time and, with four or more circles in operation in some units, the position of quality support manager was created to coordinate their activities.

The original objective of the quality-circle programme had been threefold: (i) to spread the word of the corporate commitment to TQM; (ii) to ensure that the employees at unit level did not regard TQM as just a passing fad; and (iii) to convince them that the senior management wanted their direct input in the running of their unit. By offering the employees an opportunity to tackle basic problem-solving issues within their unit, it was hoped that frustration levels could be reduced in preference to increased interdepartmental communication. This, in turn, introduced the need for a training programme to equip the employees with the tools necessary to take on basic problem-solving issues. Sessions on communication, team dynamics, monitoring and observation techniques, and brainstorming and data analysis techniques, were held to help the employees strengthen the quality circle foundation and to help them begin to contribute their own ideas for improving the operation of their unit.

With a strong top-down commitment to TQM, and a growing level of support at unit operative level, the only weakness in the programme appeared in middle management, where many more traditional managers were having trouble in aligning their personal management styles with the new TQM philosophy. The transition from supervisor/controller to coach/facilitator was proving to be difficult for some of the older managers, and so a further training commitment was required from senior management to help the middle managers develop more supportive management styles.

THE 'WHEEL OF FORTUNE' MODEL OF TQM

The linchpin of the TQM programme is the 'wheel of fortune' training model (Figure 11.1) which is designed to provide leadership and structure for the programme whilst being broken down into separate training initiatives. The model depicts quality as a process of continuous improvement – this is symbolized by the use of a wheel to represent continual motion. The model is built around five separate modules.

- The concepts of TQM
- Retention of people
- Retention of customers
- Profitability
- Plan for action

At the centre of the wheel, the three words 'Total Quality Management' denote the three key features of Scott's commitment to service quality. *Total* indicates that it is the responsibility of everyone in the organization, either individually or through teamwork, to satisfy the needs of the customer. *Quality* denotes that the service received by Scott's' customers at the very least meets their expectations and, ideally, exceeds those expectations. *Management*, and in particular the phrase 'organize not supervise', denotes the belief that the company should be organized such that everyone has a say in how it is run, rather than managers simply passing directives on to employees.

Every employee in the organization has received the 'wheel of fortune' training, and with an investment of over 25,000 training hours (around twelve hours for each employee), the programme carries a very strong message that the commitment to quality goes far beyond simple initiatives to improve attitude and motivation. The emphasis is placed on achievement through teamwork.

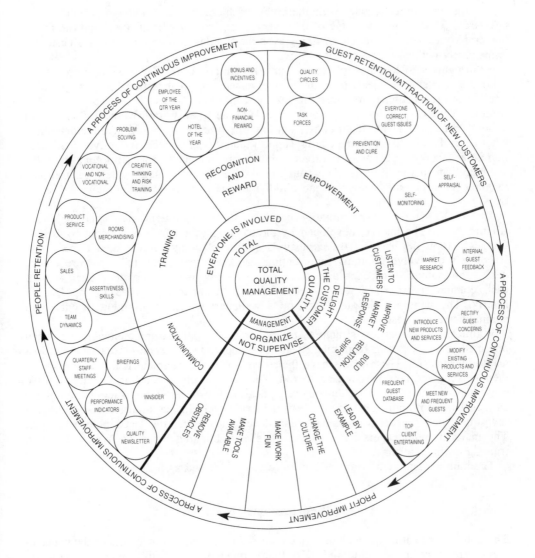

Figure 11.1 Scott's Hotels: Wheel of Fortune

QUALITY TEAMWORK

Scott's have recognized that the problems that can arise in service or production environments are typically not the result of one specific department or discipline. Almost inevitably, it is the result of a weak link in a service-delivery process that usually crosses over several different departments. As such, finding a solution to that weak link must require the input of a representative from each department involved. This, in turn, overcomes the traditional management hierarchy problem of the middle managers being unaware of a problem (by virtue of their separation from the front line), and the front-line employees being incapable of fixing even the smallest problem to satisfy a customer immediately without management approval.

By bringing staff together to work towards a common goal of improving a process or solving a problem, the messages of total involvement and total responsibility are emphasized. The organizational structure for quality within Scott's develops at corporate level from the Total Quality Steering Group (TQSG) to the Quality Improvement Team (QIT) at hotel level. The TQSG itself consists at any one time of the board of directors, three hotel general managers, and the quality support manager, who meet monthly. Their function is, as inherent in the title, to direct and develop a planned approach to quality in the company. On an annual basis, the group would develop and communicate a general plan for the company, under whose guidance individual units would develop their own initiatives.

The TSQG's most recent initiative has been the development of a Quality Matrix (Figure 11.2). The matrix, developed by the steering group from a concept by British Gas, will form the basis of the company's quality planning for the next three years. It consists of twelve columns representing the key focal areas of a comprehensive quality programme. For each area there are ten steps to be completed. Each step of each column is broken down in detail in the accompanying guide to the Quality Matrix. The steps are also displayed on a wallchart which is provided to chart and communicate progress.

Within this organization structure, the belief in the benefits of teamwork has been reflected in the evolution from quality circles – departmental teams – to a new multiple team environment. These teams have their own particular characteristics depending on their makeup and how they are organized. They can be organized horizontally to solve cross-departmental issues, or diagonally to deal with broader issues such as communication. The team approach has also featured extensively in the significant and ongoing investment in the process of management development over the last eighteen months. The majority of managers have spent well over a hundred hours each in team-based training during that time.

The multiple team environment can be further described as follows:

Quality Improvement Teams (QITs)

These are formed at hotel level and are comprised of designated members of the management team of the hotel, including heads of department and specialist quality role holders, such as action team facilitators and quality circle facilitators. The team is maintained on a full-time basis, meets monthly, and is led by the general manager. They support the corporate Total Quality Plan – using the Quality Matrix – to develop a planned approach to improvement in the hotel. They are responsible for guiding, communicating, measuring, and monitoring all quality initiatives within their property.

Hotel Action Teams (HATs)

Also called Quality Action Teams, HATs comprise employees who work together towards a common mission to improve a process or solve a problem. The team may be formed for several reasons: to implement quality improvement for a particular process that crosses functional lines; to solve a specific problem; or to carry out a specific task.

HATs are responsible for:

- Establishing improvement goals with the Quality Improvement Team.
- Following an improvement process plan that is consistent with the division's philosophy, such as PDCA (Plan, Do, Check, Act), a recognized cycle of continuous improvement.
- Developing measures and collecting data.
- Applying quality improvement tools and techniques.
- Finding out the root cause of a problem and recommending a solution.
- Improving a process to produce higher quality products and services that meet customers' requirements.
- Communicating results to the quality leaders of the hotel, managers, other teams, employees, and the quality support manager at head office.
- Requesting additional resources and support from the Quality Improvement Team as needed to effect quality improvement.

The HATs are generally brought together in one of three forms:

Task force teams

Formed at corporate, regional or hotel level, these teams are typically brought together to address system-wide issues. Employees involved may be assigned full time for the life of the project, or on an 'as needed' basis. System-wide issues would include such things as: improving compensation and benefits packages, or education and training procedures.

Cross-functional teams

Formed at hotel unit level, these teams, as the name suggests, are brought together to solve a problem with a process or improve a process for a multi-departmental product or service. Team members would include anyone who is representative of those who have a stake in the process and will be affected by any changes or improvements to the process – this could include management only, operative employees only, or a combination of both. Project issues would include such problems as: checking guests into dirty rooms (reception/housekeeping/laundry), or improving service standards in the restaurant (restaurant/kitchen). Cross-functional teams are usually brought together only for the life of the project.

Quality circles

Formed at departmental level, these teams comprise people brought together from the same work area to identify, analyse and solve work-related problems or make improvements. Membership of the quality circles is voluntary; meetings are held in company time; and projects are identified by the team members themselves.

The success of the action-team approach was exemplified by the team which came together to address the growing problem of car park security across the company. Comprised of a combination of operational and head office management personnel, the team followed a structured 'project' process in which it defined its objective as the

	MANAGEMENT COMMITMENT	RECOGNITION AND REWARD	QUALITY TEAMS	QUALITY TRAINING	DEVELOPMENT OF PEOPLE	HEALTH AND SAFETY MANAGEMENT
10	QUALITY PRINCIPLES ARE AN ACCEPTED MANAGEMENT STRATEGY, BEING CONTINUALLY USED AND REVIEWED BY MANAGERS	RECOGNITION AND REWARD SYSTEMS ARE REGULARLY EVALUATED AND REVIEWED	QUALITY TEAMS ARE AN ON-GOING PART OF THE QUALITY PROCESS	QUALITY IS A CONSISTENT COMPONENT OF ALL TRAINING PROGRAMMES	TRAINING AND DEVELOPMENT NEEDS ARE REVIEWED AND UPDATED REGULARLY	A CULTURE OF CONTINUOUS IMPROVEMENT IN HEALTH AND SAFETY STANDARDS IS ACHIEVED
9	MANAGERS REGULARLY TUTOR THE PRINCIPAL TRAINING COURSES AND HOLD QUALITY AUDITS IN OTHER ORGANISATIONS	EMPLOYEES AGREE RECOGNITION PROGRAMMES ARE WORKING	QUALITY TEAMS ARE OPERATING IN KEY AREAS AND MEET REGULARLY	TRAINING NEEDS AND RESOURCES ARE REVIEWED REGULARLY	75% OF VACANCIES AT SUPERVISORY AND MANAGEMENT LEVELS ARE FILLED INTERNALLY	HIGH LEVEL OF PERFORMANCE IS ACHIEVED AS MEASURED BY EXTERNAL AUDIT
8	QUALITY IMPROVEMENT IS INTEGRAL TO PERFORMANCE	HOTEL IS RECOGNISED WITH AN AWARD AT THE ANNUAL AWARDS FUNCTION	75% OF EMPLOYEES HAVE EXPERIENCED WORKING IN A QUALITY TEAM	TEAM PROJECTS ARE REVIEWED AND REFOCUSED	THE HOTEL HAS REGULAR TEAM BUILDING ACTIVITIES	EXTERNAL AUDIT FINDINGS ARE REVIEWED AND USED TO IMPROVE ACTION PLAN
7	QUALITY IMPROVEMENTS ARE MEASURED ON AN ON-GOING BASIS	HOTEL REPRESENTATIVE TEAM ATTEND AND FEEDBACK ON ANNUAL AWARDS FUNCTION	FIRST PROJECTS HAVE BEEN PRESENTED AND THE RESULTS ARE REGULARLY MONITORED	QUALITY TRAINING PROCESSES ARE REVIEWED AND REDEFINED	HOTEL BASED ACTIVITIES CARRIED OUT AS PER PLAN	GOOD LEVEL OF PERFORMANCE IS ACHIEVED MEASURED BY EXTERNAL AUDIT
6	QUALITY ISSUES ARE DISCUSSED AT ALL APPROPRIATE MEETINGS AND EMPLOYEES ARE AWARE OF THE CRITICAL ISSUES AND HOW THEY CAN INFLUENCE THEM	NOMINATIONS FOR 'DEPARTMENTAL MANAGERS OF THE YEAR' SUBMITTED	ACTION TEAMS ARE ESTABLISHED AND WORKING ON PROJECTS	PROBLEM SOLVING TRAINING IS COMPLETED FOR ALL EMPLOYEES	INDIVIDUALS' DEVELOPMENT NEEDS ARE INCORPORATED INTO THE HOTEL TRAINING PLAN	ACTION PLAN IS IMPLEMENTED

	MANAGEMENT COMMITMENT	RECOGNITION AND REWARD	QUALITY TEAMS	QUALITY TRAINING	DEVELOPMENT OF PEOPLE	HEALTH AND SAFETY MANAGEMENT
5	MANAGERS 'CHAMPION' QUALITY TEAMS	'EMPLOYEE OF THE YEAR' AWARDED BY THE QIT	ACTION TEAM FACILITATOR APPOINTED AND TRAINED	TEAM LEADER AND FACILITATOR TRAINING IS COMPLETED	EMPLOYEES HAVE DETAILED DEVELOPMENT PLANS	ACTION PLAN IS PRODUCED TO FULLY MEET SAFETY OBJECTIVES
4	MANAGERS HAVE PARTICIPATED AS A TEAM MEMBER	'EMPLOYEE OF THE QUARTER' RELAUNCHED AND OPERATING SUCCESSFULLY	QUALITY CIRCLES ARE ESTABLISHED AND CIRCLE LEADERS TRAINED	EMPLOYEES UNDERSTAND THE PRINCIPLES OF TOTAL QUALITY	HOTEL SUCCESSION PLANS AGREED	RESULTS OF ASSESSMENT ARE REVIEWED AND ANALYSED
3	MANAGERS ACTIVELY ENCOURAGE THE FORMATION OF QUALITY TEAMS AND MAKE RESOURCES AVAILABLE	RECOGNITION AND REWARD SYSTEMS IN PLACE	FIRST PROJECT IS SELECTED	SENIOR MANAGEMENT UNDERSTAND THE PRINCIPLES OF TOTAL QUALITY	APPROPRIATE INDIVIDUALS ATTEND MARRIOTT LEADERSHIP TRAINING	FIRST ASSESSMENT IS CARRIED OUT
2	MANAGERS UNDERSTAND, PRACTICE AND CAN TEACH TOOLS AND TECHNIQUES	RECOGNITION AND REWARD SYSTEMS ARE UNDERSTOOD BY EMPLOYEES	QUALITY CIRCLE FACILITATOR IS APPOINTED AND TRAINED	INTRODUCTION TO QUALITY TRAINING IS COMPLETED. QUALITY PRESENTATIONS AT INDUCTION	EMPLOYEES AND MANAGERS RECEIVE REGULAR PERFORMANCE RECOGNITION	ASSESSOR IS APPOINTED AND TRAINED
1	MANAGERS HAVE ATTENDED THE KEY TRAINING COURSES AND UNDERSTAND THE QUALITY PRINCIPLES	RECOGNITION AND REWARD SYSTEMS ARE UNDERSTOOD BY QIT	QIT MEMBERS ARE SELECTED AND TRAINED	QIT MEMBERS HAVE COMPLETED RELEVANT TRAINING	EMPLOYEES AND MANAGERS TRAINED IN RECOGNISING PERFORMANCE PROCESS	HEALTH AND SAFETY POLICY KNOWN AND UNDERSTOOD BY ALL EMPLOYEES

Figure 11.2 Quality matrix: Scott's Hotels

	EXTERNAL CUSTOMER STANDARDS	QUALITY ORGANISATION, DOCUMENTATION AND STRUCTURE	BENCHMARKING	QUALITY PERFORMANCE INDICATORS	SUPPLIER QUALITY	COMMUNICATION
10	EMPLOYEE AND CUSTOMER FOCUS GROUPS ARE INTRODUCED	MECHANISMS ARE IN PLACE TO ENSURE CONTINUITY OF QUALITY ACHIEVEMENTS	ONE PROJECT OUTSIDE THE HOTEL IS COMPLETED	QUALITY ACHIEVEMENT MEASURES AND COSTS USED AS STANDARD AT DEPARTMENTAL LEVEL	HOTEL SUBMITS SUPPLIER(S) FOR NATIONAL NOMINATION	EMPLOYEE FEEDBACK CONFIRMS THAT COMMUNICATION IS EFFECTIVE
9	QUALITY TEAMS ARE USED TO DEFINE CUSTOMER DRIVEN SERVICE INITIATIVES	THE QUALITY STRUCTURE HAS BEEN MODIFIED TO SUIT THE REQUIREMENT OF THE HOTEL	THE USE OF BANCHMARKING IS ON-GOING AND SELF MANAGING	DEPARTMENTAL LEVEL OF REPORTING OF QUALITY MEASURES AND COSTS IN PLACE	QUALITY REVIEW TAKES PLACE WITH 100% OF SUPPLIERS	HOTEL MANAGEMENT REVIEW AND UPDATE COMMUNICATION PROCESS
8	GSS AND OTHER MARKET RESEARCH PROCESSES ARE USED TO IDENTIFY AREAS OF SERVICE SHORTFALL	THE QUALITY PLAN IS REVIEWED AND AMENDED AS NECESSARY	THREE FURTHER PROJECTS HAVE NOW BEEN COMPLETED	DEPARTMENTAL TARGETS HAVE BEEN SET FOR QUALITY ACHIEVEMENT AND NON-QUALITY COSTS	THERE IS SIGNIFICANT IMPROVEMENT IN LONG TERM RELATIONSHIPS WITH SUPPLIERS	SYSTEMS ARE IN PLACE TO SUCCESSFULLY PROMOTE THE HOTEL WITHIN THE LOCAL COMMUNITY
7	QUALITY TEAMS ARE USED TO PRODUCE CUSTOMER DRIVEN LOCAL SOPs	PROCEDURES ARE IN PLACE TO ENSURE SUCCESSFUL ADOPTION OF SOPs	FIRST NON-COST BENCHMARKING PROJECT IS NOW COMPLETED	EMPLOYEES UNDERSTAND CROSS-DEPARTMENTAL MEASURING METHODOLOGY	QUALITY REVIEW TALES PLACE WITH 75% OF SUPPLIERS	EXTERNAL CUSTOMER COMMUNICATION IS INCLUDED IN THE HOTEL'S BUSINESS PLAN
6	AREAS NOT COVERED BY SOPs ARE IDENTIFIED THROUGH PROCESS ANALYSIS	AN ANNUAL TOTAL QUALITY PLAN IS PRODUCED BASED ON THE QUALITY MATRIX	FIRST NON-COST BENCHMARKING PROJECT AGREED	QUALITY PERFORMANCE MEASURES ARE ESTABLISHED AT DEPARTMENTAL LEVEL	ON-GOING SEARCHING FOR NEW SOURCES OF SUPPLY TAKES PLACE	QUALITY TEAMS INCLUDE EXTERNAL COMMUNICATIONS AS PART OF THE PROJECT PROCESS

	EXTERNAL CUSTOMER STANDARDS	QUALITY ORGANISATION, DOCUMENTATION AND STRUCTURE	BENCHMARKING	QUALITY PERFORMANCE INDICATORS	SUPPLIER QUALITY	COMMUNICATION
5	A PROCESS FOR UPDATING SOP MANUALS HAS BEEN ESTABLISHED	A SYSTEM IS ESTABLISHED FOR THE DISTRIBUTION AND MONITORING OF GSS RESULTS	BENCHMARKING ACTION TEAM IS ESTABLISHED AND TRAINED	PERFORMANCE MEASURES REPORTING MECHANISM IS ESTABLISHED AT CORPORATE LEVEL FOR ALL HOTELS	QUALITY REVIEW TAKES PLACE WITH 50% OF SUPPLIERS	HOTEL REPRESENTATIVE APPOINTED TO COMMUNICATE HOTEL INFORMATION TO HEAD OFFICE
4	ALL SOPs ARE IMPLEMENTED	EACH QUALITY MATRIX COLUMN HAS A 'CHAMPION'	FIRST COST COMPARISON PROJECT IS COMPLETED AND CHANGES IMPLEMENTED	QUALITY ACHIEVEMENT MEASURES ARE IDENTIFIED AT HOTEL LEVEL	RESULTS RECORDED AND ANALYSED	HOTEL FINANCIAL PERFORMANCE AND GSS RESULTS ARE PRESENTED REGULARLY TO ALL EMPLOYEES
3	ALL EMPLOYEES BRIEFED ON THE SPECIFIC SOPs IMPACTING THEIR WORK AREA	QUALITY FACILITATORS ARE APPOINTED	FIRST COST BENCHMARKING PROJECT IS AGREED	EMPLOYEES KNOW AND UNDERSTAND PERFORMANCE INDICATORS	SUPPLIER PERFORMANCE MONITORED	DEPARTMENTS REGULARLY DISCUSS THEIR FINANCIAL PERFORMANCE AND GSS RESULTS
2	ALL EMPLOYEES BRIEFED ON THE PURPOSE AND SCOPE OF SOPs	THE QIT HAVE COMPLETED THE NECESSARY QUALITY TRAINING	INTER-HOTEL COST COMPARISON PROCESS IS ESTABLISHED	MANAGERS IDENTIFY APPROPRIATE PERFORMANCE INDICATORS FOR THEIR QUALITY PLANS AND ON-GOING QUALITY PERFORMANCE	PERFORMANCE REQUIREMENTS ESTABLISHED	PROCESSES ARE IN PLACE TO ENSURE DISPLAY OF CURRENT COMPANY INFORMATION
1	METHOD OF IMPLEMENTING SOPs ESTABLISHED	THE QIT ARE ESTABLISHED AND MEETING REGULARLY	THE QIT UNDERSTANDS THE PRINCIPLES OF BENCHMARKING	MANAGERS UNDERSTAND PERFORMANCE INDICATORS	KEY SUPPLIERS SELECTED FOR QUALITY REVIEW	DEPARTMENTS PUBLISH A CALENDAR OF MEETINGS

Figure 11.2 Quality matrix: Scott's Hotels (cont'd)

prevention of theft from hotel car parks. Appropriate quality tools and techniques such as flowcharting were used to identify the key elements to be considered, with a project goal of creating a cost-effective and secure car parking environment, which would, in turn, give the company a competitive market advantage.

It carried out extensive research, both internally and externally, to establish the extent and the nature of the problem. Detailed questionnaires were sent to the British Airports Authority (BAA), Wrexham Hospital, Mars, and ICI in order to add their experience to a growing database on vehicle security devices, the predominance of thefts on particular days of the week, and the relative merits of different types of car park lighting. A detailed statistical analysis was carried out, and the team then brainstormed possible solutions.

The Business Research Unit was then commissioned to research customer reactions to the teams' ideas. Two focus groups were conducted with business customers who regularly travel to hotels by car. The resulting twenty-four page report on this research enabled the team fully to develop their outline into a list of action proposals. These were presented to the quarterly business planning meeting – with all company senior management present – after a total of some eight months of hard work since the team had first been brought together.

As a result of its efforts, comprehensive procedures were implemented across the company, including training programmes and improved signage. In addition, the security aspects of several car parks in the company were revised and improved, including capital investment where necessary. The situation has been monitored on an ongoing basis with extremely encouraging results. With the task achieved, the action team was disbanded, but each team member was left with a great sense of personal satisfaction of a job well done, and the company continues to benefit from such customer comments as: 'Such a professional approach is rare to find and is very much appreciated.'

The success of Scott's commitment to teamwork has been brought about through their service strategy of linking employee empowerment and continuous improvement in customer service. Constantly examining and questioning the way things are done, rather than simply taking existing procedures for granted, keeps everyone aware of the importance of delivering a quality service to the customer. In addition, by enabling employees to contribute ideas for improvement and to feel confident in solving a guest complaint immediately, rather than seeking the permission of a manager, Scott's can show their trust and confidence in the abilities and experience of their employees.

WORKING WITH MARRIOTT

By the end of 1991, Scott's commitment to the TQM philosophy had developed into a corporate quality programme that operated at all levels of the organization, with the underlying message that everyone in the company was responsible for creating 100 per cent guest satisfaction. Having devoted so much time and financial resources to convincing the staff that TQM was here to stay, the 1992 announcement of the changeover from Holiday Inn to Marriott (a little known brand name in the UK at that time) brought questions about whether the TQM programme would survive the transition.

The decision to reconsider the working relationship with Holiday Inns (a partnership that had been operating for over 20 years) was not taken lightly. As Jan Hubrecht explains:

Scott's own market research indicated that the customers' future use of a hotel brand would be determined by the satisfaction/quality rating of their most recent stay. The evidence pointed to the need to be affiliated with a globally recognized brand offering consistency in all its hotels and a company which had a system in place for ensuring total quality for its customers.

The initial talks with Marriott indicated that both companies shared a commitment to the TQM philosophy, and to the principles of both listening to customers, and continuously improving the products and services being offered to those customers. As the introduction to Marriott's Success Kit for New Managers explains:

> Our success at Marriott is largely a function of our service to the guest. Quality service depends on you and the successful management of your people. If you treat your people well and guide them in a positive manner, they in turn will handle the guests with the warmth, friendliness, and efficiency that are our trademarks. If you remember little else, please remember that we are all at Marriott to make our guests' visits as comfortable as possible.

While this compatibility helped to allay fears that the fifteen units in operation at that time would be swallowed up by the 700-plus Marriott International network, Scott's still felt that directly involving everyone in the transition process would not be enough to answer all the questions about the impending changeover. As a solution, an internal public relations campaign was developed to provide information about the Marriott organization, and in particular its business values and methods of operation. This internal PR campaign culminated in giving each unit the authority to decide how to dispose of their new Marriott key on 15 July with some interesting results. (The ceremony of disposing of the key is a Marriott tradition that signifies that the hotel is always open to receive guests.) The Gateshead Marriott team buried their key in a time capsule in the hotel grounds, and the Slough/Windsor Courtyard by Marriott team decided to eat theirs by presenting a cake in the shape of a key to a local children's hospital.

By tackling the questions and concerns of their staff in such a direct manner, Scott's were able to overcome the problem of unsubstantiated rumours undermining the high level of teamwork and communication that would be needed to handle the changeover in such a short time. The demonstration of the similarities between Scott's business values and those of the Marriott organization also emphasized the message that this changeover was a positive move towards improved customer service. Once the physical conversion was achieved, embracing the Marriott quality culture was straightforward. The similarity in the approach of both companies required only minor operational adjustments. Scott's decided to retain their own organizational structure and terminology for quality as they were comfortable with it and, quite simply, it worked.

GUEST SERVICE INDEX (GSI)

One of the Marriott operational tools which has been taken on board is the Guest Service Index (GSI). What the GSI programme represents is an extensive collection of customer response data to provide unit managers with a running readout of their service quality levels.

As Scott's Personnel and Training Director Tim Savage explains:

> The GSI data comes in on a monthly basis on a rolling three-monthly aggregate total. We now use it as a target area where unit managers and their employees can identify which areas in the hotel are not meeting customer expectations. We can then select the quality tools and techniques to address the problem. The GSI is a very practical application which we now link directly to the bonus structure for our general managers.

EMPOWERMENT

The quality cultures of both Scott's and Marriott feature the concept of employee empowerment – giving employees the authority and responsibility to solve guest problems on the spot rather than automatically seeking a decision from a manager. Marriott International has taken this commitment to empowerment one step further by making it a prominent issue in their international advertising campaign. Stories of hotel concierges sending forgotten briefcases by cab to reach guests at the airport now serve to bring home the message of the conscientiousness of Marriott staff.

Scott's are only too willing to provide their own stories for this campaign:

- A guest at the Bristol Marriott asked Marlene Abbott, a guestroom attendant, to arrange for some items of clothing to be laundered. The timing of the request meant that it would be difficult to fulfil, so rather than telling the guest this, she took the guest's laundry home and did it herself.
- Syd Pitcher, a hall porter at the Swindon Marriott, gave a guest directions to the nearest golf course. Not long afterwards, however, the guest returned disappointed because the clubs he was offered were not good enough. Syd promptly came to the rescue. 'Why not borrow mine?'
- Jean Murphy, a banqueting beverage supervisor at the Bristol Marriott, overheard a young woman guest inquiring about the nearest Chinese take-away. It was late one miserable night and the guest was on her own. The take-away was near where Jean lived and, thinking it unwise for the guest to venture out alone, she telephoned her husband Terry and asked him to fetch a take-away and bring it to the hotel.

Encouragement of this kind of performance from their people is achieved through recognition in the corporate newsletter and frequent exceptional service awards. However, Scott's operational policy on empowerment remains a little more focused. As Tim Savage explains:

> We do want our people to feel confident in solving problems themselves, and we make every effort to ensure that they are comfortable with the concept of empowerment and what it means for them. As a result, the topic is a key feature in the 'Whatever it Takes' training programme, and the forthcoming 'Whatever it Takes To ...' programme. In line with working towards greater service consistency, as measured by the GSI, we are striving to educate our employees to understand the concept of 'a customer', and that each customer has different needs. By recognizing their needs they can react to each of them appropriately – thereby each employee becomes a business

person in their own right, dealing with market segments of one. We are therefore getting quality by personal commitment not coercion, by shared values rather than by standards, and by motivation rather than by mandate. We are creating an environment where we treat mistakes as a learning opportunity which will result more often than not in the guest's problem being resolved with sincerity and a smile rather than something material.

BS 5750 AND IIP

Despite the serious concern for customer recognition of consistent quality service via a globally recognized brand, Scott's has chosen not to pursue the British Standard's BS 5750 Kitemark as a public demonstration of their commitment to service quality within the industry. The Kitemark was considered, but it was felt that it suggested conformance to a predetermined specification. Scott's view of quality is one of customer individuality rather than a rigid quality standard.

Investors In People, on the other hand, has been adopted. After forming a cross-functional HAT to look into the programme, it was decided to make the means available for hotels to pursue the award on an individual basis. To date, two hotels have already achieved IIP – Bristol and Aberdeen – and five other properties have submitted a letter of intent to participate in the programme. The main reason for choosing to participate in IIP but not in BS 5750 would appear to be that IIP is more aligned with Scott's commitment to their employees on an internal level, with the external recognition being a secondary issue. In addition, the reputation for consistent service quality that the Marriott brand name carries offers equal, if not greater, external recognition than the Kitemark.

THE SYNERGY OF THE FRANCHISE RELATIONSHIP

The partnership with Marriott International has brought tremendous synergy and benefits. Marriott's structured programme of research and development, combined with their considerable financial resources, has brought advantages in systems development, product and process re-engineering, training, and development.

The nature of the operating relationship on training, for example, is that it is a two-way street, with initiatives being shared by and with both sides for mutual benefit. Scott's integrate programmes developed and offered by Marriott into their own comprehensive corporate training plan. These, along with programmes written and designed by the Scott's human resource teams, combine to meet identified needs in a balance, varied, and appropriate way.

One example of a Scott's programme that served to reinforce the conversion to Marriott was a training programme called 'Whatever it Takes' (WIT). The objective of the WIT programme was to encourage employees to evaluate the hotel from the guest's perspective. Using a series of role-playing exercises, the WIT training focuses on six rules:

1. Please acknowledge that you have seen me and know that I am standing/sitting here waiting to be served.

2. Please make me feel important and like a real individual.
3. Please find out what my needs are.
4. Please look as though you enjoy working here.
5. Please know what you are doing and do it promptly.
6. Please don't bring any more hassle into my life.

By emphasizing the importance of making a good first impression, and of understanding what exactly the guest is looking for in terms of service performance, the WIT programme serves to underline the message that each employee has an individual responsibility to ensure that the guest's stay at a Marriott hotel is as perfect as it can be.

Marriott's three phase TQM development programme covers employee empowerment (TQM1), problem solving and communication skills (TQM2), and advanced problem solving and leadership skills (TQM3). Scott's made the decision to modify the programme slightly under the title of 'Leading and Organizing Quality Improvement Initiatives', to address what they saw as a weakness in the commitment of middle managers within the organization who were experiencing difficulties in defining their contribution to the new TQM environment. A tutor team made up of Jan Hubrecht, Managing Director, hotel general managers and the central human resource team, led 184 managers through a total of five programmes during one year.

Evidence of the two-way operation of the training issues can be found in Scott's participation in Marriott's leadership training programmes. Marriott operates their courses based on a group of people from different locations but from a similar management level – general managers and executive committee members, for instance. Scott's preferred to have the whole management team from one unit attend the course at the same time. As Tim Savage explains: 'It costs more and takes more time, but we have found that the way they can move forward is incrementally greater than sending one person who comes back with new ideas which no one else wants to know about because they don't know anything about it'.

A total of 166 managers have been through the two-tier leadership programme, with Scott's trainers working with Marriott personnel on the delivery of the 'Foundations to Leadership' programme itself. Marriott found the team-based approach to be an exciting further development of the programme that merited consideration, despite the additional costs involved.

THE FUTURE OF THE TQM INITIATIVE

The Quality Matrix

The Quality Matrix, one of the earliest examples of successful benchmarking, will be the dominant influence on Scott's TQM initiative over the next three years, as it serves to pull all the key elements of activity together into one focused plan that is both self-directing and self-monitoring. In addition, the initial quality training programmes used to launch the TQM initiative have been revised to reflect progress to date, rewritten, and re-launched. This education process is now defined in the 'Quality Training' column in the matrix (Figure 11.2). The 'wheel of fortune' has reappeared as the 'Introduction to Quality' – the essential first step of TQM knowledge for everyone. This is then followed by the renewed 'Whatever it Takes' programme, and finally the 'Leading Quality' programme which defines the role of management.

This comprehensive commitment to training and team-based quality initiatives has succeeded in passing the primary momentum for the TQM initiative down from the senior management level to the individual unit level. Equipped with an exceptionally detailed guide to the future in the shape of the Quality Matrix, the way forward is clear. As an indication of the importance attached to the Matrix, it has had the centre-page spread in the company magazine *Focus on Scott's* devoted to it in its entirety.

Quality Support Manager (QSM)

Scott's have been without a quality support manager for most of the last year since the departure of the previous incumbent to her own business. By virtue of their leadership position in TQM in the hospitality industry, they feel it is unlikely that they will find a candidate there to fill the vacancy. As a result, they have been talking to candidates from other industries with the view of attracting them to join in the capacity of quality support manager, or as non-executive director within the TQSG, or in a position that combines them both. It is anticipated that this will help broaden the outlook of the company by bringing in new and different ideas and a fresh way of looking at the industry from a quality perspective.

THE FUTURE WITH MARRIOTT

In the past two years, Scott's has concentrated on developing an efficient working relationship with Marriott International. The considerable similarities in business values and methods gave them a significant head start. Both parties appear to regard the relationship as a partnership of equals, and have established a very strong two-way communication network. For the immediate future, a closer integration with the Marriott network is the goal – an ongoing relationship of continuous improvement for mutual gain. The franchisor/franchisee relationship is a difficult one, but with both parties sharing the same values and ideals, the relationship can only go from strength to strength.

TWELVE

Sutcliffe Catering Group Ltd.

Andrew Ghillyer

Acquired from P&O in 1993, the Sutcliffe Catering Group now forms part of the Services to Business Division of the Granada Group plc, alongside Granada Contract Services, and Granada Vending Services.

Sutcliffe has doubled in size over the last five years, and is now Britain's second largest food service management company. In 1992 the company began operating in Eire, and it is now Eire's largest contract catering company. The company is divided into five separate divisions operating from ten offices around the UK (excluding Eire and the Fairfield Catering Company, which is operated as a specialist education division within the group). Turnover for 1993 was around £400 million.

Customers are drawn from across a wide range of activities from boardrooms and staff catering requirements to independent and grant-maintained schools, training and conference centres, hospitals (both in the private and NHS sectors), nursing homes, public authorities' requirements in town halls and the Ministry of Defence, and other government departments. Sutcliffe caters for 83 of *The Times* top 100 companies, and customers include the Law Society, Lloyd's Bank, the Cabinet Office, P&O, British Airways, IBM, Rolls Royce, Oundle School, Charing Cross Hospital, the Inland Revenue, Oxford Brookes University, and Belfast International Airport. To service those markets, 20,000 staff are employed across a nationwide client base of approximately 2300 catering contracts serving over one million meals per day.

Since the purchase by Granada, the profile of Sutcliffe's operations has changed considerably. In February 1994, the civil service catering organization Forward was purchased for £4.6 million, beating off the challenge of Aramark, Compass, and a management buyout team. The purchase of Forward added 250 catering outlets around the country, including GCHQ at Cheltenham, the Welsh Office, and the Cabinet Office, employing a total of around 1,800 staff with an annual business turnover of around £25 million. Complete integration of those 250 outlets into Sutcliffe's divisional structure was accomplished in only seven months, with the conversion of each restaurant being achieved without any disruption of service to the client.

A COMMITMENT TO EXCELLENCE

Sutcliffe has maintained an average growth rate of 20 per cent per annum over the last five years. A large part of that success is due to its commitment to excellence in the range of services which it offers to its clients:

- Full management of client catering requirements, including recruitment and employment of staff, menu planning, budgeting, purchasing, production control, legal responsibility for all aspects of hygiene and health and safety.
- Sutcliffe site managers set, monitor and maintain the highest catering standards within closely controlled financial parameters for clients based on stringent reporting, self-assessment and auditing systems.
- The company spends approximately £1.5 million annually on staff training (the company employs 14 full-time training staff and 1000 of their managers are qualified as on-job trainers).
- A specialist Environmental Services Team is on call to advise and provide assistance, make regular and stringent checks on suppliers, and maintain the highest standards of hygiene and safety in Sutcliffe's kitchens and restaurants at all times.
- Hotel services are available for residential contracts, such as corporate training centres, hospitals, schools, colleges and marine contracts.
- Other specialist services include:
  Purchase only
  Consultancy only
  Corporate hospitality
  TFM – management of all facilities.

SERVING TWO MASTERS

Quality is seen as the key element in Sutcliffe's competitive strategy for the long-term development of their customer base. In this context, it defines quality as: 'achieving the highest possible standards of food and service within the policy and financial targets agreed with our clients.'

The achievement of those aims is made more complex by the fact that Sutcliffe must strive to satisfy the expectations of two masters (as do all contract caterers). The first master is the client, Customer A, who provides some, if not all, of the funding for the catering service and specifies the contractual parameters within which Sutcliffe must operate. The second master, or Customer B, consists of the employees of Customer A who consume the food produced. With Customer A usually seeking to minimize costs, and Customer B typically regarding company catering as part of their benefit package, the two parties can often develop very different viewpoints about what standard of food and facilities should be made available. In seeking to satisfy both sets of expectations simultaneously, Sutcliffe focuses on the development of a strong working relationship with their clients as a 'customer partnership'. The formal contracts are used to establish the clients' aims, objectives and standards from the outset, but it is the proactive nature of the working relationship, through regular dialogue, 'open-book' finances, and a highly visible local management team, which allows Sutcliffe to achieve and maintain high service standards and, over the long-term, to generate significant referral business from its existing client base.

The strength of this 'customer partnership' has enabled Sutcliffe to cope with a marked change in its client profiles in recent years. As Quality Services Manager, Mike Batchelor explains:

> Over the last couple of years, our client profile has shifted from being typically the personnel manager – because catering was considered to be a relatively 'soft' issue within the overall staff benefits package – to a new situation where the responsibility now falls to the finance or purchasing manager. What this means for us is that, in general terms, the judgement on whether we are performing well has gone from the relatively flexible view of the personnel manager, who probably judges us on the basis of how many of his/her staff pick up the 'phone and complain about the shepherd's pie being cold, to the far more 'black and white' view of the finance manager who judges us based on 'you told me it would be £2,000 and it isn't'.
>
> If this trend towards a greater financial emphasis continues, we can foresee a change in the way the catering budget will eventually be made up, as the client company puts less into the cost of catering with the expectation that their staff are going to pay more – that is a difficult game to be in the middle of, as the perception from the employees is typically that Sutcliffe are the ones raising the prices.

QUALITY SELF-ASSESSMENT

The linchpin of the 'customer partnership' is the site catering manager. He or she is the primary point of contact between Sutcliffe and the client, and the level of performance achieved is very much dependent on that manager's interpretation of the informal needs of the client which may not have been expressed in the contract document. In this context, the catering manager is also the primary element in Sutcliffe's quality control programme – the Quality Self-Assessment (QSA).

Towards the end of the 1980s, under the guidance of former Quality Services Director Christopher Page (now Managing Director of Granada Contract Services), the decision was made to formalise the issue of quality within the organization, and to develop a system which would ultimately make Sutcliffe the best at what it does – namely in bringing about the criteria which meet the 'food-on-the-plate' requirements of the customer, and the financial and operational parameters of the client. Before that, Sutcliffe's approach to quality had been the use of a checklist by which the area manager periodically inspected each unit within his designated region. The general perception of the checklist was fairly negative – it did not reflect the wide variations in unit sizes and service levels, and it was so time-consuming to complete that there was rarely any time left for the area manager and the catering manager to discuss the results and really learn something from the exercise.

After undertaking a comprehensive review of the operation (and listening to the negative feedback about the quality checklist), the QSA audit was introduced. In contrast to the 'inspection from above' process, the QSA focused on providing the necessary documentation for the catering manager to assess his/her own performance and the performance of his/her unit staff.

In simple terms, the QSA document consists of two parts. The first is a minimum standards manual which breaks down the job description of a site catering manager into six principal areas of operation:

1. Menu planning, purchasing, food production
2. Merchandising, customer relations, service standards
3. Staff and training
4. Hygiene, health and safety
5. Finance and administration
6. Vending.

The perspective taken is that of meeting the necessary legal requirements of unit operation – primarily hygiene, health and safety regulations – as well as meeting the clients' expectations. There is still an element of checking performance against predetermined criteria, but the difference lies in the trust and confidence being placed in the catering manager – 'this is not an inspection, but a reminder to help you make sure that your unit is running at peak performance'. The purpose of the manual is not to define cooking methods or even presentation methods. As Chris Page commented:

> That flexibility is left to the experience of craft and management skills on site. We are not aiming to be a McDonald's or a Little Chef where meals are identical in all 2,000 locations. Each of our clients has different needs and we must match those to meet individual client requirements.

The second part of the QSA audit is the self-assessment document. It is designed to allow the catering manager to assess his/her own performance quarterly against the minimum standards set out in the first part of the audit. The document matches, in general, the six sections in the standards manual, and the assessment points are geared to those numbered standards (Table 12.1).

Table 12.1   Examples of self-assessment questions from the QSA Audit

1. How much time do you spend talking to customers during service times and understanding and responding to their needs?
2. How well briefed are your serving staff on:
   - the daily menu?
   - the use of servery equipment and utensils?
   - portion control?
3. How skilled are your staff in promoting the sale of food items?
4. How well do your staff handle customer complaints/problems?
5. To what extent do your staff project a friendly professional image?
6. How interesting and imaginative is your use of professionally prepared point-of-sale material to complement and support your food and beverage sales?
7. To what extent do you make use of special days/promotions to create interest in the restaurant, stimulate sales, and improve customer loyalty?

Between 1990 and 1992, £1.25 million was invested in the appointment of 24 quality services managers (QSMs), among whose responsibilities was the introduction of the new QSA programme to the organization and to bring home the message that quality was now 'the responsibility of the individual'. At the time, there was one QSM assigned to each operations director within the group. In contrast to initial suspicions, the role of the QSM remained that of an advisor to area managers on the implementation of the

QSA programme. For the catering managers, the emphasis of the QSA remained on 'self' and has always done. The natural scepticism about how accurate and honest a 'self-assessment' can be has been dispelled by performance. The quarter-on-quarter gradual increases over the two-and-a-half years that the programme has been running show such solid performance increases that it would be unreasonable to think that the results are being 'fixed'.

For the first year, the QSA was run without the direct involvement of the area managers. Over time, the nature of that involvement has changed to a point where the area manager may become involved in the QSA at the first and last quarters of the year to monitor accurately the development of the catering manager and his/her unit. The continued 'fine-tuning' of the QSA document has simplified its use as a progress monitor, an appraisal document and, where necessary, an inspection sheet. As Mike Batchelor commented: 'I can't think of a more efficient way to get a good fix on the position within any unit than to run through a QSA – it addresses every single facet of the operation that a catering manager and an area manager need to know'.

It is important not to underestimate the significance of the QSA audit to Sutcliffe's operations. The document is actively promoted as a sales tool, and the clients themselves are encouraged to participate in the quarterly audit as a means of developing the 'customer partnership'. Many clients take advantage of this invitation, and some even tie Sutcliffe's income from the contract to performance levels achieved on the QSA.

BS 5750

Sutcliffe's growing interest in formalizing quality procedures within its organization coincided with growing interest among its clients in the BS 5750 quality standard (now called BS EN ISO 9000). As many of its client companies achieved registration, it became inevitable that registration for BS 5750 would become a key element in contract requirements. In this context, the minimum performance criteria established in the QSA audit laid the groundwork for the accreditation process, and it became the responsibility of the QSMs to address the issue of BS 5750/ISO 9002 and to guide their units towards registration. The company's initial response to the issues of BS 5750 was a very proactive one. Plans were developed to guide all 2,000 units in operation then through the accreditation process, under the leadership of the QSM team. In addition, Sutcliffe became directly involved with the British Standards Institute, and produced some pioneering work in devising accreditation guidelines which would be acceptable to the hotel and catering industry.

As questions began to arise as to the applicability and industry-specificity of the BS 5750 quality standard, however, Sutcliffe's role changed somewhat. The company remain committed to it, but future registrations are likely to be driven by commercial need rather than idealism. At present, each division has 'a toe in the water' with at least one unit registered for BS 5750 or under consideration for registration, and the learning process of those accreditations has adequately prepared Sutcliffe for future registrations, should the individual client contract demand it. As Mike Batchelor explains:

> In our South West and Wales Division, for instance, we have four sites out of a total of about 450 registered. In essence, there is nothing different in the way in which those

four sites are managed compared with the way the other 446 in the division are managed. We simply upgraded their operations manuals to meet the requirements of BS 5750, checked that we'd got it right by registering them, and then subsequently upgraded everybody else's operations manual – so there is really very little difference between what those four units do and what the core business does.

By upgrading the operations manual for the core business, it has made our life that much easier, in so far as, if a client rings up today and says 'we're going to tender, I want you to get registered for BS 5750', then the procedures are already in place and it's almost a formality of inviting in the assessors – obviously I don't want to downplay the achievement of the four registered sites, but we have learnt so much from their accreditation experiences that registering any of the other sites would be relatively straightforward.

Sutcliffe's commitment to the quality standard remains a positive one, but because of the paperwork and expense involved there are no plans to seek registration for all 2500 units at this time. Management feels that the experience gained from their registered units, and the continued refinement of the QSA audit leaves them adequately prepared, and if a client does bring up the subject of BS 5750 registration, the response is: 'We are more than happy to do it, but who is going to pay for it?'

As to the reputation of BS 5750 itself, Mike Batchelor has his own views on the subject:

Our commitment to QSA made it easier for us to move up to BS 5750, but we're no more nor less organized than the rest of the industry. The big cultural divide to cross is actually getting the disciplines of measurement, self-assessment and management in place – it's instilling the desire to be disciplined in the first place. I do feel that it's a sad thing that 5750 as a standard has had such a bad press over the past couple of years, but this, in my view, results from a lot of misunderstanding. You have to go into it with as open a mind as you can, and sadly too many people don't do that, or they will hire an expensive quality consultant who may feel it's part of their job to make it sound difficult to justify their fees.

We haven't gone out of our way to achieve registration as a sales gimmick – any company looking at 5750 as a way of attracting new business is going to have a very prejudiced view of it, because there's not that much new business around in the current climate. If you're going to grow your business by 5–10 per cent, all of the effort that you are putting into registration is being offset against 5 per cent of your business – the other 95 per cent is going to look at it as a major inconvenience. If you look at BS 5750 as a way of improving the way *all* the business operates, then the reception, I think, will be much more positive.

INVESTORS IN PEOPLE (IIP)

Participation in IIP is regarded as coming under the remit of the Human Resources Department. Sutcliffe's involvement in the programme has not been as prominent nor as active as BS 5750, arguably because the requirement for IIP accreditation has not, yet, been showing up in client tender documents. Many of their client companies already have IIP registration, and Sutcliffe has been involved in many discussions and evaluations as to the benefits of IIP but, because of their commitment to QSA, any further involvement is likely to be prompted by commercial need rather than idealism. Given the comparative disciplines involved in both BS 5750 and IIP, the view taken is that IIP is very much a logical step beyond BS 5750.

THE CHANGING FACE OF SUTCLIFFE

One result of the comprehensive review of operations was the realization that Sutcliffe's management structure caused some confusion to its clients. The role delineation of area supervisors and area managers was not immediately apparent, for instance, and so a complete reappraisal of the line management structure was undertaken to both eliminate this confusion and to flatten the organizational hierarchy and enable the company to become more responsive to its clients. Since some additional structural changes have taken place after the change in ownership from P&O to Granada, some have argued that the reorganization was primarily a cost-based rationalization but, in reality, the plans for the restructuring were already in place and in progress before the Granada purchase, and were prompted more by a commitment to service excellence and continuous quality improvement than a simple financial decision.

The reappraisal has resulted in some dramatic changes in the way Sutcliffe operates. The position of Operations Director has been changed to Director of Food Service, with responsibility within that position increasing from a norm of 80–90 contracts to more than 120 contracts. The role of Area Supervisor has been removed completely, so that the Area Managers now represent the senior management level above Catering Managers. The typical area manager is now responsible for 20–22 contracts, up from a previous norm of 13–15 contracts. The role of the QSM has also changed and their numbers have declined considerably. As Mike Batchelor explains:

> The job description for a QSM was, to be honest, fairly 'woolly' in the early days. As the role developed, some of the QSMs found that it was not particularly what they wanted to do for the rest of their lives; some were sidelined back into operations as the needs and opportunities arose; the team was gradually shrinking as the task became a bit more clearly defined.

The key mechanism which has allowed this dramatic restructuring to take place is the QSA. The continued fine-tuning of successive versions of the QSA document reflects the extent to which the quality message has been 'taken on board' by the Sutcliffe organization, and also the extent to which the achievement of those quality goals now rests with the site catering managers. With area managers now responsible for 50 per cent more contracts, there is a greater dependence on the skills and experience of the catering managers to ensure that the needs and expectations of the client are being met. In this respect, the minimum standards manual no longer needs to spell out the basics – it is assumed that every one of the 2,500 operations is already running far above that. The legal requirements are still there, of course, but the QSA audit now focuses even more strongly on meeting client expectations as the key to service excellence.

PROSPECTS FOR THE FUTURE

Having become part of the Granada Group in 1993, totally restructured its organizational hierarchy, and completely integrated the 1,800 staff and 250 unit sites of the Forward catering company, Sutcliffe has been rather busy of late, and there appears no signs of that momentum slowing down. The launch of 'Choices', a range of five food- service concepts, in the spring of 1994, marked the company's move into branded food offerings. Designed to help provide a catering service at a lower subsidy and to offer a higher perceived value for money, the 'Choices' range enables Sutcliffe to bring more of a 'high-street feel' into the employee feeding market, while meeting the demand for more modern eating patterns (lighter meals and snacks). The five food-service concepts are as set out below.

1. *ZEFFERELLI'S*
    A range of freshly baked pizzas and pasta meals. Pizzas can be sold whole or by the slice to eat in or take away.
2. *JACKETS ... NO TIES*
    Freshly baked potatoes in their skins served with a range of hot or cold fillings. Healthy, nutritious and filling meals offering great value for money.
3. *STRIPES AMERICAN DINER*
    A fast-food/burger bar serving all-day breakfasts, burgers, fries and nuggets with a range of hot and cold beverages – fast!
4. *HAMPERS*
    A sandwich bar offering a wide range of packaged and made-to-order sandwiches, snacks, confectionery and drinks to eat in or take away. With a choice of breads and fillings, any combination can be made to order.
5. *LA BONNE BAGUETTE*
    A French-style baguette and patisserie bar offering items such as croissants, pain au chocolat, filled baguettes and croque monsieurs, all freshly baked on the premises and complemented by a range of quality coffees and bottled drinks. 'La Bonne Baguette' is particularly suitable for a retail/public catering kiosk.

A NEW OPERATING ENVIRONMENT

Within the contract catering industry, there is a trend towards the development of 'fixed price' (everything provided for one price) rather than 'cost plus' (food/labour/equipment costs plus a management fee) contracts for catering services. For Sutcliffe, the transition into this new operating environment is anticipated to be a smooth one. Its whole quality programme is geared to providing what the client wants at the price the client wants to pay, and if the client's requirements change, systems are designed to keep closer to that change than its competitors. With the contractor's income being made up from a number of sources, such as a direct management fee, or volume discounts on food purchases, this change in contract policy is regarded simply as a change in the way the numbers add up – the company is still in the same business of meeting the 'food-on-the-plate' requirements of the customer, and the financial and operating parameters of the client.

As for the QSA system itself, the short-term goal is to continue to update and refine what is already in place. Individual units will continue to be registered for BS 5750 on an 'as needed' basis – several applications are in progress, and by the end of 1995, it is anticipated that Sutcliffe will have doubled the number of units registered for BS 5750. The commitment to service excellence, continuous quality improvement, and the strength of the 'customer partnership' remains paramount as the long-term strategy of the organization.

THIRTEEN

The Tussaud's Group

Andrew Ghillyer

The Tussaud's Group Ltd, part of the international media group Pearson plc, runs the UK and Europe's top attractions, including Madame Tussaud's, the London Planetarium, Rock Circus, Madame Tussaud Scenerama Amsterdam, Warwick Castle, Chessington World of Adventures, and Alton Towers, with nearly ten million visitors a year. The continued advance in attendance figures at Madame Tussaud's and Alton Towers ensures that the Tussaud's Group own Britain's two most popular paid attractions. In May 1994 the Group took on a £32 million, 40 per cent equity stake in, and a management contract of, Port Aventura, a superb new theme park in Spain. Situated at Salou, the park is an hour drive south of Barcelona, and opened in the Spring of 1995. This significant further expansion in Europe reflects the Tussaud's Group's strategy for developing as a major force in the international entertainment market.

At the end of 1994, the Group undertook a company-wide climate survey to find out how the company was perceived by its employees, and how well they were doing as managers. The senior management team was pragmatic enough to expect some unpleasant surprises from the survey, but in view of its market leadership position and their expanding interests across the globe, the exercise was a very necessary one. As well as providing feedback on its performance, one of the other outcomes of the survey was a clearer picture of what quality should mean for the company as a whole, and what commitments would have to be made to achieve an agreed quality standard.

In operating terms, quality remains very much an issue for each profit centre, and we were able to look at two interpretations of it – Alton Towers, Britain's No.1 paid visitor attraction, and Warwick Castle, the finest mediaeval castle in England.

ALTON TOWERS

Developed as a relatively small-scale attraction – 'a little park in the middle of the countryside with some rowing boats and a chuffer train' – in 1979, Alton Towers has grown into a major international player in the theme park market. Since its acquisition by Tussaud's in 1990, the park has seen the best four years in its history, year on year, with the 1994 season breaking all records. Visitor numbers between March and November were up more than 25 per cent on 1993, smashing the three million barrier for the first time at a total of 3.25 million. With overall revenue also up by 30 per cent, 1994 exceeded even Alton Towers' own expectations.

When it is considered that Disneyland Paris (formerly EuroDisney), which was widely predicted to end Alton Towers' leadership in the European market, is still experiencing difficulties in emerging from near bankruptcy, the success of the Alton Towers organization appears even more exceptional. As Europe's busiest and most successful theme park, Alton Towers has proved that it not only understands what the customer wants, but that it can also deliver the kind of variety and quality that brings customers, of all ages, back to the Staffordshire hills time and time again.

A COMMITMENT TO QUALITY

In light of the commitment of the Tussaud's Group to gaining recognition as a provider of quality visitor experiences at all their attractions, it is surprising that Alton Towers is, to date, the only operation that has a designated quality manager. The position was first created in 1992, at the height of quality buzzwords in the leisure industry. The initial interpretation of the role was one of being 'a nice guy' who was there to support and motivate other members of staff into 'doing their best' in the performance of their daily tasks. However rudimentary such an approach may now appear, that season produced the lowest number of guest complaints that Alton Towers had ever had.

Before the Tussaud's purchase, the park had been operated as a classic entrepreneurial organization, with the consequent development of individual 'fiefdoms' within it. In this context, the issue of quality became a question of how well it was supported by a particular fiefdom. The security department, for instance, currently holds the BS 5750 quality standard – it is the only department in the park to do so, which shows the extent to which a public commitment to quality was left almost to personal choice (in this case the security team).

With record volumes over the last four years it has, until recently, been difficult to move the issue of quality beyond that stage – 3.25 million visitors in only eight months has demanded that the management team be 'fire fighters' on some days rather than long-term quality strategists. For the organization as a whole, however, quality has now become a more central issue. Over the past twelve months, under the direction of Clive Stephens, their new Quality Manager, the initial rudimentary approach to quality has been replaced by a new desire to learn exactly what quality means for Alton Towers, and what commitments will have to be made to achieve a definitive quality standard.

The last four years have seen a predominance of 'product quality' capital investment both in bringing the park up to the same high standard as the other Tussaud's attractions, and in the development of large-scale signature rides such as 'Nemesis' in 1994 and 'Energizer' in 1995. With £12 million invested in new attractions in 1994 alone, and a further £17 million budgeted for 1995/6 (including a 175-bedroomed themed Alton Towers hotel opening in 1996), this commitment to providing top-quality attractions at Alton Towers (and to remaining Britain's No. 1 paid visitor attraction) is likely to continue. However, with this closer examination of the issue of quality has come the realization that simply providing bigger and better rides every year will not, in itself, guarantee the long-term viability of the park. As Clive Stephens explains:

> What we are trying to achieve is a clear vision of where we would like to be in ten to fifteen years time, and to really begin to coach our workforce in sharing that vision. We have a wonderful product – undoubtedly a product which can aspire to be one of the greatest theme parks in the world. Quality offers us the opportunity to embrace our workforce in the realization of that. If we can develop a common set of values and a sense of real ownership and pride in a harmonious workforce who really enjoy what they are doing, then the service they deliver to our customers will be a lot better – this, in turn, will benefit our end product which, over the longterm, will provide us with an even stronger competitive edge.

'DELIVERING THE MAGIC'

The first step in the achievement of those goals has been to avoid the use of the word 'quality'. After examining the issue in detail at senior levels for six months before launching the new quality programme at the end of the 1994 season, it was decided that the word 'quality' has too many buzzwords attached to it and too much of a history of other companies pursuing it directly and failing in that pursuit (not that the management team are unaware of the likelihood of making a few mistakes themselves along the way).

In place of 'quality', the phrase being used is 'delivering the magic'. The word 'magic' features very strongly in both the vision and the brand values of the Tussaud's Group, in particular at Alton Towers, which uses the advertising strapline, 'Where the wonders never cease and the magic never ends'. As to a basic definition of the products and services being delivered to the customer, the term 'magic' is used to denote the series of good memories that customers gain at Alton Towers from the moment they drive through the gates to the moment they leave the park. The concept has been further developed here to introduce the idea of both internal and external customers receiving good memories when the 'magic' is delivered.

At first, the link with the advertising strapline meant that the phrase 'delivering the magic' was regarded as nothing more than marketing jargon, but by introducing the idea of good memories being delivered at the point of service – the classic 'moment of truth' – the management team has been able to put the message across that every employee is capable of making a contribution to adding magic to the end product by becoming involved in the creation of good memories for the customers.

SPREADING THE WORD

With a workforce of 245 full-time employees and up to 1250 seasonal employees at peak season, getting the quality message across is very difficult. Consequently, the introduction of the new quality programme has been undertaken very gradually. Six months of detailed examination and consideration preceded the public launch at the end of the 1994 season. At that stage the presentation consisted of nothing more than half-a-dozen bullet points qualifying exactly what 'quality' will mean for Alton Towers. A basic refresher article was published in the *Alton News* company newsletter in January 1995, and the training sessions began in earnest in February, prior to the 1995 season opening. The training modules lasted between one and three days, depending on the employee's role within the organization and the extent of their level of customer contact. In total, almost 100,000 hours of training were committed to spreading the 'delivering the magic' message.

The quality programme may be in its infancy at this stage, but the training policies for a general assimilation of the quality message into daily operations over the long-term are already in place. The Investors In People (IIP) accreditation process is already underway – the programme will come under the remit of the personnel department with an ongoing input from the quality manager and, where necessary, external consultants.

BS 5750, however, is regarded as having limited potential for a competitive edge – in reality, the Kitemark bears little relation to the atmosphere of thrills, excitement and magic that Alton Towers is trying to create to attract more visitors. Thus, the perspective being taken by the management team is that rather than attempting to climb the paperwork mountain of BS 5750 to achieve accreditation, the focus will remain, in the short-term, on developing their internal systems to deliver their own predetermined quality standards. It is an interesting point that the members of the security team who were responsible for their BS 5750 accreditation have now been exposed to Alton Towers' vision of quality as 'delivering the magic', and in their opinion, BS 5750 has little to do with the customer's perspective of quality, and that, after all, is the person whose viewpoint counts the most.

The use of prepackaged 'add-on' quality initiatives or designated 'quality consultants' is unlikely to feature in the Alton Towers programme. During the six-month planning period, the quality initiatives of several other companies – including Rolls-Royce and D2D (winner of the 1994 European Quality Award) – were analysed in detail, and the important elements – continuous improvement, the costs of quality, and the tools of quality (flow charting, pareto analysis, statistical process control) – were drawn from them. As a leader in its field, Alton Towers considers itself to be in something of a unique situation when it comes to benchmarking ideas from other organizations – it does not want to be doing what everyone else is doing. In this respect, it has taken what it considers to be the best elements of other initiatives and aligned those elements to its own programme.

COMPARISONS WITH DISNEY

Disney's highly systemized approach to quality – employees are 'cast members' and they are 'on stage' when they are delivering their closely scripted presentations to customers – has some relevance here. Comparisons between Alton Towers and Disney are inevitable. When EuroDisney (now Disneyland Paris) first opened in 1992, sceptics predicted that it would steal a large portion of Alton Towers' customer base. With a 'pathetic' marketing budget in the face of Disney's 'mega marketing bucks', it was felt that there would be no contest between the two theme parks. Fortunately, those fears have not been realized, and the infallible money machine appears to have stumbled for once.

Nevertheless, there is still a great deal to be learned from the Disney example, although consensus within the Alton Towers organization appears divided. Some feel that they do not want their employees to become 'scripted robots', while others feel that there is some benefit to be gained from consistency of performance. In the short-term it is likely that the consistency argument will win out. Every department in the park is already flowcharting its work performance, and for those job descriptions with a high degree of customer contact, scripting the customer encounter represents the fastest way to achieve a higher standard of performance.

A 'WORK-IN-PROGRESS'

At this early stage, Alton Towers' quality programme remains very much a 'work-in-progress'. Having taken the time to analyse exactly what quality is all about and what it will mean for the park in real terms, the organization feels well prepared for many of the problems that have proven to be stumbling blocks for other companies – unrealistic expectations, lack of financial support, lack of employee involvement, etc. The final word on what it hopes to gain from all this must go to Clive Stephens:

> We are looking to develop a longer-term relationship with our customers. By improving the level of service and continually upgrading our product, we can begin to develop that relationship whereby, if they visit one of our competitors – i.e. American Adventure or Drayton Manor – they'll come away feeling dissatisfied with what they've just experienced. In terms of visiting a theme park, there will be only one place to go for value for money and a magical experience, and that will be Alton Towers.
>
> I don't think we can just invest in bigger rides – the tangible elements of our product – to achieve that. We must really enhance those products by improving our service. That can only be done by making sure we have the right people here in the first place to deliver that service, and the right systems, management styles, management philosophies, visions and values in place to complement what we are trying to aim for.
>
> We are riding on the crest of a wave at the moment but if we don't continue to improve then this situation will not last. We know our competitors are investing in their products all the time, and we have to continue to find ways to differentiate our product. Alton Towers already has a unique location and some very unique rides, but if we could also differentiate ourselves by the level of service that we can deliver to our customers, then it just adds to the overall competitive edge that we are developing in the marketplace, and will hopefully lead to a healthy and sustained future.

There is still a great deal of ground to be covered, however. In the comparison with Disney, for instance, which can draw on a truly global catchment area for its employees, Alton Towers, in the face of an astronomic growth rate over the last 15 years, still draws on the same limited catchment area. Plans for the provision of employee accommodation and, perhaps, even an Alton Towers University will have to wait on the drawing board for a while yet.

WARWICK CASTLE

Standing on the banks of the River Avon, a few miles from Shakespeare's Stratford, Warwick Castle is widely regarded as the finest medieval castle in England. The site was first selected and fortified by William the Conqueror in 1068, and over the centuries it has been home to the Earls of Warwick, who were to play key roles in the Wars of the Roses, the Hundred Years War with the French, and the English Civil War. Over the years, generations of earls developed the Castle into the most outstanding of England's ancient fortresses. Capability Brown was commissioned to landscape the grounds and raise the level of the courtyard, while the Castle's living quarters were transformed into a residence of the grandest style; famous visitors included George IV, Queen Victoria, Prince Albert, Edward VII, and Winston Churchill. The Castle contains an outstanding collection of furnishings, paintings, tapestries and armour, including the personal belongings of Queen Elizabeth I, Oliver Cromwell, and Marie Antoinette; and yet it retains its medieval character, complete with commanding battlements, parapets, towers and dungeon.

A UNIQUE COMMERCIAL ENTERPRISE

The Castle has been open to the public, to varying degrees, for over 200 years, but it is only in the last 17 years that it has been allowed to flourish as a commercial enterprise. In November 1978, the year when visitor numbers first exceeded half a million, Lord Brooke, the eighth Earl of Warwick, sold the Castle, most of its contents, and 40 hectares (100 acres) of grounds to Tussaud's for £1.5 million. His reasons for doing so lay both in the tremendous financial burden of maintaining a 900-year-old castle, and in the uncertain political and economic climate of the time (taxation for the wealthy was running at 98 per cent and inflation had reached as high as 26 per cent). The choice of Tussaud's was a recognition of the commercial management abilities and experience of one of the leading names in the leisure field. The acquisition of Tussaud's in February 1978 by Pearson, and the financial stability that the new ownership offered, no doubt added to Lord Brooke's conviction that the long-term viability of Warwick Castle would be assured in the hands of Tussaud's.

In operating terms, being owned by a public company places Warwick Castle in a unique situation since most equivalent properties are either privately owned by the family which has an historic claim to the property, or are owned by the National Trust or English Heritage. As such, the management objective for Tussaud's is not only to maintain and preserve the property for future generations but also to turn a sufficient profit to warrant continued investment by the parent company. Thus, while the Castle, as a commercial enterprise, has access to financial resources that other privately-owned properties may not, the money is only made available when there is a specific return on investment to be achieved. One major feature in Warwick Castle's continued success has been the willingness of its parent company to invest for the longterm.

DELIVERING A QUALITY PRODUCT

In addition to the purchase price of £1.5 million, Tussaud's approached the Warwick Castle project with a further commitment of another £1.5 million for immediate restoration and refurbishment. Over the last seventeen years, this commitment has increased to £10 million, with a further £10 million invested in additional capital investment. A large portion of that restoration has taken place on non-show elements such as leaking roofs and rusting pipes (much to the chagrin of the sceptical soothsayers who foresaw Warwick Castle being turned into a medieval wax museum). The number of projects undertaken based on these funds is too many to be listed here in detail, but some of the largest projects were:

1. Transforming Lord Brookes' former private apartments, after three years of detailed research and reconstruction, into The Royal Weekend Party 1898 Exhibition (which subsequently received several national awards).

2. The construction of a footbridge to a 8-hectare (20-acre) island in the River Avon, giving visitors access to a view of the whole river front of the Castle.

3. Complete restoration of the late-eighteenth-century gothic conservatory.

4. Restoration of the stables to form the main visitor reception area (later extended to include a 125-seat restaurant).

5. Redevelopment of parking facilities to achieve a sixfold increase in site capacity while, by virtue of a new entrance, diverting potential traffic congestion from the town centre.

Underpinning all this activity has been a guiding principle of remaining true in spirit and in context to the original. As Ralph Armond, General Manager, explains:

> We have a shopping list of things to do on Warwick Castle that could go on for fifty years for both show and non-show items. Every year we allocate additional funds for restoration and refurbishment and we will continue to do so. We have always taken a long-term view of the brand and its strategy – we're always looking for ways to give our visitors an improved experience, but never at the expense of detracting from the magic of the Castle itself.

The directive of maintaining the 'magic' of the Castle is applied equally to the large-scale projects and the day-to-day operations – and the application of that directive is often manifested in ways that would not immediately come to mind.

Representatives from each of the nine operating departments within the Castle have been brought together on a Quality Committee, chaired by Ralph Armond, to ensure that 'every experience that our visitors have here, whether it's in relation to the product, a member of staff, or even down to the signs that they read, doesn't break the magic of a special trip to our medieval castle.' The Committee is given a budget to spend on quality improvements – last year thirty-five improvements were carried out, including putting real flowers in some areas of the exhibitions rather than plastic ones; changing the type of paint on toilet doors to overcome a graffiti problem; putting a baby-change unit in the men's toilets – all quite small improvements, but, in relation to the visitor experience, they are all regarded as solutions to potential negative experiences that could 'break the magic' of a trip to the Castle.

DELIVERING A QUALITY SERVICE

Over the first 12 years of Tussaud's ownership of Warwick Castle, the emphasis on quality remained predominantly directed towards the physical product, not only in terms of basic restoration to bring the Castle up to standard, but also in developing the infra-structure needed to support the visitor numbers that Tussaud's believed that the Castle could generate. In the last five years, with a fully restored and refurbished product now in place, the emphasis has moved towards putting the customer first and emphasizing the quality of his/her interaction with every aspect of the Castle – the exhibitions, the staff, and the visitor facilities. As Ralph Armond explains:

> In the past there seemed to be a feeling that Warwick Castle was a private house, and since you were coming to someone's home, it was almost as if the family came before the visitors – it was almost a privilege to be allowed in. Although all our staff are highly skilled and very loyal, I think that attitude rubbed off on them a bit.
>
> We've now come to the realization that, as a business, that is an attitude which we can no longer live with – we are here to serve our customers, to give them the best possible visitor experience, and to make sure that they leave thinking that Warwick Castle is good value for money.

To monitor their progress in achieving those objectives, the management team at the Castle spends over £50,000 a year on market research to find out their value-for-money ratings, customer satisfaction levels, and customer expectations. Since Warwick Castle's ticket price places them at the higher end of the stately home market, much of the research is finance-led to ensure that visitors are experiencing value for money; but the Castles' management team is equally attentive to the non-financial measures that reflect the overall quality of the visit. The attitude taken at the Tussaud's Group level is that while the financial measurements, for reporting purposes, must be consistent for the Group as a whole, the individual operations are free to design operational measures to suit their own requirements. Many of these measures can be related to theme-park management – criteria such as dwell times, queue length, service times, interaction times. Benchmark performance levels have been established for each criterion, and these form the basis of the standard operating procedures (SOP) manuals for each department.

QUALITY THROUGH PEOPLE

Without a highly trained and totally customer-focused workforce, Warwick Castle would simply be an expensive museum. Every member of the 200 full-time and 100 seasonal staff is regarded as being a key element in the delivery of the 'Warwick product' to the customer – whatever their designated job title, they are held responsible for helping visitors to experience fully the best of the Castle. The management philosophy here is one of open communication, minimal bureaucracy, and intensive training. Each of the nine departments is team based, with department heads reporting directly to the general manager. A 'news update' meeting is held every Monday morning at 9 a.m. to discuss the previous week's business from both a financial and customer viewpoint, and plans for the forthcoming week are also reviewed. By midday the minutes of that meeting have been typed up and distributed so that every member of staff is kept informed of how things are going.

Training is a top priority, but it is handled as an internal issue rather than using any external programmes such as Investors In People (IIP). As Ralph Armond comments:

We are not a chain of hotels or shops where there are a lot of skill courses to choose from – as far as we are concerned, we are the best people for designing the training courses for our staff in what we expect them to deliver to our customers. We are, perhaps, rather arrogant in thinking that we understand our business better than anyone else outside of our organization, but we have yet to be convinced otherwise. We have a well-developed personnel and training department here, and we have access to an extensive head office training resource if we need it.

We did look at IIP, and we had quite a few meetings with our local TEC about it, but in the end we found it to be too bureaucratic for our needs. We have taken a different route by putting together our own courses – in specialist areas and general customer-focus training – both at Group level, and in working with a couple of consultants for our individual staff training courses.

The pursuit of BS 5750 as an external quality accreditation was regarded as equally bureaucratic and insufficiently industry specific for a service establishment. As Armond concludes: 'If we employ the right staff here, with the right vision and the right approach to business, then we should be able to exceed the standards that any external qualification would give us.'

'KINGMAKER!': THE FUTURE OF WARWICK CASTLE

Over the past 17 years, Tussaud's have sought to bring the Castle to life for their visitors. Its aim has always been to provide a professional quality product and therefore differentiate themselves from other stately homes. In this respect, the management team is trying to enhance the visitor experience by providing interactive exhibitions where the visitor can become more involved with the exhibits rather than simply looking in on them. During Easter 1994, Warwick Castle introduced the first of these – 'Kingmaker – A preparation for battle'. Situated in the fourteenth-century undercroft, the exhibition tells the story of the Castle's most notorious earl – Richard Neville – who, as the most powerful nobleman in England during the Wars of the Roses, became known as 'Warwick the Kingmaker'.

In comparison to the more traditional use of Tussaud's wax figures in 'The Royal Weekend Party 1898', the Kingmaker exhibition represents a marked advance in the use of appropriate modern technology within an historical setting. To quote the brochure:

People are encouraged to touch the figures; to feel the weight of fifteenth-century chain mail; and to smell the rich variety of aromas, from the unmistakable smell of the horse in his stable to the distinctive aroma of the leather worked on by the cobbler. Through a combination of realistic scenes, wax figures, sounds, smells and special effects, visitors feel as if they are actually answering Kingmaker's call to arms!

The opening of the exhibition coincided with an increase in the admission price by 12 per cent. However, the response to 'Kingmaker' has been so positive that not only have dwell times increased but also the value-for-money ratings have improved, even with the price increase. While the transformation of the former storage rooms and workshop into a first-class medieval attraction was a triumphant achievement, the management team remains aware that there are very specific limitations to what they can do in a Grade I listed building. Fortunately there is still sufficient space within the Castle and the grounds to take the product enhancement programme into the next century. Another exhibition on the scale of 'Kingmaker' is already planned to be opened within the next two to three years, and the River Mill site is currently under consideration for refurbishment.

In the summer of 1995 Warwick Castle introduced its very own jousting team – The Lions – in an authentic recreation of a 1358 jousting tournament that took place at the Castle. This use of re-enactments is seen as a further enhancement of the basic product and another means of bringing the castle to life for their visitors. As Ralph Armond explains:

> These events extend dwell times, they can take pressure off the Courtyard when it's congested, and they do bring the time period to life more effectively than simply looking in on an exhibition. We are looking at more re-enactments and historical events to portray more of how the Castle 'fitted in' to events in history.

With a 40 per cent increase in visitor numbers during the 1980s, and annual numbers now exceeding 750,000, Tussaud's commitment to continuous quality improvement at Warwick Castle, both in capital investment and staff training, appears to be paying off. The only downside to their product enhancement programme, however, is that the older exhibitions are starting to show their age alongside the new attractions, which is indicative, perhaps, of the constant pressure to improve which exists once any commitment to excellence is made.

FOURTEEN

Conclusion

Michael Baker and Andrew Lockwood

RECIPES FOR SUCCESS

This is not a management cookbook. The case studies are not a selection of recipes recommended by the editors. It is however worthwhile reviewing the reasons for their choice.

In selecting examples for study, we were encouraged to look for 'best practice'. The choice of Rombalds, for example, was made because of the innovative idea of giving staff vouchers so that they could experience the product as customers. Sometimes this means of selecting a subject for study simply produced an account of what had originally attracted us to the firm. For example the Copthorne, Cardiff, was chosen because it had attracted attention as an early ISO 9000 registrant; the case study is a straight account of how Simon Read and his team achieved this, and a review of what it meant at the time and subsequently. In other cases we were initially attracted by one aspect, but subsequently found other issues of interest. Haven Leisure was chosen because of the way the company managed quality when the vast majority of the employees is seasonal and temporary; but the firm revealed itself to contain many other useful lessons in how to manage quality in the hospitality and leisure industry.

We recognize that the case studies have all the disadvantages of their breed: selective choice of evidence on the part of the subject; partial selection of witnesses; and selective reporting on the part of the researcher. To minimize the effect of these factors, we employed a standard format in our research approach and a semi-structured questionnaire for the interviews. The case studies, however, tended to resist the attempt to straitjacket them, and managed to impose their own logic on the account. The consequence is one that we make no apologies for – a series of rich pictures with moments of entertainment and drama as well as serious management study. Examples are the obvious pleasure and pride in her job taken by Haven Leisure's Mrs Joan Thomas ('Mrs T.'), and the heritage of Bob Payton in the form of 'Bobisms' at My Kinda Town.

Because these are rich pictures, readers are encouraged to draw their own conclusions from the case studies. However, as editors, we feel a responsibility to draw some conclusions from the body of case studies as a whole, looking for common themes and issues that the studies raise.

QUALITY ISN'T DIFFERENT

The first theme that stands out from the case studies is that managing quality into an organization, and keeping it there, is no different, and not separate, from management of the organization as a whole. This means that the laws of good management are not suspended for quality initiatives, and mistakes are punished by the market as well as success being rewarded. Well-managed firms tend to be good at managing quality. Haven Leisure, for instance, emphasizes good management and is fostering it through its Career and Personal Development Programme (CAPD), whilst other firms such as Gleneagles and My Kinda Town wrestle with the problems of a career ladder in a delayered organization. Alan Parker, at Country Club Hotel Group, has called in the consultants Hay Management Group to develop profiles for selection and training general managers, with particular emphasis on 'impact skills'.

MANAGEMENT PERCEPTIONS

The case studies demonstrate that quality is viewed by these companies as an integral part of their product offering. At Tussaud's, for instance, the company sees it as imperative to invest in both the physical aspects of the product and the service aspects. Each is clearly seen as complementary to the other. So the investments in new rides at Alton Towers and in new attractions at Warwick Castle are now being matched by the attention to the service elements that combine to provide the total experience of the customer. At Haven Leisure, which sees itself an 'old-fashioned' business, there is a recognition that the quality of the physical environment and the quality of the service are two sides of the same coin. At English Lakes, the management believes that 90 per cent of the success of the enterprise depends on the people in the organization and 10 per cent on the hardware – the fabric and the property. This reinforces the view that competitive advantage cannot be delivered by continual investment in physical facilities alone. While physical facilities can be copied, investment in service is not as easy to reproduce.

Management's perceptions of the nature of the business and the place of quality in it are important. At Alpha Flight Services, the company sees quality a matter of logistics and statistical quality control, rather than as some grand vision of customer service excellence. Its approach to the task is to manage the process, including working with both clients and suppliers to achieve the necessary results. The Sutcliffe example also points up the importance of working with the client in a partnership, with frankness extending to 'open-book finances'.

Looking after the fundamentals is the key to My Kinda Town's success, according to the Managing Director, Peter Webber. 'Serve the hot food hot, and the cold food cold, and everybody smiles'. He sees a mature business as harder to manage; the novelty of the product wears off in the market, costs have to be more tightly controlled and forgiveness on the part of the customer for mistakes becomes harder to secure.

RESPONSE TO THE MARKET

The case studies highlight how quality is, in the successful firm, integrated into the product offer, and shows how the approach to quality is closely linked to a realistic perception of what the market wants. At Warwick Castle, the current emphasis on quality has been a part of a shift from ensuring that the physical aspects of the product are satisfactory to a concentration on the interaction with the customer and a consequent focus on the customers' experience. In contrast, Alpha Flight Services seem to be separated from their final customers but their relationship with their direct customers – the airlines – is very close. Its emphasis is on differentiating the product through consistency of process, with the quality built into the offer entirely to meet the identified client airlines' needs. Sutcliffe, working with a different type of client, has seen the requirements of these clients change dramatically in recent years. The tendency for the responsibility for contracting catering in the client organization to shift from the personnel director to the finance or the purchasing function is an interesting reflection of this. As a result, with a much closer attention being paid to value for money, quality has to be managed into the offering.

In the case of the Country Club Hotel Group, the new emphasis on quality of service as well as reducing overheads to provide a value-for-money offering was part of a strategic move to transform a poorly performing subsidiary, moving the firm into a market segment where it could operate profitably. Gleneagles has also undergone a dramatic change, and again the management has a clear vision of what the product offering should be and how this meets the requirements of the hotel's market.

Haven Leisure is another company whose clear view of who its customers are and what they want is evident. A close and realistic understanding of the company's customers and how their requirements and expectations are changing has led to the steady change in the quality element in the product offering. In the same way, the company has responded to the trend of increasing on-site spending by developing more extensive on-site retail facilities. My Kinda Town similarly reveals a straightforward approach to service quality, in the same way as the company's whole approach is deceptively simple: focus on what the customer expects.

At Scott's Hotels, Jan Hubrecht, unlike Alan Parker at Country Club Hotels, had not had to engage in a process of dramatic change to catch up with rapidly changing market needs. However, over the last five or so years change has been reasonably rapid, and, again, the deep changes in company culture to improve service quality have been a response to the competitive environment. At Copthorne, the acquisition of ISO 9000 registration can be seen as market research. It was viewed by the senior management as a trial, to see if registration would be a market plus. As it turns out, the Copthorne Group has not pursued registration in other hotels in the group.

MEASUREMENT

'If you can't measure it, you can't manage it.' The case studies reveal many examples of managers who, on the evidence, believe this.

Tussaud's has undertaken a company-wide climate survey. The company employs a wide range of service level measures: for instance, it monitors dwell times, service times, interaction times and queue lengths against benchmarks. Warwick Castle spends £50,000 a year on market research to determine its value-for-money ratings, customer satisfaction levels and customer expectations.

At Country Club Hotels, accurate measurement of performance is seen as fundamental. Customer satisfaction is tracked through the STARS system, which is questionnaire-survey based, and includes rating the hotels against their competitors. Quality service and cleanliness are measured through incognito visits by an AA Hotel Inspector, or with a mystery guest programme. At Haven Leisure, the number of repeat bookings, the level of complaints, and a customer satisfaction questionnaire provide measurement of customer satisfaction.

At My Kinda Town, performance criteria are tightly specified, as is necessary if franchise contracts are to be specific enough to protect the reputation of the franchiser. The company has a fully specified set of operating policies and over the years the operating manuals have been developed to ensure this is the case. The company has followed its US counterparts in putting everything down on paper. The result of this that the company can, and does, monitor and thus control the process effectively. The measurement of outcomes is not, however, neglected. As well as comment cards, the company operates a programme of secret or mystery diners. Scott's has adopted Marriott's Guest Service Index (GSI). This provides a monthly analysis of a range of customer response data collected over the previous three months. Scott's also employ benchmarking to provide target levels of performance.

Of the contract caterers, Sutcliffe's Environmental Services Team make regular and stringent checks on suppliers and monitor hygiene and safety. Sutcliffe's main innovation is the Quality Self-Assessment Audit, by which the catering manager assesses his or her own performance across all the areas of responsibility, on a formal basis each quarter, against the minimum standards laid down for each site. At Alpha Flight Services, the monitoring is specification based, employs statistical process control and employs a detailed unit audit, which is integrated into the appraisal system, based on a zero defect philosophy.

CONTROL

Control is also an important management function no less important in the delivery of quality than in other aspects of management activity. Indeed, to the extent that the essence of quality is consistency, much of the delivery of quality is a matter of good control. None of the companies seem to have followed the Disney approach of achieving consistency through scripted encounters. At My Kinda Town the training outlines the key issues to be covered during the service encounter but relies on this as a framework to ensure that the delivery is adjusted to the customers being served – families, teenagers, senior citizens and so on. At Alton Towers opinions on scripting of the service encounter remain divided and it is not widely used.

A number of the case studies – for instance Haven Leisure and My Kinda Town – show how focusing on service quality quickly leads to establishing tighter control over recruitment. However powerful the training programme, it is always worthwhile trying to start off with a round peg for a round hole. Another aspect of control is illustrated by the use of labour scheduling methods to ensure sufficient (but not too many) staff are on duty to deliver the service required.

MANAGEMENT STYLE AND CORPORATE CULTURE

The subject of control raises questions about management style, corporate culture and motivation. Much of the discussion of service quality has been in the context of 'empowerment' and specific approaches to motivation. In these case studies, corporate culture and management style vary widely. One distinction that is apparent is that between the companies that have changed incrementally, and a smaller number (Country Club Hotel Group, Gleneagles, Scott's Hotels and Copthorne, Cardiff) which have made substantial changes over a relatively short length of time. The distinction is, of course, arbitrary, and it could be argued that, for instance, My Kinda Town is changing rapidly too. We consider the incremental changers first.

Tussaud's seek open communication and minimum bureaucracy. Its approach to quality appears to have been a combination of analysis – reviewing the quality initiatives of other companies and taking the best from them – and attempting the inspirational – through the advertising strapline 'delivering the magic'. General managers of the individual sites have considerable discretion. At Warwick Castle the emphasis is on teamwork. The interdepartmental quality committee, with its budget for discretionary expenditure, is an example of that commitment to teamwork.

Haven Leisure takes the time to do things properly. The company sees its organization as lean and responsive, with a focus on management team building. It has been able to benefit through assimilation and inheritance from the organizations it has acquired, as well as from internal change. The company's organizational structure is the traditional 'line-and-staff'; the main responsibilities lie with the line managers. Line managers are responsible for training the seasonal staff, although the human resources department has developed the procedures.

English Lakes is an example of a traditional family firm facing up to the challenges of the 1990s. The management has been prepared to 'walk the talk', with an emphasis on IIP and developing a training culture. At My Kinda Town, it is the clarity about objectives that is striking. The company is another that has few layers of management. Peter Webber's view is that, 'Head Offices don't make money, they spend it'. Nevertheless, the business is in transition. Under its founder's 'hands-on' management style, employees burned out quickly; now the business is more mature, the staff turnover is down. At Sutcliffe the flattening of the organization has been accompanied by a delegation of responsibility to the catering managers. At Alpha Flight Services, the way the company tackles the issue of quality is a result of long-term development in a tightly controlled organisation making incremental changes to meet market requirements. The approach is methodical, and empowerment is a matter of how much freedom is needed to do what is required. An example of this is the elimination of inspectors and the corresponding responsibility laid on each individual for the quality of the product as it passes through their area of responsibility.

MANAGEMENT AND CORPORATE CHANGE

Corporate change demands team-leadership skills, attention to motivation and usually a change in corporate culture. The case studies illustrate these points.

At Country Club Hotels, Alan Parker's intention to achieve a culture change was explicit. The crash course of improvement included shedding people and properties to cut costs and develop a more focused product portfolio; it also concentrated on employees at the sharp end as the deliverers of quality. Performance on quality delivery is measured like other aspects of the business, and pay and other rewards are linked to performance.

Peter Lederer's perception, at Gleneagles, was that too much time and resources were expended in bureaucratic functions and maintaining interdepartmental barriers. The organization has been flattened, and the responsibility and the authority for service delivery forced down the chain of command to departmental teams. The culture change that is being pursued is to focus on the people at the sharp end, and to develop a cross-departmental, team-oriented approach to quality. The 'people-oriented' approach is being reinforced by a training initiative – 'Breakthrough' – delivered by outside consultants.

Scott's Hotels have taken a more deliberate approach to organizational change and, arguably taking longer over it, has enabled the organization to absorb the new culture more thoroughly. Jan Hubrecht has led the development of a comprehensive and fully-fledged TQM system in Scott's. The case study might have come straight out of the TQM manual. There is a strong emphasis on empowerment and teamwork, and there are quality circles, cross-functional team working, and continuous improvement. There is strong top–down commitment to the system. The emphasis for management is 'organize not supervise' and to achieve through teamwork.

Simon Read, at the Copthorne, Cardiff, did not so much have to change a culture but to develop one from scratch. Introducing ISO 9000 into a new hotel has the advantage that it does focus management's attention on the control systems the hotel ought to have (but which it might not systematically install without such a stimulus). At English Lakes, gaining ISO 9000 registration in a new hotel was seen as avoiding adopting a three-star mentality from the start. No doubt, too, the experience of working together to achieve a goal helped weld the core members of the team into a cohesive group.

All the culture-change case studies raise the issue of how to maintain the momentum; motivation will depend on a sense of ownership, and on implicit or explicit bargains struck between the staff and the management. Management that fails to deliver, to 'walk the talk', can expect to see the culture revert to its old form. And, of course, one of the most effective ways of achieving this motivational failure is to replace the person at the top by someone not committed to the previous leader's approach. For this reason, if for no other, the issue of leadership in change management continues to be crucial after the change has apparently been effected.

TRAINING

Every one of the case studies demonstrates the importance placed on training by organizations committed to service quality. The organizations that have made substantial changes, like Gleneagles and Scott's Hotels, look to training to inculcate new values. Haven Leisure has created a new human resources department over the past seven years to put in place stronger and more defined personnel and training functions. The major task at Haven is to train the army of seasonal workers at the start of the season, treating seasonal workers as professionals.

Some lessons can be drawn from the choice of training providers. Whilst larger companies can draw on or develop their own resources, although they may choose to use outside help, smaller firms may not have the resources to do the job properly. English Lakes obtained general training advice from its local Training and Enterprise Council (TEC). Other companies have drawn on the Investors in People programme, which is also administered by the TECs.

INVESTORS IN PEOPLE

Most of the case study companies have found that IIP complements their strategies. This is not surprising. IIP sets out to develop in the firm's employees the abilities they need to achieve the company's business goals. In service industries particularly the employees' performance can make a critical contribution to the customers' experience of the product. Consequently, training can change significantly the customers' perception of value for money.

At English Lakes the objective in gaining IIP recognition was to develop a more formal framework for personnel and training initiatives. With IIP the company follows through on commitments to achieving high quality through staff performance. It finds IIP supports corporate objectives to provide good working conditions in which staff can develop, and be respected for their contribution to the team. IIP also helps English lakes to attract and retain staff, keep staff turnover low and morale high.

At My Kinda Town, Peter Webber sees IIP as a way of dealing with some of the problems of the company's growing maturity. Over the past eight years, he has shifted responsibility for training from the training and personnel departments down to the general managers at unit level. At the same time the focus of training has moved from simply teaching the bare essentials to recruits who were expected to burn out quickly, to developing individuals over the longer term with a view to fostering their development as continuing members of the workforce.

It is instructive to look at the reasons why the minority of companies in our case studies have decided, for the time being at least, not to go for IIP. At Tussaud's, although at Alton Towers accreditation is under way, at Warwick Castle this was considered and rejected. There they take the view that they know their business better than anyone else, and have the resources to design training programmes that are specifically targeted at the needs of the business. At Rombalds, too, the smallest firm in our case studies, Ian Guthrie had no patience with IIP.

A further clue to the reasons for these rejections of IIP may lie in Haven Leisure's approach. Haven Leisure is piloting IIP at Harcourt Sands, and finding it hard work, despite the enthusiasm of the local management. The experience prompts them to think that the five larger, all-year-round parks will eventually adopt IIP, but the smaller ones would not cope with the paperwork. Could it be that the medium-sized enterprise is the most likely to be able to benefit from IIP? Perhaps the larger ones can fashion their own programmes, and the smallest ones cannot cope with the burden of compiling written evidence?

ISO 9000

Experience of ISO 9000 seems to suggest that despite changing its name and considerable efforts on the part of BSI and its technical committees to tailor the system to the needs of the hospitality, tourism and leisure industries, there is more to be done. The experience of the Copthorne, Cardiff supports the view held by many people in the industry in the early 1990s that ISO 9000 clearly demonstrated its manufacturing origins, and had failed to adapt sufficiently to meet many of the requirements of the hospitality industry. The case study also identifies a consequence of this, that both the consultants who supported the implementation, and the external assessors, had little or no experience of the hospitality industry, and this added to the difficulties and costs. Although there is also some evidence that things are changing, the jury is still out on whether ISO 9000 is appropriate for use in hotels.

What emerges from the case studies at English Lakes, Copthorne and Sutcliffe is that the benefits of ISO 9000 lie in its being a potential vehicle to install the disciplines of measurement, monitoring and control in place, to achieve consistency of performance. The experience of Sutcliffe is interesting. The company was initially enthusiastic, but now takes the view it can gain all the benefits the system has to offer by having a small number of sites registered, and thus avoid much of the cost. The lesson of these case studies seems to be that companies contemplating registration to ISO 9000 must have a realistic understanding of what they expect from the system. It is clear that its possession is not on its own a sufficient marketing advantage to be worth the cost and effort.

This point is underlined by the Copthorne Cardiff case, where it is far from clear whether the effort of getting ISO 9000 was worthwhile. It seems that rather than measuring before-and-after performance to identify the market pay-off, the hotel group embarked on the project with the main criterion of success being ISO 9000 registration. Perhaps a lesson from this experience is the need to monitor carefully from the start both costs and benefits of what will be a considerable investment in both management time and hard cash.

In this context it is worth referring to other initiatives which were in hand during the researching of these case studies. In 1993 the CBI formed its Tourism Action Group under the chairmanship of Sir John Egan. This group initiated a benchmarking exercise in 3- and 4-star hotels, comparing British establishments with those in France and Germany. *World Hosts* was published in 1995 (CBI, 1995).

The Department of National Heritage also commissioned KPMG and MVA Consultants to undertake a complementary benchmarking exercise in smaller hotels (3-star or below), guesthouses and B&Bs. This was published in March 1996 (DNH, 1996a); with it was published a do-it yourself benchmarking kit for smaller hotels (DNH, 1996b) available from the Department of National Heritage (Tel: 0171 211 6328). This gives hotel proprietors a simple and quick way of seeing how their establishments measure up, and of identifying any areas of weakness.

TQM IS NOT ROCKET SCIENCE

A final message that emerges strongly from looking through the cases reported here is that there is no one way to develop quality within an organization. The journey towards total quality will be different for every organization, depending on where it is coming

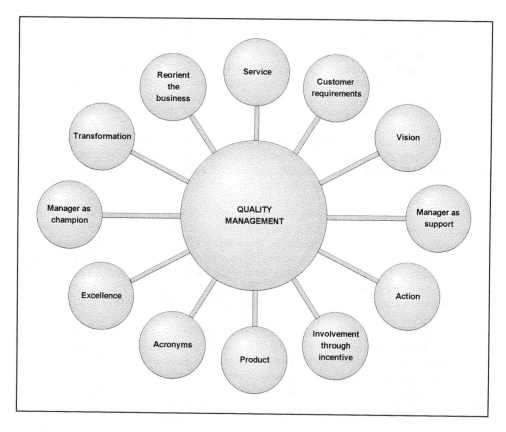

Figure 14.1 Dimensions of quality management

from and where it wants to end up, but will cross roughly the same terrain. The main dimensions of the complex set of decisions that companies face, as identified through our best practice examples, are illustrated in Figure 14.1.

It can be seen in the descriptions of the dimensions below that the extremes are not mutually exclusive. A company may have different departments or functions that operate in different ways and will therefore need a different approach. A company may even give importance to both ends of the dimension at the same time. What emerges is a multi-dimensional space with equally successful profiles being found throughout it, but with a distinct sense that gravity is pulling in an identifiable direction. The dimensions are:

- Service ↔ Product. Some of the companies described have placed a heavy emphasis on investment in the product aspects of their operations. Other companies, having decided that they cannot sustain the necessary capital investment over a long period, and that product quality can be undermined in the short term by a poor service encounter, have placed their faith in service to provide sustainable market advantage.
- Vision ↔ Process. Some of the companies described have developed a grand vision of product and service excellence which they are disseminating throughout their organization. Others have placed their emphasis on maintaining control over the product and service-delivery process.

- Transformation ↔ Action. Some companies have decided that in order to deliver long-term success they must transform the culture and character of their whole organization. Others have decided that they need to be seen to be taking action for change in the short-term in order for quality to be taken seriously.
- Customer requirements ↔ Acronyms. Some companies have pursued a policy of developing easy-to-remember slogans, or acronyms, in order to provide a focus for action. Others have seen the exacting requirements of their customers as the only focus they need.
- Reorient the business ↔ Involvement through incentive. Some companies have taken the view that quality management is a whole new way of doing business and have set out to bring this about. Others have seen the involvement of everyone in the organization as the key facilitator and have used incentives to encourage this involvement.
- Manager as a support ↔ Manager as a champion. There is clear evidence that managers must be seen to have a dual role. While a successful quality programme must be carried forward by the commitment of the front-line staff, the original impetus for and championing of quality must be from the top down. At the same time managers must act as a support, providing the resources people need to meet the objectives of quality management. The role moves from one of being a supervisor and controller to being more of a coach, facilitator and guide.

At the end, however, the message is very simple. Quality is a matter of looking after the fundamentals: it is knowing what your customers want, paying attention to the detail of providing it, giving clear guidance in the expectation of, and the encouragement and support of, consistently high performance. For Sutcliffe's it is 'achieving the highest possible standards of food and service within the financial targets agreed with our clients'. For My Kinda Town, it is even more straightforward – 'you serve the hot food hot, the cold food cold, and everybody smiles'. While delivering quality is essentially straightforward in concept, the case studies eloquently demonstrate that it isn't easy in practice.

REFERENCES

CBI (1995) *World Hosts: International Benchmarking in the Hospitality Industry* London: CBI.

DNH (1996a) *Tourism: Competing With the Best: 2. Benchmarking for Smaller Hotels* London: DNH.

DNH (1996b) *Tourism: Competing With the Best: How Do You Measure Up? Hotelier Self-assessment Test* London: DNH.

INDEX